OPTICAL SWITCHING AND NETWORKING HANDBOOK

McGraw-Hill Telecommunications

Ali	*Digital Switching Systems*
Ash	*Dynamic Routing in Telecommunications Networks*
Azzam	*High-Speed Cable Modems*
Azzam/Ransom	*Broadband Access Technologies*
Bartlett	*Cable Communications*
Bates	*Broadband Telecommunications Handbook*
Bayer	*Computer Telephony Demystified*
Bedell	*Wireless Crash Course*
Clayton	*McGraw-Hill Illustrated Telecom Dictionary*, 3/e
Collins	*Carrier Grade Voice over IP*
Davis	*ATM for Public Networks*
Gallagher	*Mobile Telecommunications Networking with IS-41*
Harte	*CDMA IS-95*
Harte	*Cellular and PCS: The Big Picture*
Harte	*Delivering xDSL*
Harte	*GMS Superphones*
Heldman	*Competitive Telecommunications*
Lachs	*Fiber Optics Communications*
Lee	*Lee's Essentials of Wireless*
Lee	*Mobile Cellular Telecommunications*, 2/e
Lee	*Mobile Communications Engineering*, 2/e
Louis	*Telecommunications Internetworking*
Macario	*Cellular Radio*, 2/e
Muller	*Bluetooth Demystified*
Muller	*Desktop Encyclopedia of Telecommunications*
Muller	*Desktop Encyclopedia of Voice and Data Networking*
Muller	*Mobile Telecommunications Factbook*
Pattan	*Satellite-Based Cellular Communications*
Pecar	*Telecommunications Factbook*, 2/e
Richharia	*Satellite Communications Systems*, 2/e
Roddy	*Satellite Communications*, 3/e
Rohde/Whitaker	*Communications Receivers*, 3/e
Russell	*Signaling System #7*, 3/e
Russell	*Telecommunications Pocket Reference*
Russell	*Telecommunications Protocols*, 2/e
Shepard	*Optical Networking Demystified*
Shepard	*Telecommunications Convergence*
Simon	*Spread Spectrum Communications Handbook*
Smith	*LMDS*
Smith	*Practical Cellular and PCS Design*
Smith	*Wireless Telecom FAQs*
Smith/Gervelis	*Cellular System Design and Optimization*
Turin	*Digital Transmission Systems*
Winch	*Telecommunication Transmission Systems*, 2/e

Optical Switching and Networking Handbook

Regis J. "Bud" Bates

McGraw-Hill
New York Chicago San Francisco Lisbon
London Madrid Mexico City Milan New Delhi
San Juan Seoul Singapore Sydney Toronto

McGraw-Hill

*A Division of The **McGraw-Hill** Companies*

1 2 3 4 5 6 7 8 9 0 DOC/DOC 0 7 6 5 4 3 2 1

ISBN 0-07-137356-X

The sponsoring editor for this book was Stephen S. Chapman and the production supervisor was Sherri Souffrance. It was set in Century Schoolbook by MacAllister Publishing Services, LLC.

Printed and bound by R. R. Donnelley & Sons Company.

This book is printed on recycled, acid-free paper containing a minimum of 50 percent recycled de-inked fiber.

CONTENTS

PREFACE

Before you begin to read this book, please take a moment to read these introductory comments. The title of the book may be misleading for many people:

For the engineering person, this may sound like the bible of optical networks and switching systems. Not so! This is not an engineering book and will not dig into the gory details of bits and bytes, ohms and lamdas, and so on. It will help an engineering person to understand the marketplace for the products and services that will be designed. It will also show you the application that the optical networks will satisfy. As I said, however, this is not a technical book. Read it for what it is worth. If you want the gory details, other books can meet that need. I would suggest that you log onto McGraw-Hill's Web site to find the many choices available.

For the financial and business person, the title may have a tendency to scare you away, thinking that it is a technical book. Please persevere and read on. This book was written for you so that you can understand the various developments and challenges to use or invest in the optical networks. I tried to write this with the simplest of terms and with some storyboards to make concepts more understandable. I also spent a significant amount of time in developing and shaping the business market strategies. If you are an investor or a VC who needs to understand the future demand for the products, then I have addressed that. If you are a telecommunications manager who is looking for the services from providers, I have addressed that too!

This is all about the demystification process of the technologies. This optical networking book is being branded as part of a continuing series of books that are geared toward a specific market niche. The *Voice and Data Communications Handbook*, the *Broadband Telecommunications Handbook*, and the forthcoming *Broadband Wireless Handbook* will all be a part of a series. These will aid you in understanding the technologies without the techno-geek jargon that is so common in our industry. Unfortunately, we are a part of a communications industry that has a very difficult time communicating ideas.

I personally hope that this series will make up for that and clear the way for your understanding.

—REGIS J. "BUD" BATES

ACKNOWLEDGMENTS

Before proceeding too far with this document, I want to personally express my thanks to the two people who are responsible for this book. The first is the person who is most responsible for this accomplishment, Gabriele, my wife. Gabriele has always been the drive in front of me, providing the encouragement and the support to continue. No matter how much effort was necessary, she continued to encourage me to keep going. The weekends and vacation time that I used to work on this book robbed her of our free time together. Moreover, Gabriele is also the person who completed the graphics by taking my raw pictures (drawings and scribbles) and creating some of the best graphics we have produced to date. Her constant support, assistance, and encouragement made this book a reality.

The second person who deserves much of the credit is McGraw-Hill's senior editor, Steve Chapman. Steve came to me with an idea of creating this book and asked me to do what I do best. His roadwork got this book approved in record time by the acquisition committees. Steve also gave me the room to write in my personal style without trying to encroach on the style, content, or timing. Steve and I have developed a respect for each other's ability to produce and make it happen.

Finally, I want to thank all the companies that have produced products and services that helped me to learn more about the overall concepts of the new world of optical communications. There are too many organizations to list here; however, they know who they are.

CHAPTER 1

Introduction to Optical Communications

Welcome to this next installment of the telecommunications made simple writings! When I first started to write in the early 1990s, I was overwhelmed with the amount of work necessary to produce the first book. That was the original *Disaster Recovery Planning for Telecommunications, Data and Networks*, and it was a rather short book. However, immediately after completing the final edit, I swore never to write another book. Well, here we are 10 books later, still saying the same things, but releasing a new one. This time the topic is fiberoptics, fiber networking, and optical switching for your reading enjoyment and understanding. The intent here is to make the technology easy to understand while giving you facts and applications in the state of the industry. Similar to the past books, if you are an engineer looking for technical discussions in the goriest detail, this book is *not* for you. However, if you fall into the following categories, then this is for you:

- Financial analysts trying to understand the cost implications of a fiberoptic network for investment or funding purposes
- Telecommunications administrator trying to understand what everyone is all excited about
- Salesperson in a telecommunications company trying to "walk the walk" and "talk the talk"
- Data processing person trying to get the most bang out of the data revolution
- Supplier of bandwidth needing to understand what the manufacturers are all saying
- "Newbie" in the industry trying to understand the technologies

What is this all about? I keep being asked to do things in my own simple way. I enjoy public speaking, and I enjoy watching people learn. You can tell when they are learning by that expression on their face when the revelation of a concept finally becomes clear. Therefore, I undertook this book on optical networking and switching to try to simplify the overall process of what is going on. Too often the vendors and standards bodies are busy writing standards documents or documentation on how equipment works. They know what they are talking about, so they assume that the readers in the industry also will know what they are saying. Unfortunately, that is *not* true! Probably all of us have picked up a trade magazine and seen a feature article written by some VP of engineering at a local manufacturer. The article presents several different acronyms and offers several opinions about the product or service. Yes, there is merit in the article, but too often there is so much jargon that readers have a tendency to put the article aside. What a sad thing it would be to have a communications industry that cannot communicate. It is for this reason that McGraw-Hill keeps asking for help in offering some semblance of understanding of industry techniques. One hopes that such understanding will result from this book as it has with the past ones.

Transmission System Terms

Before discussing the fiberoptic world, I should at least describe some very basic terms. These will help you to understand the world of fiber. There are many other ways of describing the use of fiber, but these definitions will aid in rudimentary understanding.

Amplifier This device increases the power of an electromagnetic wave, such as sound or light, without distorting it, as shown in Figure 1-1. Your stereo amplifier takes the weak radio signals from the air and boosts them so that they are strong enough to drive the speakers. Amplifiers in fiberoptics systems do almost the same thing—they brighten the light passing through the fibers.

Coaxial cable Coaxial cable is a high-frequency transmission line that is used to send telephone and television impulses. The CATV companies use a single cable to deliver multiple channels of TV by employing a multiplexing technique that separates the signals by frequency. See the representation of coaxial cable in Figure 1-2.

Modulator A modulator is a change agent. This device converts (changes) electrical on/off pulses into sound pulses for voice telephone calls. The modulator in a fiberoptic system does the same thing, except that it converts the electrical pulses into pulses of light, as shown in Figure 1-3. A modulator-demodulator (called a *modem*)

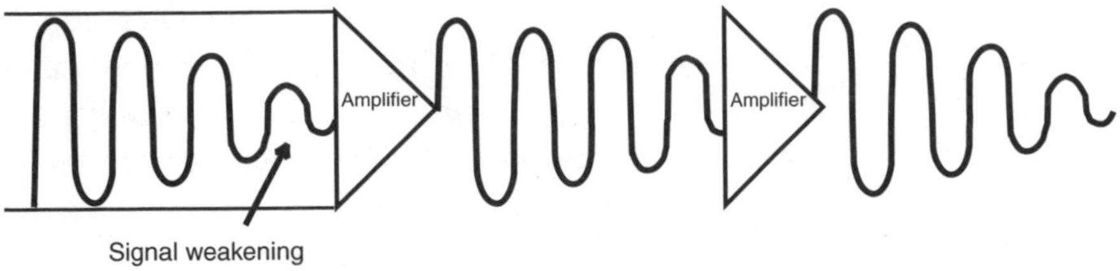

Figure 1-1
Amplifiers boost weak signals.

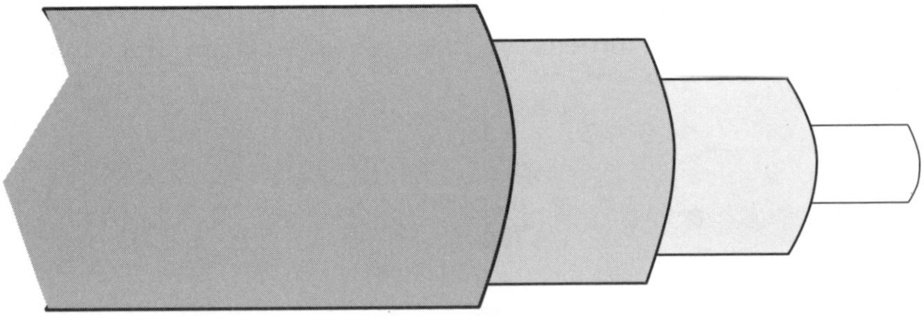

Figure 1-2
Coaxial cables handle high-frequency transmissions especially for TV.

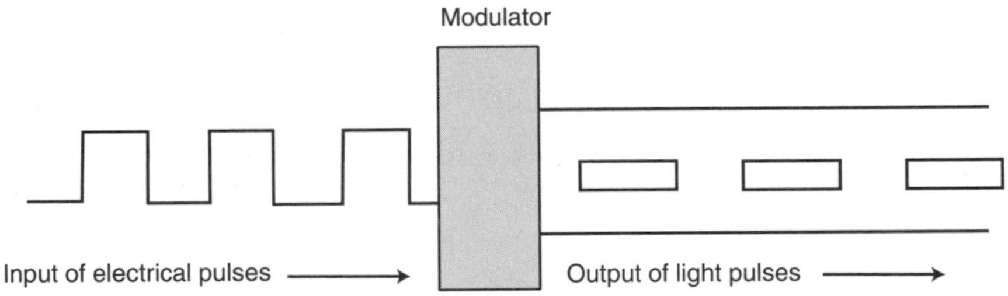

Figure 1-3
A modulator converts the electrical pulses into light pulses.

converts information from one form and back again, depending on the direction.

Laser (*l*ight *a*mplification by *s*imulated *e*mission of *r*adiation) A light source created by exciting atoms, causing them to emit light of a specific wavelength (frequency) in a focused beam. Think of a group of people who are all trying to lift a very heavy object, one at a time. Nothing happens because they individually have little strength. However, if they all get together and lift at the same time, their concentrated strength creates the result. Violà! They lift the heavy object. Doing the same thing with light, by exciting a single light particle individually, the beam is barely visible. However, if you concentrate and excite all the light particles at the same time, you create a very intense light beam.

Multimode fiber This type of fiber is used for hauling traffic over short distances, such as within a building. In optical fiber technology, multimode fiber is optical fiber that is designed to carry light rays on different paths or modes concurrently, each at a slightly different reflection angle within the optical fiber core. Multimode fiber transmission is used for relatively short distances because the modes tend to disperse over longer lengths (this is called *modal dispersion*). Multimode fiber has a larger center core than single-mode fiber. Figure 1-4 offers a comparison between multimode (thick) and single-mode fiber.

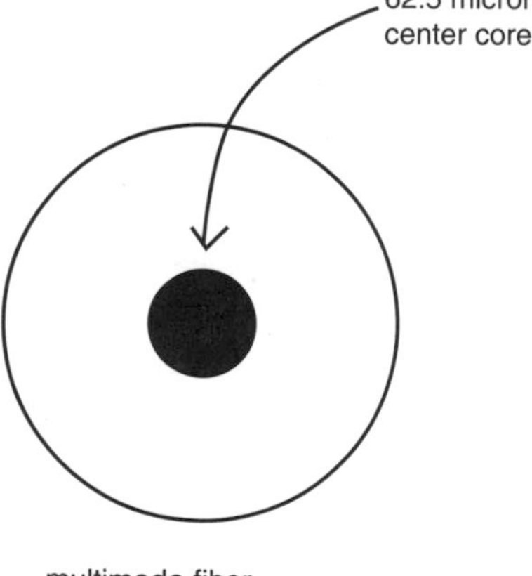

Figure 1-4 Comparison of the fiber types

Receiver A receiver is an electronic device that converts optical signals to electrical signals. Your antenna receives radio signals. A fiberoptic receiver—usually an electronics component called a *diode*—similarly receives light signals.

Single-mode fiber This type of fiber is used typically for long distances. Single-mode fiber is optical fiber that is designed for the transmission of a single ray or mode of light as a carrier and is used for long-distance signal transmission. Single-mode fiber has a much smaller core than multimode fiber.

Time-division multiplexing (TDM) A scheme in which numerous signals are combined for transmission on a single communications line or channel. Each signal is broken up into many segments, each having very short duration. The circuit that combines signals at the transmitting end of a communications link is known as a *multiplexer.* It accepts the input from each individual end user, breaks each signal into segments, and assigns the segments to the composite signal in a rotating, repeating sequence. The composite signal thus contains data from all the end users. At the other end of the long-distance cable, the individual signals are separated out by means of a circuit called a *demultiplexer* and routed to the proper end users. Think of a road system where you have a six-lane highway. Suddenly you come to a single-lane bridge. Protocol states that politely, each lane will in turn enable one vehicle to cross the bridge. Therefore, each input (lane) grabs the entire bandwidth (the lane) and passes its traffic (the cars) one at a time. This is shown in Figure 1-5 with the single-lane bridge analogy.

Transmitter Just as a radio transmitter sends out radio signals, an optical transmitter—usually a *light-emitting diode* (LED) or a laser—sends out optical signals.

Wavelength-division multiplexer (WDM) A fiberoptic device used to separate signals of different wavelengths carried on one fiber. Imagine two people talking on the phone at the same time, one with a deep male voice and the other with a high-pitched female voice. You can focus on one person or the other by listening for the deep sounds or the high ones. Similarly, several signals can be sent along an optical fiber using different frequencies (colors) of light. At the receiving end, the WDM "listens" to the different frequencies and separates the different signals. This is shown in Figure 1-6.

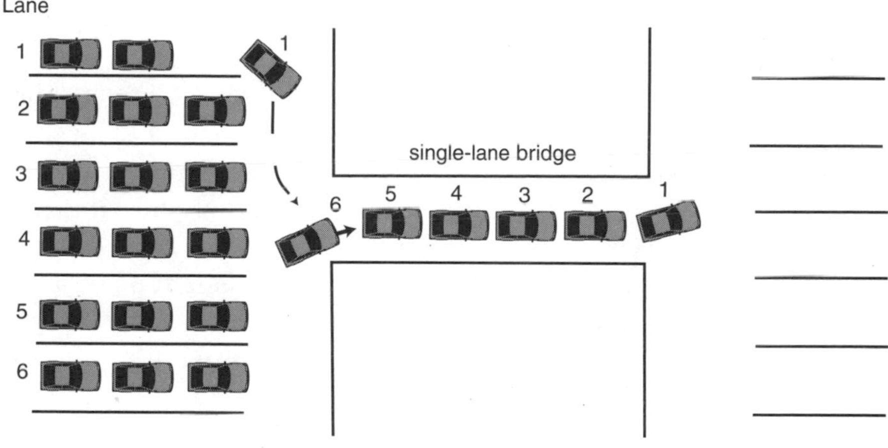

Figure 1-5 Time-division multiplexing enables each input to seize the entire bandwidth for a short duration in rotation.

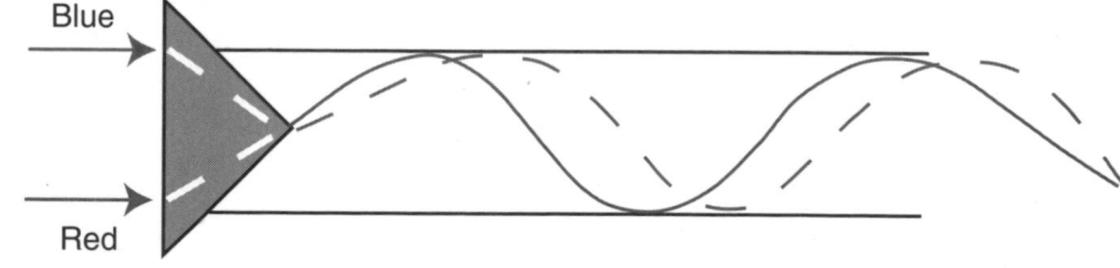

Figure 1-6 Wave-division multiplexing uses different wavelengths (frequencies) of light.

History of Optical and Fiber in Telecommunications

Let's take a trip down memory lane and discuss the use of optical communications in the telecommunications industry from its inception to the development of the various types and modes of fiberoptic systems. The beginning of optical communications is rather interesting. It has always been a belief that if you want to know where things are going, you have to understand where they have been. A little history will help.

Optical communications systems date back to the "optical telegraph" invented by French engineer Claude Chappe in the 1790s. He used a series of semaphores mounted on towers, with human operators relaying messages from one tower to the next. Of course, in order for this to work, the people had to be close enough together to visually see the other messenger's motions. This was not a great service for evening transmission and had some problems with weather conditions (for example, fog, heavy rain, heavy snow, and so on). The system depended on a line-of-sight operation; hence, the towers needed elevation to extend the coverage (albeit, a limited distance between repeaters) and close proximity.

However, the optical telegraph did perform better than hand-carried messages. Alas, by the mid-nineteenth century the system was replaced by the electric telegraph, leaving a scattering of "telegraph hills" as its legacy. The use of electrical transmissions was better suited for communications over distances.

In 1880, Alexander Graham Bell patented an optical telephone system, called the *photophone.* His earlier invention, the telephone, was far more practical and widespread. Bell dreamed of sending signals through the air. Unfortunately, the atmosphere did not carry transmitted light as reliably as wires carried electricity. Light was used for a few special applications, such as signaling between ships, but otherwise, optical communications did not achieve the expected results.

Later, a new technology began to take root that ultimately would solve the problem of optical transmission. It took a long time before it was finally adapted and accepted for voice and data communications. This new development relied on "total internal reflection" that confines light in a material surrounded by other materials with a lower refractive index, such as glass in air. Chronologically, the events leading up to the use of glass began with several steps, as shown in Table 1-1.

Today, more than 90 percent of long-distance data traffic in the United States is transmitted through fiberoptics. More than 15 1/2 million miles of fiberoptic cable has been installed already, all of it using the original design of Maurer, Keck, and Schultz.

Fiberoptics work by using light pulses traveling along glass fibers that are less than the thickness of a human hair to transmit data. These cables are much smaller than conventional copper wires and are able to transmit data at very high speeds, making them ideal for video and audio.

The Demand for Bandwidth

Meanwhile, telecommunications engineers were seeking ways of delivering more transmission bandwidth. Radio and microwave frequencies were already in heavy use. Therefore, the engineers looked to higher frequencies to carry traffic loads, which they expected to continue increasing with the growth of television and telephone traffic. Telephone companies thought video telephones lurked just around the corner and would escalate bandwidth demands even further. In 1964, during the World's Fair in New York, AT&T introduced an experimental model of the PicturePhone that required a T3 line[1] to transmit motion video across a telephone link (Figure 1-7). The other end of the connection was at Disneyland (in California). The commercial version was introduced in 1970 in Pittsburgh. Despite all the hopes and predictions, the cost and bandwidth demands of this device made it impractical. Moreover, the device was bulky and not user-friendly. However, the seed was planted for the future use of a video conferencing system that would transmit real-time pictures.

---

[1]A T3 is a multiplexed transmission that delivers 44.736 Mbps of information.

Table 1-1

Timeline for Development of Fiber-Based Systems

1840s	Daniel Collodon and Jacques Babinet showed that light could be guided along jets of water used for fountain displays.
1854	John Tyndall created interest in guided light by displaying light guided by a jet of water flowing from a tank.
1900s	Various inventors realized that bent quartz rods could carry light and patented them as dental illuminators.
1920s	John L. Baird and Clarence W. Hansell patented the idea of using arrays of hollow pipes or transparent rods to transmit images for television or facsimile systems.
1930s	Heinrich Lamm demonstrated image transmission through a bundle of optical fibers. He used his to look inside inaccessible parts of the body in a medical application. He also documented that he could transmit an image through a short bundle of fibers. However, the unclad fibers transmitted the images poorly.
1940s	Many doctors used illuminated Plexiglas tongue depressors.
1951	Holger Møller Hansen applied for a Danish patent on fiberoptic imaging. The Danish patent office denied his application, based on Baird and Hansell's patents.
1954	Abraham van Heel, Harold H. Hopkins, and Narinder Kapanyin separately announced imaging bundles. None of these people made bundles that could carry light very far, but their reports popularized the fiberoptics revolution. The primary innovation was made by van Heel. Early use of fiber was with "bare glass," with total internal reflection at a glass-air interface. Van Heel covered a bare fiber with a transparent cladding with a lower refractive index.
1956	The next step was the development of glass-clad fibers by Lawrence Curtiss while working part time on a project to develop an endoscope to examine the inside of the stomach.
1960	Glass-clad fibers had attenuation of about 1 decibel per meter, which worked well for medical imaging. This was much too high for use in telecommunications.
1970	Maurer, Keck, and Schultz made the first optical fiber with data losses low enough for wide use in telecommunications. It is now capable of transmitting data 65,000+ times faster than regular copper wire methods.

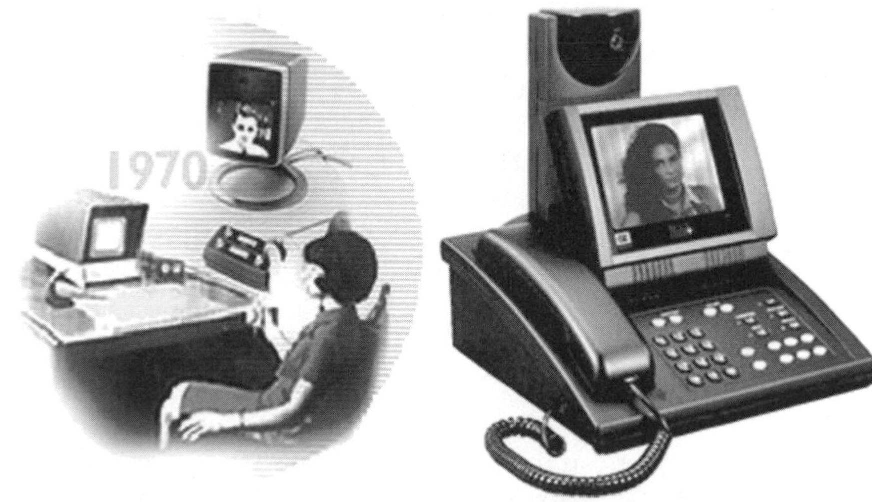

Source: AT&T

Source: Picturephone

Figure 1-7 The PicturePhone was introduced by AT&T in 1964 (AT&T). (For comparison, a 1970s Picture-Phone and a more recent one.)

Serious work on optical communications had to wait for the continuous-wave helium-neon laser. Although air is far more transparent at optical wavelengths than to millimeter waves, researchers soon found that rain, haze, clouds, and atmospheric turbulence limited the reliability of long-distance atmospheric laser links.

By 1965 it was clear that major technical barriers remained for both millimeter-wave and laser telecommunications. Millimeter waveguides had low loss, but only if they were kept perfectly straight; developers thought the biggest problem was the lack of adequate repeaters. Optical waveguides were proving to be a problem. Design groups at Bell Telephone Labs were working on a system of gas lenses to focus laser beams along hollow waveguides for long-distance telecommunications. However, most of the telecommunications industry thought the future belonged to millimeter waveguides.

Optical fibers had attracted some attention because they were analogous in theory to plastic dielectric waveguides used in certain microwave applications. In 1961, developers demonstrated the similarity by drawing fibers with cores so small they carried light in only one waveguide mode. However, virtually everyone considered fibers too "lossy" for communications; attenuation of a decibel per meter was fine for looking inside the body but not for long-haul communications. Telecommunications operated over much longer distances and required loss of no more than 10 or 20 decibels per kilometer.

At the Corning Glass Works (now Corning, Inc.), Robert Maurer, Donald Keck, and Peter Schultz started with fused silica, a material that can be made extremely pure but has a high melting point and a low refractive index. They made cylindrical performs by depositing purified materials from the vapor phase, adding carefully controlled levels of dopants to make the refractive index of the core slightly higher than that of the cladding without raising attenuation dramatically. In September 1970, they announced that they had made single-mode fibers with attenuation at the 633-nanometer helium-neon line below 20 decibels per kilometer.

The Corning breakthrough was among the most dramatic of many developments that opened the door to fiberoptic communications. In the same year, Bell Labs and a team at the Ioffe Physical Institute in Leningrad made the first semiconductor diode lasers capable of emitting a continuous wave at room temperature. Improvements over time allowed for dramatically less fiber loss, aided both by improved fabrication methods and by the shift to longer wavelengths where fibers have inherently lower attenuation.

Early single-mode fibers had cores several micrometers in diameter, and in the early 1970s, this bothered developers. They doubted it would be possible to achieve the micrometer-scale tolerances needed to couple light efficiently into the tiny cores from light sources or in splices or connectors. Not satisfied with the low bandwidth of step-index multimode fiber, they concentrated on multimode fibers with a refractive index gradient between core and cladding and core diameters of 50 or 62.5 microns. The first generation of telephone field trials in 1977 used such fibers to transmit light at 850 nanometers.

These first-generation systems could transmit light several kilometers without repeaters but were limited by loss of about 2 decibels per kilometer in the fiber. A second generation soon appeared using new lasers, which emitted at 1.3 microns. Fiber attenuation was as low as 0.5 decibel per kilometer, and pulse dispersion was somewhat lower than at 850 nanometers. Development of hardware for the first transatlantic fiber cable showed that single-mode systems were feasible, so when deregulation opened the long-distance phone market in the early 1980s, the carriers built national backbone systems of single-mode fiber with 1300-nanometer sources. This technology has spread into other telecommunications applications and remains the standard for most fiberoptic systems.

However, a new generation of single-mode systems found application in submarine cables and systems serving large numbers of subscribers. They operate at 1.55 microns. Fiber loss is 0.2 to 0.3 decibel per kilometer, enabling even longer repeater spacing. More importantly, erbium-doped optical fibers serve as optical amplifiers at this wavelength, avoiding the need for electro-optical regenerators.

Submarine cables with optical amplifiers operate at speeds up to 5 *gigabits per second* (Gbps). These can be upgraded from lower speeds simply by changing terminal electronics. Optical amplifiers also are attractive for fiber systems delivering the same signals to many terminals because the fiber amplifiers can compensate for losses in dividing the signals among many terminals.

The biggest challenge remaining for fiberoptics is economic. Today, telephone and cable television companies can cost-justify installing fiber links to remote sites serving tens to a few hundred customers. Terminal equipment remains too expensive to justify installing fiber all the way to the home, at least for now. Instead, cable and phone companies run twisted-pair wire or coaxial cable from optical network units along the side of the road to individual homes. Time will see how long this lasts, although many people believe that *fiber to the home* (FFTH) is already upon us.

Fiber Justification

Many reasons exist for the initial introduction of fiber, but some of the strongest reasons are as follows:

Bandwidth compared with copper Taken in bulk, it would take 33 tons of copper to transmit the same amount of information handled by 1/4 pound of optical fiber.

Strength The tinsel strength of the fiber is greater than that of steel.

Speed of transmission Fiberoptic networks operate at speeds up to 10 Gbps, as opposed to 1.54 *megabits per second* (Mbps) for copper. Soon, a fiberoptic system will be able to transmit the equivalent of an entire encyclopedia of information in 1 second. Fiber can carry information so fast that you could transmit three television episodes in 1 second.

Immunity to electrical and radiofrequency interference Fiberoptic cables have a greater resistance to electromagnetic noise from items such as radios, motors, or other nearby cables. Because optical fibers carry beams of light, they are free of electrical noise and interference.

Less weight in installation Fiberoptics have a greater capacity for information, which means that smaller cables can be used. An optical fiber cable the size of an electrical cord can replace a copper cable hundreds of times thicker.

How It Works

A glass tunnel through which light travels is created. When the light hits the cladding, it interacts with and reflects back into the core. Because of this design, the light can "bend" around curves in the fiber, and this makes it possible for the light to travel greater distances without having to be repeated. This is illustrated in Figure 1-8.

The light that travels along the fiber is made up of a binary code that pulses "on" and "off" and determines what information a given signal contains. The advantage of fiber is that these on/off pulses can be translated to video, computer, or voice data depending on the type of transmitter and receiver used.

A fiberoptic cable has two parts: the core (center or inside) and a cladding (outside covering). These two parts of the fiber work together to cause something called *total internal reflection*, which is the key to fiberoptics. The light beam is focused on the core of the fiber, and it begins its journey down the fiber. Soon, because of a turn in the fiber or the direction at which the light originally entered the

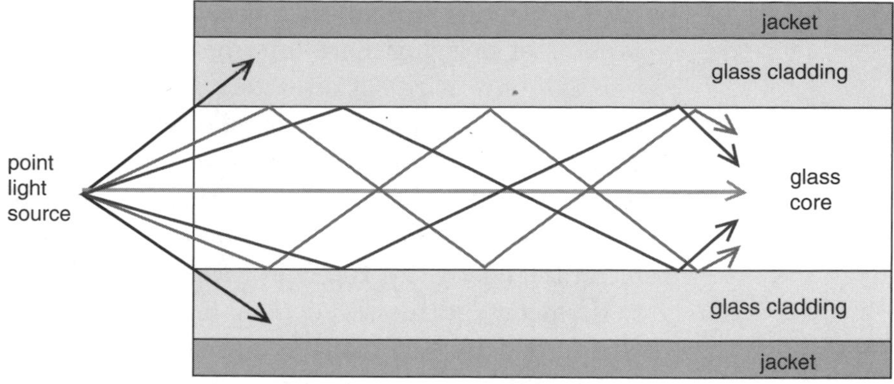

Source: Corning

Figure 1-8 Light travels down the glass.

fiber, the light reaches the outside edge of the core. Normally, it would simply exit the fiber at this point, but this is where the cladding helps. When the light hits the cladding (which is made of a material selected especially because it reacts differently to light than the core material), instead of going on straight, it reflects. This creates a tunnel effect in which the light bounces its way down the fiber until it exits at the other end of the fiber.

Facts about Fiberoptics

Everyone has a story to tell when asked about fiber. Many of the myths and facts get confused and confusing. Thus we should understand just why everyone is so excited about the use of fiberoptics. Let's start with the facts first:

1. Optical fiber will be the backbone of the information superhighway, transporting voice, video, and data to businesses, schools, hospitals, and homes. Demands for information continue to increase so much that the maximum available transport rates are doubling approximately every two years. Because of this rapid growth, electronic functions in communications networks eventually will be replaced by photonic functions, which provide higher information-carrying capacity.

2. Fiberoptics are needed because coaxial television cables are capable of carrying more information than copper wire (unshielded twisted-pair wire). Computer and telephone companies need something with which to compete with the CATV companies. This also means that the fiber wires will allow the telephone companies to offer newer services. A new service being offered to consumers known as *very-high-bit-rate digital subscriber line* (VDSL) will bring telephony, TV, Internet access, and high-speed future services to the door. Yet this will depend on fiber to really achieve the result. Currently, the telephone companies are using a *hybrid fiber and coaxial* (HFC) service to offer VDSL.

3. Currently, all new undersea cables are made of optical fibers. This is crucial to the economic installation of high-density transmission systems. The cost of the fiber as opposed to the cost of copper makes the undersea cable more attractive and readily available. Look at the cost reductions in getting a trans-Atlantic circuit since the introduction of fiber. Costs literally dove down to more affordable communications for corporate connectivity internationally.

4. Many believe that 98 percent of copper wire will be replaced by fiberoptic cable, including at the local loop to the residence. This belief is one we can all take to the bank. Copper has many problems in distribution and maintenance. Fiber becomes far more economical. Logic, therefore, points to the deployment of more fiber to every facet of communications. Fiberoptic cable installed in place of copper wire that already requires replacing is less expensive. Because it only needs repeaters to amplify the signals every six miles instead of every mile for copper, the cost of installation is much less.

5. Optical fiber phone lines cannot be bugged or tapped easily. If one were to attempt to tap into the fiber, the cable would be broken in the process. This would trip alarms on the link and cause maintenance and surveillance personnel to take notice. Moreover, to rejoin the cable is more difficult, eliminating the novice from the process of tapping into a fiber system. By breaking into the cable, the light flow is disrupted (Figure 1-9). By splicing the cable improperly, loss and transmission impairments become highly

problematic. Actually, the light's reflections and refractions can be changed significantly, causing character changes in the cable. Therefore, only skilled personnel today can splice the cables properly.

6. A fiber is thinner than a human hair. Fibers are 8 to 10 microns or 50 to 62.5 microns thick. One micron (1 μm) is 1/250th the thickness of a human hair. This thickness (thinness) represents the advantages of the glass itself. It is lighter and easier to handle. It is immune to the mechanical problems of copper. It carries thousands of times the information of copper wire.

7. As radio spectrum becomes more scarce and the need for more information-carrying capacity increases, many utility companies are finding it cost-effective to install fiberoptic communications networks.

Fiber Myths

Many common misconceptions about optical fiber technology slip into any discussion. Optical fiber, optical systems, optical networks, optical technology—What does this "opto" jargon mean? It means optoelectronic technology: the transmission of voice, data, and video using pulses of light instead of electricity. Because we discussed the facts earlier, we should now clear up some of the misconceptions related to fiber and consider "the facts" about fiber's technical merits and capabilities. The myths include the following:

1. *Fiber is the most expensive wiring option.* Actually, fiber is exceptionally cost competitive when compared with coaxial cable and copper twisted-pair cable for most applications. Over the long term, fiber is actually the least expensive option.

When considering fiber, it is important to look at the total picture. Factors to consider when projecting network costs are the life of the network, the life of the system, the need to upgrade the system for future capacity requirements, and the possibility of generating revenue by leasing reserve capacity to other carriers. Compared

Figure 1-9 Breaking the fiber disrupts the flow of light along the cable.

with copper twisted-pair cable, optical communications systems exhibit a much lower *bit error rate* (BER) while operating at much higher data rates. As a result, data transmission is both faster and more reliable over optical fiber systems. In fact, installing extra fiber provides a bigger bang for the installation buck by preventing disruption and additional expense when it is time to upgrade. Optical fiber is not *hardware-dependent,* which means that fiber systems can be upgraded as new transmission technologies become available.

The biggest chunk of new network costs is usually installation, so it makes sense to take advantage of the opportunity to meet tomorrow's requirements by installing fiber today.

2. *Unshielded twisted-pair cable can be used for high-speed data applications.* When you transmit above 100 Mbps, fiber is the only medium that can be used confidently. As a stopgap measure, some high-speed copper wire systems are being offered today. However, these systems may require rewiring with special wire, such as a specially rated version of shielded twisted-pair cable. Even with

this special copper wire, questions still remain as to whether the system can transmit 100 Mbps over typical distances.

3. *Only high-speed systems need fiber.* Fiber can be used effectively for any system. When demands dictate, new electronics can be installed as upgrades to higher speeds. Error-free transmission capability is a critical aspect of any modern communications system. Many present-day and virtually all future communications networks will require the extensive bandwidth and flexibility of optical fiber.

4. *Fiber is highly technical and very difficult to handle.* Installing fiberoptic networks is predictable and standardized. Because fiber cable is smaller, lighter, and more flexible than other types of cable, some installers feel that it is actually easier to install fiber.

5. *Fiber is extremely fragile.* Glass fiber is actually stronger than steel. With an average tensile breaking strength of 600,000 pounds per square inch, fiber exceeds the strength requirements of all of today's communications applications.

Types of Fibers

The differences among fibers are their core sizes (the light-carrying region of the fiber). Multimode cable is made of multiple strands of glass fibers and has a much larger core than single-mode fiber.

Multimode cables have a combined diameter in the 50- to 100-micron range. Each fiber in a multimode cable is capable of carrying a different signal independent from those on the other fibers in the cable bundle. These larger core sizes generally have greater bandwidth and are easier to couple and interconnect. They enable hundreds of rays of light propagate through the fiber simultaneously. Multimode fiber today is used primarily in premise applications, where transmission distances are less than 2 kilometers.

Single-mode fiber is a single strand of glass that has a much smaller core, enabling only one mode of light to propagate through the core. Single-mode fiber has a higher bandwidth than multimode and for this reason, is the ideal transmission medium for many applications. The standard single-mode fiber core is approximately 8 to 10 microns in diameter. Because of its greater information-carrying capacity, single-mode fiber typically is used for longer distances and higher-bandwidth applications.

Although it may appear that multimode fibers have higher information-carrying capacity, this is not the case. Single-mode fibers retain the integrity of each light pulse over a longer distance, which enables more information to be transmitted. This is why multimode fibers are used for shorter distances and more often in premises at corporate locations (such as, high-rise offices, campus environments, and so on).

An Application of Fiberoptics

How are fiberoptics used in every day life? A basic telephone conversation can be used as an analogy for this discussion. In the North American telecommunications system, a call is transmitted from one end through an electric cable (copper) to an encoder, which transmits a signal through a fiberoptic (glass) cable. It then travels through a repeater, back through the cable, into a decoder and through an electric cable (copper) into the phone line on the other end. This transition is shown in Figure 1-10 for the flow of communications.

The sound waves that your voice generates become waves of electricity in the mouthpiece of your telephone. Rather than electricity flowing through copper wire to the final destination, fiberoptics enables electricity to pass through the encoder, which measures the waves of electricity 8000 times each second. The encoder then converts these waves into on/off pulses of light (operating as invisible infrared light). The pulses are digitized, enabling them to be read by the telephone system. The digitized message is received at the decoder. The decoder converts the laser light back into electricity. These electrical waves are changed into the sound that you hear on the phone. This same process works not only for the telephone but also for other sources that transmit data (such as, computers, televisions, and so on).

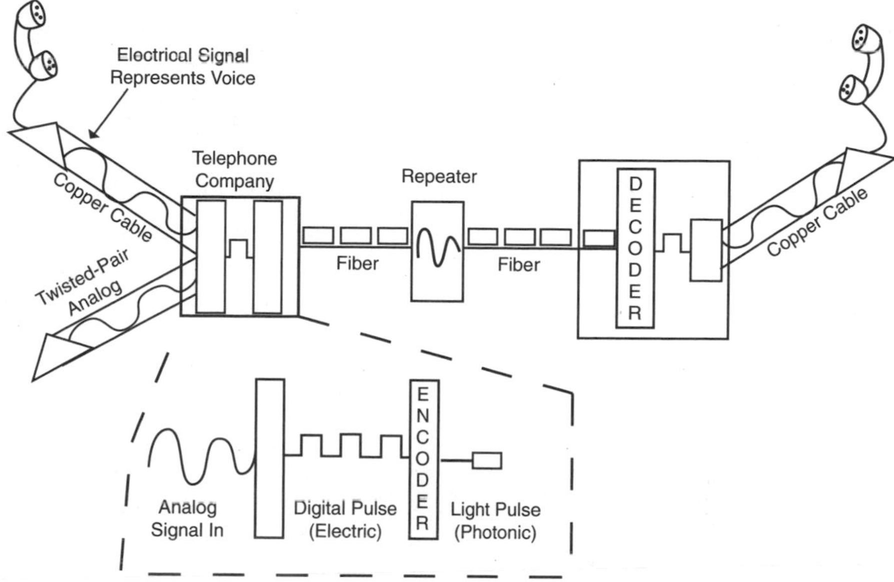

Figure 1-10 The flow of a call through the North American telecommunications system

The amount of data that can be carried is directly proportional to the transmission systems' coders/decoders used and the equipment in the middle. The higher the transport rates, the more calls or the more data that can be carried. The fiber systems use combinations of frequency- and time-division multiplexing. *Time-division multiplexing* (TDM) is used when sampling the input from telephones or computer terminals. Using this clocking (sampling) rate of 8,000 samples per second, multiplexed signals can be received from multiple inputs. From there, *frequency-division multiplexing* (FDM)[2] is used to combine the light beams operating at a certain wavelength on the fibers themselves. This is shown in Figure 1-11, where the combination of TDM and FDM is illustrated.

As mentioned earlier, AT&T Bell Labs scientists became interested in light wave communication in the mid-1960s, when it became

[2]This is also called wave-division multiplexing because different signals are multiplexed at different wavelengths together.

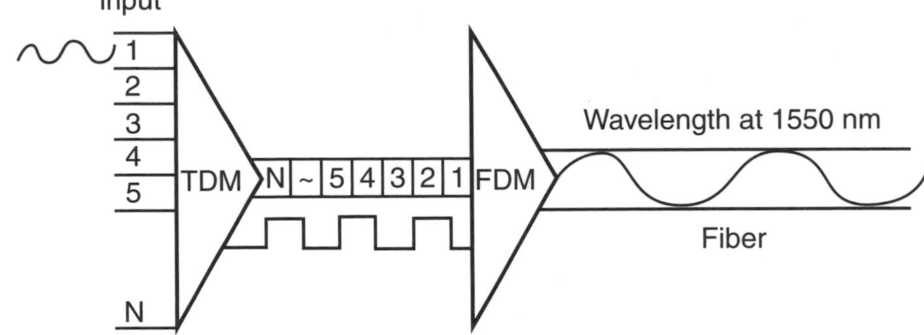

Figure 1-11 The combination of TDM and FDM on fiber

apparent that light waves had an enormous capacity for carrying information and were immune to electrical interference. Advances in lasers, light-emitting diodes, repeaters, connectors, photodetectors, and glass fibers in the following decades—and the realization that they could be fabricated and installed as integrated components—led to the installation of the first light-wave system in an operating telephone company in 1977.

This installation was the world's first light-wave system to provide a full range of telecommunications services—voice, data, and video-over a public switched network. The system, installed over about 1.5 miles under downtown Chicago, used glass fibers that each carried the equivalent of 672 voice channels (a T3).

Growth in Fiber-Based Systems

More than 15.5 million miles of fiber had been installed worldwide by the end of 1997. Construction continues growing at an endless pace that should reach 30 million miles by the end of 2001. China and the Far East market is expected to grow three times during the period of 2000-2003.

The services using fiberoptic systems are provided by all the telecommunications providers/carriers. The long-distance companies (AT&T, MCI/WorldCom, British Telecom) have been using fiberoptics for decades. Many others, such as the competitive local exchange carriers (CLECs), CATV companies, electric utility companies, and the incumbent local exchange carriers (ILECs),[3] are relatively new in this portion of the industry. The regional Bell operating companies (RBOCs) have a great deal of fiber in place within their major operating cities. They are now looking to expand their capacity as cheaply as possible because of the embedded copper plant that is rapidly becoming a liability. The newer carriers (like the CLECs) are planning to build networks based on new fiberoptics that are significantly less expensive than those used by their competitors. Their goal is to enter the market with a sufficiently attractive cost per minute for voice calls and cost per bit for data transmission to attract users to them. The cost per minute has long been the measure of data and voice transmissions.

A T3 operating at nearly 45 Mbps costs from US$80,000 to US$100,000 per month from the East Coast to West Coast. This makes the cost of transmission very reasonably priced when all things are compared. Let's look at the overall cost per minute for a 45-Mbps link. At US$80,000 per month, this can be priced as shown in Table 1-2 to keep things straight.

One can see the differences by using the T3, for example. However, prior to having the fiber-based networks, the carriers charged much more for the service on copper. Using an analogy of those costs, the costs would be far more dramatic, as shown in Table 1-3 for a copper-based architecture in the past. In this scenario, using a copper cable plant, the cost per T3 from East Coast to West Coast on the carrier networks varied between $560,000, $280,000, and $175,000 per month based on variables of length of agreement, cities connected, and so on.

---

[3] The Bell Systems LECs are more experienced in using fiber since the 1970s and 1980s.

Table 1-2

Comparing the Costs of Using a Fiber Link for T3 Access

T3 Line East to West Coast	Cost per Item
Per month	$80,000
Per day based on a 20-workday month	$ 4,000
Per hour based on a 8-hour workday	$ 500
Per minute at 60 minutes per hour	$ 8.33
Per second at 60 seconds per minute	$ 0.14
Per bit at 45 million bits per second	$ 0.000000003+

Table 1-3

Comparing the Cost of Using a Copper-Based T3 Access Link

Item	@ $560,000/ Month	@ $280,00/ Month	@ $175,000/ Month
Cost per day with 20-day month	$28,000	$14,000	$8,750
Cost per hour with 8-hour day	$3,500	$1,750	$1,094
Cost per minute	$58.34	$29.17	$18.23
Cost per second	$0.972	$0.49	$0.30
Cost per bit	$0.000000021	$0.000000012	$0.000000007

The Emergence of Wavelength-Division Multiplexing

As early as 1988, *synchronous optical networking* (SONET) and *synchronous digital hierarchy* (SDH) were the hottest discussion topic in terms of the emerging backbone fiber standards of all future telecommunications networks. Both SONET and SDH were seen as the panacea for carriers in developing multiplexing standards and techniques to reinforce the network. In 1997, *wavelength-division multiplexing* (WDM) suddenly became the big-ticket item. Managers, designers, and engineers alike saw the benefit that multiple wavelengths could add to the capacity of fiber-based networks. Many colors of light[4] increase the capacity of the installed fiber to 320 Gbps and in the future 1.6 *terabits per second* (Tbps)[5] and beyond. Theoretical limits of fiber today are around 30 to 40 Tbps, but with some changes, in the future we may see 100-Tbps possibilities.

SONET and SDH standards were designed originally for the TDM systems prevalent in the 1980s. Using TDM, a data stream at a higher bit rate is generated directly by multiplexing lower-bit-rate channels. High-capacity TDM systems operate at levels up to OC-192, or 10 Gbps. The problem comes with moving to higher bandwidth speeds at OC-768 and above. Current TDM equipment has trouble operating at these higher speeds.

WDM, in contrast, can carry multiple data bit rates, enabling multiple channels to be carried on a single fiber. The technique quite literally uses different colors of light down the same fiber to carry different channels of information, which are then separated out at the distant end by a receiver that identifies each color. All optical networks employing WDM with add/drop multiplexers and cross-connects permit this. Dense WDM (DWDM) systems multiplex 32 or more wavelengths in the 1550-nanometer range, increase capacity on existing fiber, and are data-rate-transparent.

DWDM ring systems can be connected with *Asynchronous Transfer Mode* (ATM) switches and *Internet Protocol* (IP) routers. ATM networks are expected to use SONET/SDH physical-layer interfaces with OC-12 add/drop multiplexers. ATM can carry voice, video, and data communications in the same transport and switching equipment.

---

[4]Although I refer to many colors of light, the two primary lasers used are red and blue, with variations on the wavelength of each. Variations can be considered like shades of red and shades of blue.

[5]Terabits per second is trillions of bits per second.

In the future, optical technology and advanced optical switching technologies will emerge that extend the capability of the optical layer. These technologies will include optical switching for recovery from failures as well as expansion of the add/drop multiplexing function. The first optical cross-connect systems will route a particular wavelength from one fiber route to another without conversion back to an electronic form.

CHAPTER 2

Basic Fiberoptics Technologies

As explained in Chapter 1, "Introduction to Optical Communications," fiberoptics is not new. However, the field has been ignited by several new uses and applications of older technologies. The telephone companies were deploying the basic fiber systems in their local architectures and then moved into *Synchronous Optical Networking* (SONET) architectures in local and metropolitan areas. We also learned that the long-distance carriers were moving toward a robust networking strategy using fiber and SONET in support of their networks. Corporate users also began migrating to fiber inside the walls of their office buildings on *local area networks* (LANs) or *campus area networks* (CANs). The issues that inevitably surface when discussing the use of fiber include

- Cost per foot of the fiber as opposed to copper-cable plant
- Cost of the electronics
- Cost of the repeaters and amplifiers
- Difficulty of installation

Each of these issues was, in its own right, a valid concern. The cost issues were significant several years ago. However, technology matures, and mass production begins driving the prices down to more palatable and financially justifiable levels.

Suppose that we were asked by management to rewire a building today. The first question we have to satisfy is: How much bandwidth do we think we are going to need in the backbone of the network, and what demands will exist to the desktop? The answer is going to be as complex as the question. Several congruent technologies can satisfy most of our day-to-day needs today. However, whether they can meet the demands for the future becomes the tough part. An example of this is the use of copper unshielded twisted-pair wires to the desktop. Clearly, we started out with the use of the different categories of wire to satisfy our immediate needs to the end-user terminal device. Summarily, Table 2-1 presents the original design around the categories of wire for use in a building infrastructure and the speeds that are supported. This table is a summary of the systems in place. However, several deviations and methods by which improvements can be made do exist. The assumptions used in the cable specification were that the wires would be as follows:

- Unshielded twisted pairs of wire (although you can use shielded)
- 100-ohm (100-Ω) cables
- Solid conductors in the cabling (you can use stranded wires, but solid conductor is more available)
- 24-gauge wire (24 AWG)
- 100 meters (328 feet)

Using these specifications, we then used the appropriate category of wire to satisfy our need, as shown in the table.

As one can see, the use of the wire was limited to specific speeds and applications within the LAN. When the industry decided to extend the speeds and the boundaries of the LAN into a CAN, the cabling systems became part of the problem. As a result, two different competing techniques emerged to satisfy the demand: FDDI, which supports 100-Mbps bursty data across a much larger area

Table 2-1

Comparing What Data Rates Can Be Achieved Through Categories of Wire

Category of Wire	Speeds Supported and Design Techniques
1	*Plain old telephone service* (POTS) and EIA-232 data*
2	4 *megabits per second* (Mbps) of bursty data as found in Token Ring LANs
3	10 Mbps of bursty data as found in Ethernet (10 base T)
4	16 Mbps of bursty data in Token Ring, 20 Mbps of bursty data as found in ARCNet, and now 25.6 Mbps ATM to the desktop
5+	100 Mbps bursty data as found in the fast Ethernet standard (100 base T) and copper data distributed interface (CDDI)† and now 155 Mbps ATM to the desktop

*EIA-232 (or RS-232) was a specification that satisfied 19.2 *kilobits per second* (Kbps) of data at 50 feet but was extended through the use of category 1 wires.

†This was a copper equivalent to the fiber distributed data interface (FDDI).

using a multimode fiber, and the 100 base F, which is the Fast Ethernet standard on multimode fiber in a backbone. Now the 1,000 base F standard (Gigabit Ethernet) is supported on multimode or single-mode fiber in the campus. This adds a new dimension to the use of fiber because the speeds are ever-increasing, yet the corporate user has other issues to handle. The selection of a wiring standard is usually based on a specific point in time. For example, 5 years ago, one may have selected Category 3 wiring as a norm because this was the standard for Ethernet cabling at the time. However, in a matter of months, Category 5 wires appeared, causing heartburn for administrators who had installed the older version. In 1996 and 1997, the use of 100 base T wiring became far more prevalent. This meant that the building that was prewired for lower-speed networks was not conducive to supporting the newer high-speed standard. The choices were limited:

1. Use only 10 base T on these wires.
2. Rewire the building to support the higher speeds at 100 and now 1,000 Mbps.

Figure 2-1 shows the growth rates for 100-Mbps Ethernet. This figure shows the percentage of new installations that use the 100-

Figure 2-1
Growth of the 100 base T standard

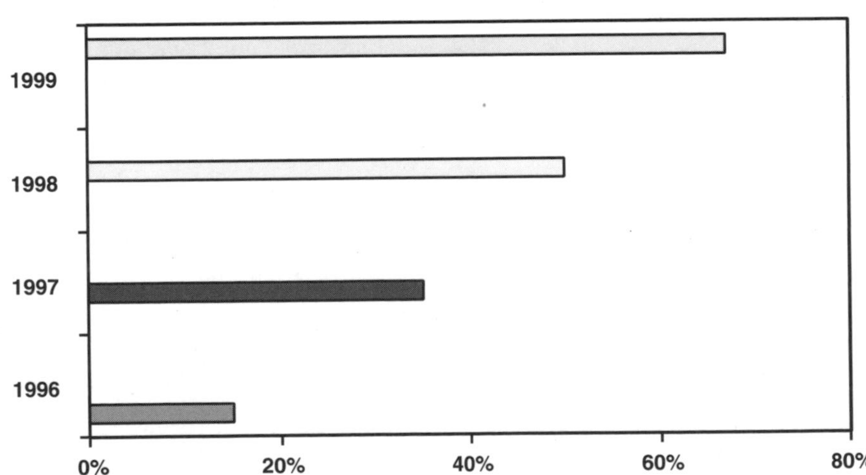

Mbps standards. In newer PCs, 10/100-Mbps n*etwork interface cards* (NICs) have been installed because of uncertainty as to what the end user's wiring supports. This will change over time.

Just as the industry started to accept use of the 100-Mbps standards for Ethernet at the desktop, the next step in the evolution arrived in 1998. Dubbed the Gigabit Ethernet (1,000 Mbps), the initial standard specified the use of fiber. The industry needed to regroup and develop a new category of wire to support 1,000 Mbps. This appeared in a higher-value (Category 6 or 7) wiring structure. However, the same problem surfaced. If the user wants support for the higher data rates, then rewiring will be necessary to the stations that will use the gigabit speeds. Recognizing this problem, the *Telecommunications Industry Association* (TIA) and the *Electronics Industry Association* (EIA) developed work-around specifications so as to use existing in-building wiring (Categories 3 and 5). This is not a specific standard to support the faster data rates. Figure 2-2 illustrates the expected growth of Gigabit Ethernet in the corporate environment.

Unfortunately, when the 10-Gbps Ethernet emerges as a standard in the new millennium, the same issues will surface. The wiring in place will not support the speeds, and some work-around techniques will be required. Creative solutions are the mainstream these days.

Fiber in the backbone and to the desktop may well be a better solution. Although the cost of the NIC for a workstation is more

Figure 2-2 Growth of Gigabit Ethernet

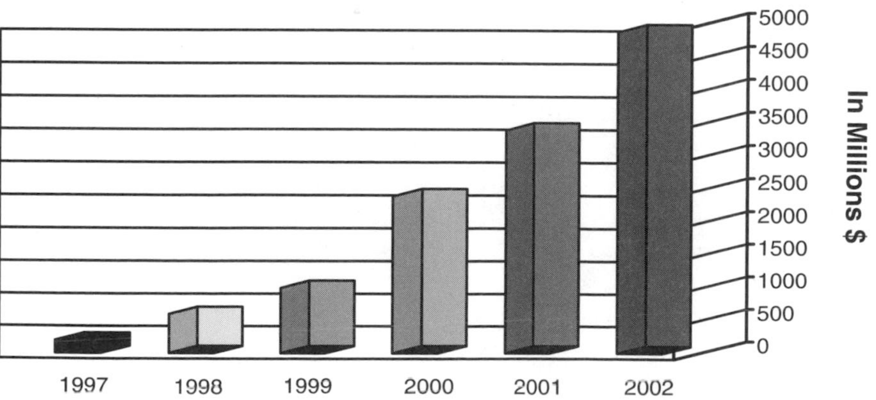

expensive and the cost of fiber to the desk is going to be higher, the need to rewire every time a new speed is achieved can be minimized. Over the longer term, the use of fiber to the desk is likely a less expensive solution. Unfortunately, local management does not see this point yet. Therefore, buildings continue to be wired with copper and rewired when speed increases are needed. Single-mode fiber to the desk will support speeds of up to 10 Gbps today without any *wavelength-division multiplexing* (WDM). Think of the possibilities *with* WDM.

Figure 2-3 illustrates the growth in capacity of fiberoptics by wavelength and the capacity potential for each of the standards-based services.

What About the Local Carrier?

If, on the other hand, a telecommunications carrier decides to build out infrastructure in the local community, the issue will be less complex. Because carriers serve many more users and charge for the

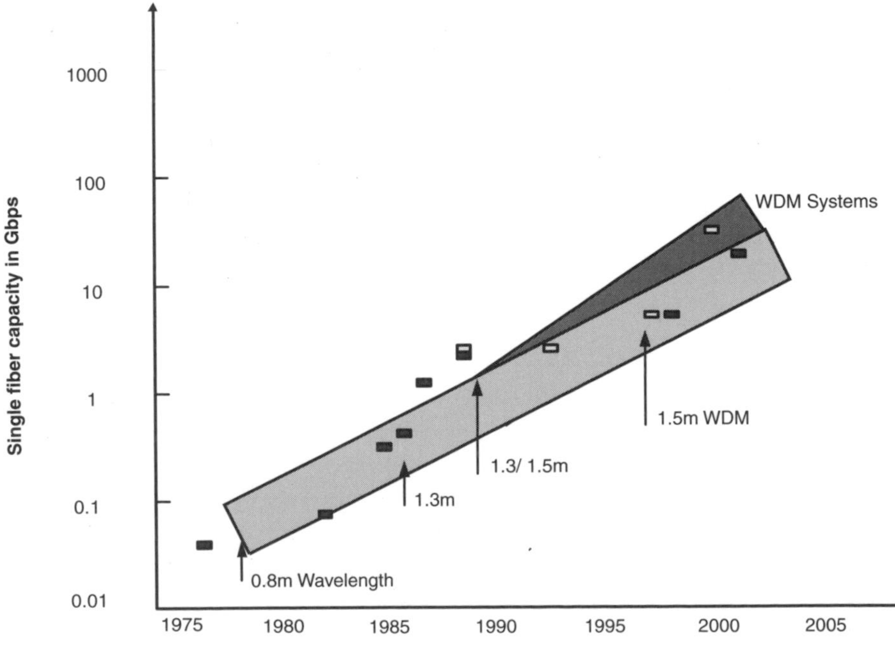

Figure 2-3 Growth and capacities of fiberoptics over time (Lucent Technologies)

usage, the cost issues are far less critical. For years now, carriers have chosen to install fiber whenever possible in their backbone. The issue they faced was which type of fiber to use: single mode or multimode. They have pretty well settled on single mode in all new installations.

The Fiber Concept

It is important for nonengineering professionals to understand the basics of fiberoptics and the use of multiplexing. However, it is not the intent of this book to make the reader an engineering wizard. Nevertheless, some technically simplified concepts are required to "talk the talk." First, it is necessary to understand the basic components of a fiber-based system. The basic pieces in an optical communications system are shown in Figure 2-4 as a means of explaining the layout.

The assumption is that at a sender's end, a serial bit stream in its electrical form is sent from the sending device to a modulator. The modulator, as shown in Chapter 1, is the change agent that will convert the electrical signal into an optical (photonic) signal. The modulator encodes the data for the fibers and sends the data to the laser or a *light-emitting diode* (LED), which focuses the light as a beam on

Figure 2-4 Optical communications system layout

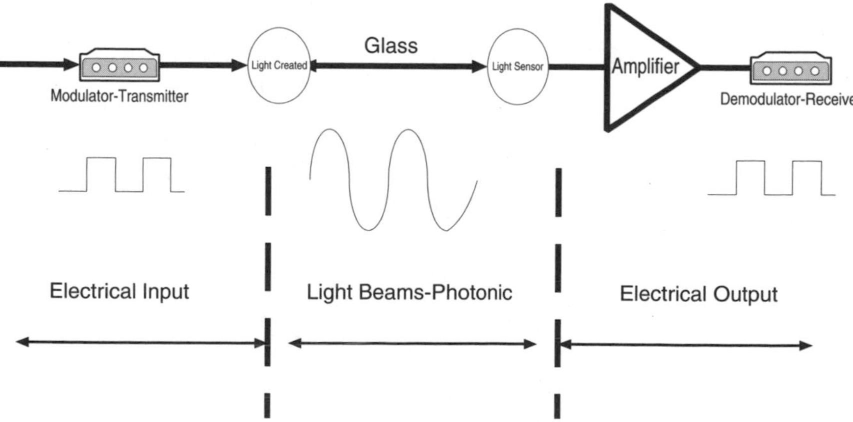

the fiber. This light beam travels down the glass. Along the way, several things could happen to the light beam:

1. It could be resisted and lose its signal strength (it gets weaker; weaker means not as bright).
2. It can be dispersed (spread out, making it less intense; spread covers a wider area; less focus is a good way to think about it).

Although these two statements sound the same, they are different.

As the signal is processed, a detector at the far end sees the light and converts it back into an electrical signal. The signal is amplified and given to a demodulator (which has a digital detector) that decodes the information back into an electrical bit stream that is passed to the end terminal. This is not a complicated system. However, the pieces must all work together to produce the desired effect of high-speed communications. At the input, the information must be processed fast enough to create the photonic output at a rate of speed consistent with the fiber. The receiving device must extract the data equally fast, otherise bottlenecks occur.

Transmitting the Signal on the Glass

As light is transmitted on the fiber, there is a common goal to understand: What kind of light are we sending? Light exists at many different frequencies (colors). The frequencies (you will hear people refer to this as *wavelength*) range from visible to invisible light in the ultraviolet range. Figure 2-5 lists the frequencies of the spectrum.

When we use these light waves for transmitting in a communications system, we use the infrared spectrum, as shown in Figure 2-5. The light is invisible and can be created with a LED or an infrared laser. Loss in the glass will be a concern; therefore, infrared is a better choice for transmission. This obviously dispels the myth that you can see the light inside the fiber, because all the communications systems today use invisible light frequencies. Ah, the glory of technology!

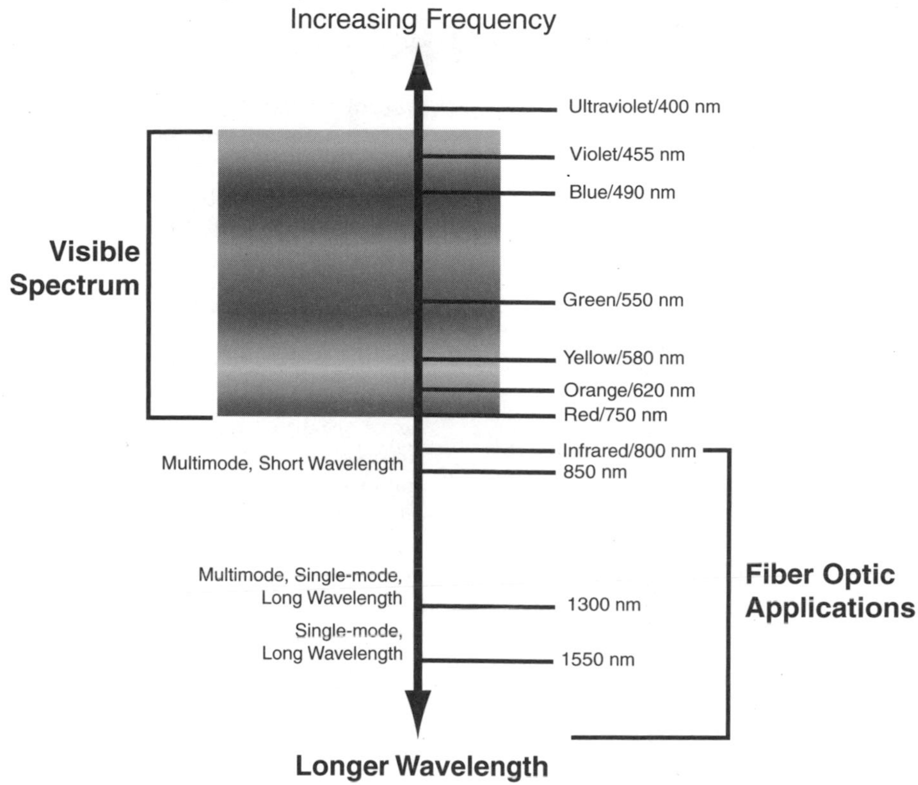

Figure 2-5 The light spectrum used in fiber (Corning)

When a short blast (pulse) of light is sent down the glass, it has the problems mentioned earlier. The light can be subject to several impairments acting on it at the same time. The light beam actually degrades quickly. The received light beam will be different from the one that entered the glass initially. It may be weaker (signal loss), smeared out across a wider frequency (time is lengthened), or dispersed (spreading it across a larger spectrum). Each of these characteristics will have an impact on the reception of the information. The impairments are shown in Table 2-2 with a summary of each of the major concerns.

Looking at the frequency spectrum, a window of frequencies is used to produce the signal in the normal operating wavelength, as

Table 2-2

Problems and Impairments Found in Fiber Systems

Impairment	Discussion
Attenuation	Like an electrical signal moving on copper, the light pulse will attenuate on the fiber. The signal gets weaker because a certain portion of the light is absorbed by the glass. The actual frequency determines the amount and speed of absorption. Attenuation is stated in the form of *decibels* (dB).
Dispersion	When the pulse is sent down the fiber, it spreads out during the transmission. The short pulse becomes longer and joins with the pulse behind it. This makes it difficult (or impossible) for the receiving equipment to separate the pulses. There are different forms of dispersion, including *Material*—A range of frequencies is produced by the LED and laser. The materials used to create the fiber cable use different refractive indices; therefore, each wavelength moves at a different speed inside the fiber cable. This means that some wavelengths arrive before others and a signal pulse disperses over a broader range. This is also called *smearing*. *Waveguide*—The center core creates the waveguide (it guides the wave inside the core). The shape and the refractive index inside the core can create the dispersion or spreading of the pulse. *Modal*—Multimode fiber creates many different modes (paths) for the light to travel down the fiber. The length of the path can be different depending on the mode taken, meaning the light beams may take different paths of differing lengths. Portions of the light may arrive out of sequence. This means that the spreading over time causes the fiber receiver to have to deal with this. The longer the route, the bigger is the problem.
Noise	Modal noise is usually associated with multimode fiber. The mismatch of the connectors and the modes in a cable can cause loss of some of the modes. This causes signal loss, which is defined as noise.
Polarization	Optical fibers in normal systems are cylindrical and symmetric. Light traveling on the fiber can change in its polarity (positive to negative). At the higher speeds, this may pose problems.

Table 2-3

Comparison of Frequency Windows and Operating Wavelength Used

Window of Frequencies	Normal Wavelength Used
800-900 nanometers (nm)	850 nm
1250-1350 nm	1310 nm
1500-1600 nm	1550 nm

described previously. The common wavelengths used in fiber systems today are shown in Table 2-3. This table indicates that a transmitter operating at 850 nanometers will produce a range of frequencies between 800 and 900 nanometers, opening the door for dispersion. The same is true with the other operating frequencies.

Types of Fiber

Already the discussion has led to differences in the actual glass. There is fiberoptic, and there is fiberoptic. The characteristics of the glass differ based on materials and manufacturer. Not all fibers are the same. When first introduced, fiber quality was less than that produced by current technology. Moreover, the chemicals used to produce the glass change the characteristics. The original glass was very "lossy" and barely suited to use in communications systems. The first fiber systems in telecommunications networks produced losses in the range of 20 decibels per kilometer. Improvements in the 1980s created glass that reduced the loss to 1 decibel per kilometer. Newer fibers have losses of 0.2 decibels per kilometer or better. The chemicals (dopants) added to the glass change the refractive index of the glass, creating more absorption, which is a problem.

Fiber is produced using silicon dioxide (glass). Silica is good for the lower end of the operating frequencies, in the range of 800 to 1,100 nanometers. Other forms of fiber use a germanium dioxide mixture in the glass. This fiber type operates better in the range of 1,300 to 1,500 nanometers. Thus one can extrapolate that the quality of the various glasses is different and that by using different glass compositions, better results can be achieved. The dopants added to the glass mix create higher speeds and less loss.

Fiber Cable Types

The differences between the fibers come down to multimode and single-mode arrangement. However, stepped-index cables use a different form of composition to create a fiber cable. The three forms of cables are

1. Multimode stepped index
2. Multimode graded index
3. Single mode

Multimode Stepped Index Fiber When fiber was first being used in the communications area, the technology was still developing. Multimode fiber was used as a means of carrying communications signals on glass more reliably. Multimode fiber, as the name implies, has multiple paths by which the light can reach the end of the fiber. Single-mode fiber, on the other hand, has only one path over which the light can travel to get to the other end. Using a large piece (chunk) of pure glass, the developers extruded the fiber into much thinner glass strands.

Multimode fibers are thicker glass by today's standards. These multimode fibers were developed in two different types, step index and graded index, both operating differently. Figure 2-6 illustrates a multimode fiber using a step index mode. In this case, the glass is very thick (by today's standards) at the center core (approximately 120 to 400 microns[1]). The thickness of the glass is crucial to the pas-

[1]A micron or micrometer is one-millionth of a meter.

sage of the light and the path used to get from one end to the other. The step index is the thickest form of fiber, using a core that is 120 to 400 microns thick; the light is both refracted and reflected inside the encased fiber. This is the concept developed in the early days, using total internal reflection. The center core, because of the density of the glass, refracts the light at different angles. At the same time, an outer cladding on the glass is used to reflect the light back into the center of fiber. This combination of refraction and reflection of the light, along with the density of the glass, causes the light to take different paths (or bounces) to the end of the cable. Different light beams inserted into the fiber will take paths of different lengths and therefore different amounts of time to get to the end of the cable.

A simple analogy to use when thinking about this concept is paddleball video games. You have all probably seen video games where you have to continue to hit the bouncing ball from paddle to some wall-like barrier. As you bounce the ball, it takes very different paths to get from the surface of the paddle to the wall and knocks out a few of the rectangular blocks. However, the return bounce can take a very different route back to the paddle, and vice versa. The ball can bounce very erratically, with several bounces off the sides, before getting to the barrier. At other times the ball seems to take a trajectory that is direct to the barrier. This difference is reflected in the width of the opening to get from one point to the next. However, if the opening is narrowed and the ball can only take a shorter path, such as when you break through the barrier, the ball takes a much straighter path and punches a hole in one spot. By narrowing the opening between the paddle and the barrier, the ball moves in a shorter path to the barrier. Moreover, the bounce back comes much quicker. Actually, the game speeds up considerably, and you have to be prepared with good hand and eye coordination as the movement speeds.

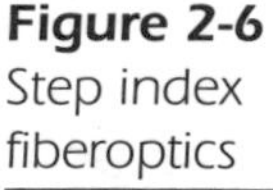

Figure 2-6 Step index fiberoptics

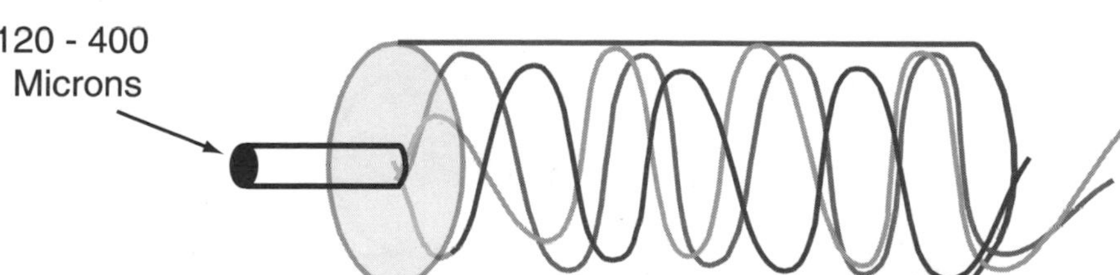

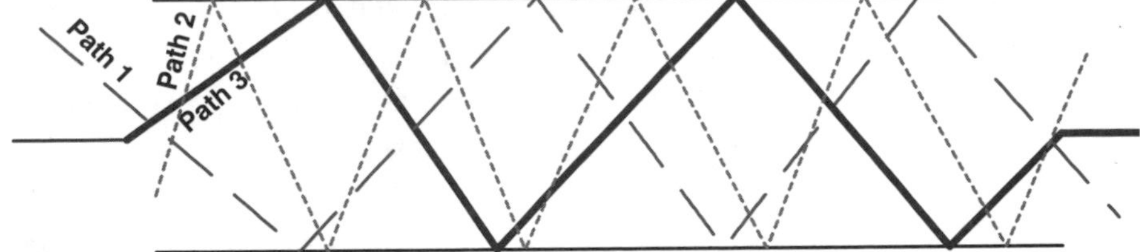

Figure 2-7 The various paths possible in multimode step index.

This same concept can be applied to fiber-based networks. Looking at this in a slightly different perspective, the light will bounce inside the glass as shown in Figure 2-7. Here, the multiple paths are shown in the geometric bounces that can take place within the glass itself.

Multimode Graded Index Fiber A second form of multimode fiber employs a graded index of the glass, as opposed to the step index. Essentially, the grading of the refractive levels of the light is changed to compensate for refraction and the density of the glass. In the step index fiber, modal dispersion (spreading out of the light), as discussed earlier, is in part responsible for a reduction in throughput on the fiber. By using a grading of the density of the glass from the center core out, the capacity of the fiber can be increased. Simply stated, the more dense the glass, the more refractive is the surface of the glass. The more refraction taking place, the longer is the path. By having a step index, the path in the outer part of the glass is longer than the path in the center of the glass. This means that light arrives at different times because the path lengths are different. Grading the center core to have a higher level of refraction and the outer parts of the glass to be thinner (and thus less refractive) can use the characteristics of the glass to get approximately the same length of a wave on the cable and therefore increase the speed of throughput. A graded index fiber is shown in Figure 2-8. The bet-

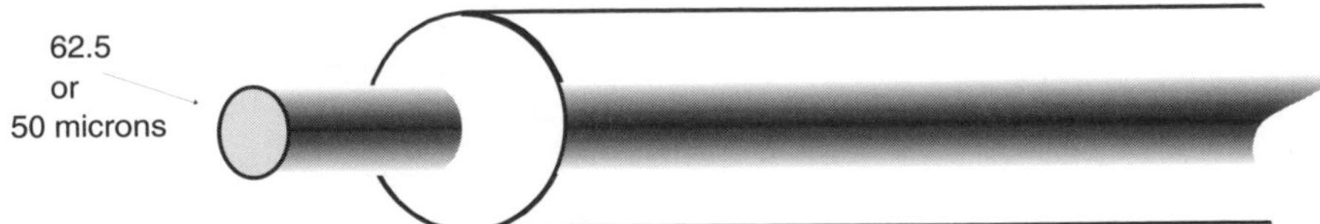

Figure 2-8 Multimode graded index fiber.

ter the grading of the index, the more throughput you can expect. Currently, the two forms of graded index fiber use either a 62.5- or a 50-micron center conductor with a 125-micron outer cladding on the glass.

Here, an analogy also will help with understanding. We can neutralize the effects of the thick and thin glass by creating a different resistance factor. If the thin glass is in the outer edge and the thicker glass is in the center, the values can be neutralized. This gives us an average speed. Think of a racetrack. The summer Olympic games use this effect when they set the stage for foot races. If you are running on the outer edge of a racetrack, the diameter of the oblong that you are running is greater than if you are running at the center of the track. To compensate for this, the runners are spaced at different points on the track, with the longest length having what appears to be a lead at the starting block, as shown in Figure 2-9. In reality, all the runners have to run the same distance; they just have to do it differently. However, the speed of the runners is what separates the racers, not the lengths of the oblong rings. These have been averaged

Figure 2-9 Geometry of the track is adjusted to equalize the distances.

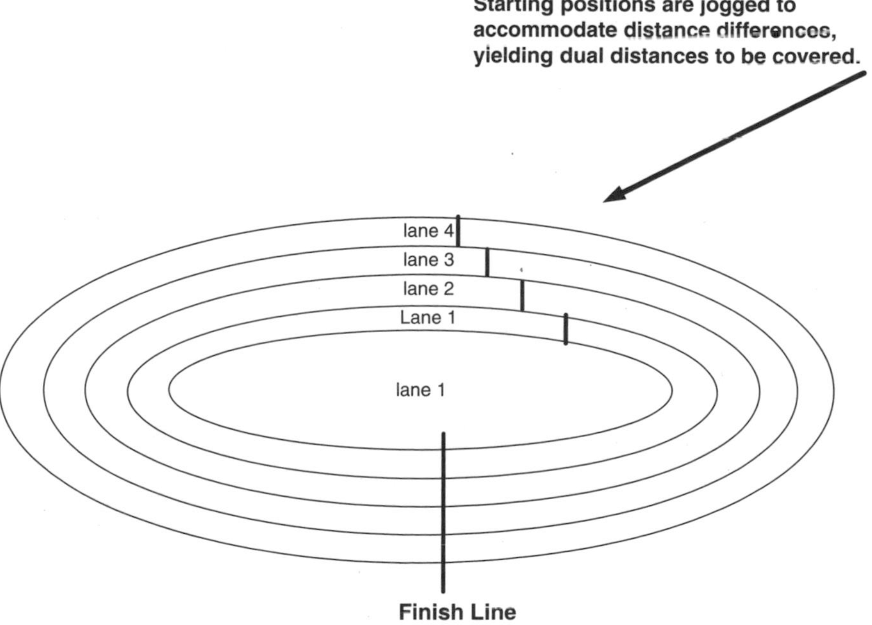

by the geometry of the track. The same holds true with multimode fibers. By adding some length to the path in the center and shortening the path on the outer edges, the playing field is leveled. This concept makes it much easier to manufacture the glass by pulling the thicknesses differently.

Looking inside the fiber, the paths look a bit different from the stepped index format. There is some symmetry to the initial look, but changes are introduced with the way the light pulses travel down the cable. Figure 2-10 illustrates these changes and the path that is used to carry the light.

Single-Mode Fiber As fiber became more popular and research was stepped up, a newer form of glass was developed. If the glass could be made very thin and very pure in the center, the light would have no choice but to follow the same path every time. A single path (or single mode) between the two ends enables the developers to speed up the input because there is no concern about varying path lengths, as shown in Figure 2-11. The thickness of a single-mode fiber today is approximately 8.3 to 10 microns at the center. An outer cladding is still present on the edges to reflect the light back into the center of the glass. The outer cladding is still approximately 125 microns thick. The single-mode fiber is the focus of most of the activity today. Many of the telephone carriers deployed multimode fibers in their networks when they were first introduced. However, over the years, multimode fiber has given way to single-mode fiber throughout the public carrier networks.

Figure 2-10 The various paths changed using graded index multimode fiber

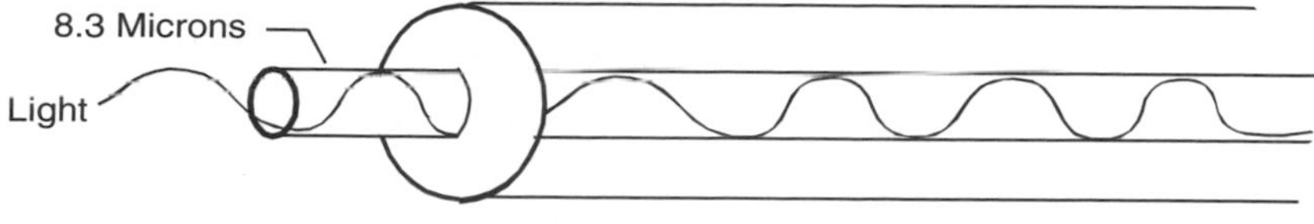

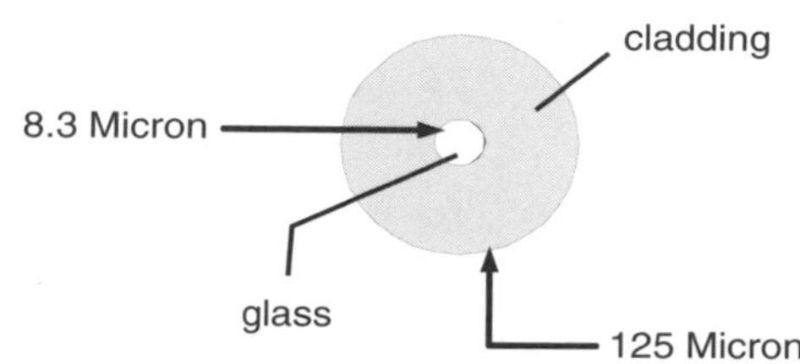

Figure 2-11 Single-mode fiber is so pure and so thin that light has only one path from end to end.

Let's try a different analogy this time. Think about a drain pipe. If you have a 6-inch outer diameter drain pipe and you start to dump water into the pipe, the water will swish back and forth on the bottom of the pipe. As the water works its way to the end of the pipe, it will have taken a circuitous route to get to there. However, if you dump more water into the pipe, the water may start to experience resistance and begin a higher motion up the sides of the pipe. The more flow you put into the pipe (without totally filling it yet), the higher up the sides the water moves. Now, the back-and-forth motion may give way to a corkscrew effect swirling down the pipe toward the opposite end. The path is lengthening to get to the other end as the corkscrew effect gets more violent. This swirling motion changes the path. Now suppose you decrease the size of the pipe to 1 inch and put the same amount of water into it. The path is restricted to a much smaller diameter opening and therefore decreases the size of the swirl (making it much tighter). The shorter path means that the water expels from the opposite end much more quickly. In fact, the appearance is that the water speeds up. It gushes out the opposite end in a jet stream instead of just flowing out.

We can achieve this same effect with single-mode fibers. Now, as the light beams are moved into the glass, they move straighter and quicker to the other end. Therefore, we can turn the spigot on faster using a “data pump” to get the flow really moving, increasing the overall throughput and data rates. The result is faster throughput and shorter distances equaling more data.

Benefits of Fiber over Other Forms of Media

The benefits of fiber over other forms of media are shown in Table 2-4. However, it is important to note that fiber has been used extensively in the long-distance telecommunications networks and local telephone company networks. It is more recent that single-mode fiber has worked its way into end-user networks (LANs and CANs). With single-mode fiber, the speeds are constantly being upped, and the error performances are being improved continually. The table concentrates on *bit error rates* (BERs) and the speed of such cabling systems.

Table 2-4

Summary of Fiber's Advantages Compared with Other Media

Lower errors	BER approximates $10^{-15,\,-16}$ for fiber, whereas copper will be in the $10^{-3,-4}$ for UTP to 10^{-8} for coaxial cable
Attractive cost per foot	Cost per foot for fiber is now approximately $0.20 compared with $0.13 for copper (Category 5+)
Performance	Immune from RFI and EMI without extra cost of shielding on copper
Ease of installation	Ease of installation due to lower weight and thickness
Distances	Greater distance with fewer repeaters. Now can achieve 30 to 200 miles without repeaters. Copper and radio are limited to less than 30 miles. UTP digital transmission systems require repeaters every mile.
Bandwidth improvements	Fiber is nearing 1.6 Tbps, copper achieves 100 Mbps, and coax can carry up to 1 Gbps
Capable of carrying analog and digital	Using TDM and WDM, the fiber is both digital and frequency multiplexed, increasing capacity

Bending Cables

As light travels along the fiber, it is reflected from the interface between the core and cladding whenever it strays from the path straight down the center. If the fiber is bent during the installation (by design or accidentally), the light only stays in the fiber because the pouter cladding reflects it back into the cable. However, total internal reflection only works under certain conditions. The angle of incidence[2] must be kept low. If you bend the fiber too much, the light can escape. The bending radius is crucial in the installation of fiber. Despite all its strong points, fiber does have some drawbacks, albeit minor. The amount of allowable bending is specific to particular cables because it depends on the difference in refractive index between the cladding and the core. The greater the difference in refractive index, the more stringent is the allowable bending radius. Figure 2-12 illustrates this bending difference.

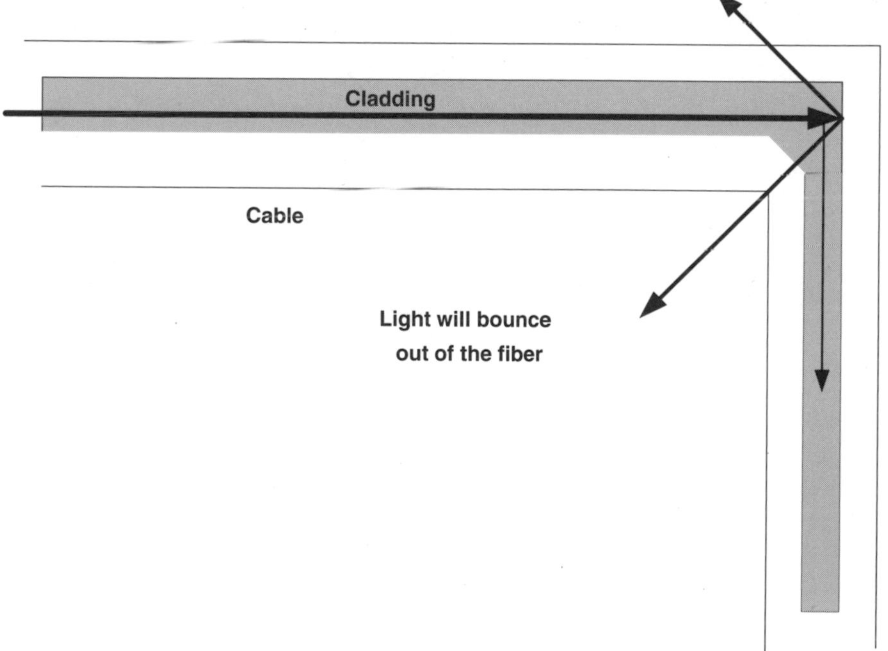

Figure 2-12 Light will bounce out of the fiber if the bend is too tight.

[2] The angle of incidence is the angle in which the light hits the cladding.

Figure 2-13 shows a bending radius that is better designed to keep the light in the fiber. This enables a smoother flow of the data around the bends when the fiber is installed properly. The amounts of reflection and refraction work better in this case so that the light makes it to the far end.

Sending Light Down the Wires

In order to send data down the fiber, a light source is needed. The two most common light sources are *light-emitting diodes* (LEDs) and lasers. LEDs are usually less expensive and are used in many corporate networks, although they are not limited to that application.

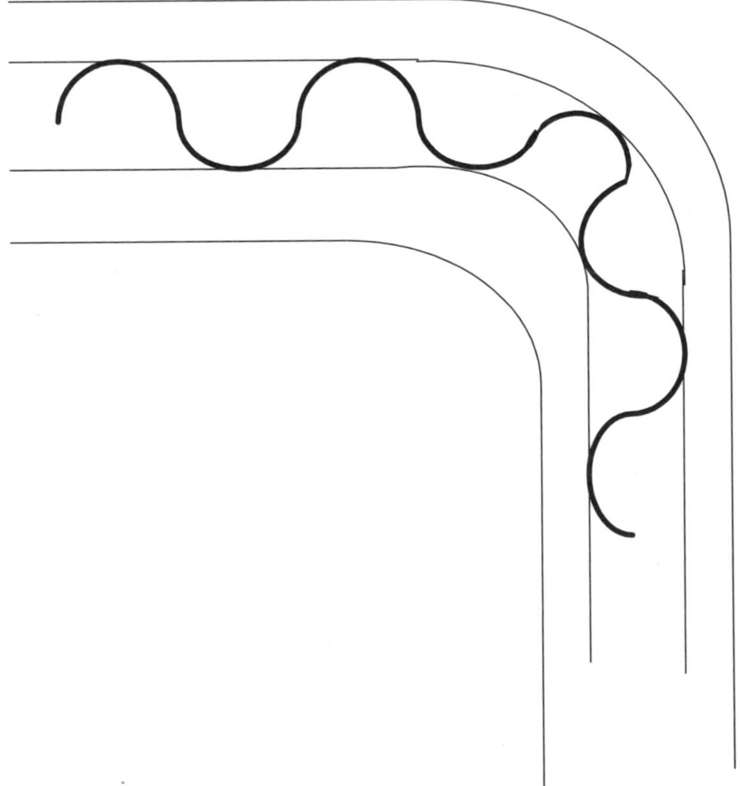

Figure 2-13 If the bending angle is correct, the light moves around the bend.

Because of cost, the LED is a favored device in LANs. Table 2-5 summarizes LED characteristics. These devices fit many communications applications.

Table 2-5

Summary of LED Characteristics

Characteristic	Description
Low cost	LEDs are much less expensive than communications lasers. This is highly controversial. Communications LEDs and lasers are not much different in structure and are comparable in manufacturing cost. However, most LEDs cannot be used with single-mode fiber, whereas lasers can be used with either single-mode or multimode fiber.
Relatively wide range of frequencies	LEDs output a band of wavelengths instead of a single wavelength. This was discussed earlier. The wavelengths can be reduced by using filters. By filtering the light, a narrow band of wavelengths can be used. Everyone probably has been exposed to a form of filtering with sunglasses, sun-blocking agents, or even in photography. The filters give the desired effect by blocking specific frequencies in the light spectrum.
Low power output	The maximum light output of a LED typically is much lower than a laser. However, a new class of LEDs with higher output has become available. The regulation of devices in production is less severe with LEDs, although things always change.
Digital	LEDs cannot produce pulses short enough to be used at high speeds. LEDs can operate at speeds of up to 622 Mbps. Digital modulation is straightforward. The device "turns on" when the voltage is strong enough to power it and turns off when the voltage drops off. This light on, light off can represent the two digital states used in communications (0 and 1).
Lenses required	A lens is needed to focus the light onto the end of a fiber. LEDs are not suitable for use with single-mode fiber because it is too hard to get the light into the narrow opening of the core and focus the light down to the other end.
Analog too	LEDs also can be analog, which is an advantage over lasers. By modulating an analog signal continuously on the fiber, the information can be carried on the analog carrier. Most people think that fibers are purely for digital transmissions.

Lasers

Laser is an acronym for *l*ight *a*mplification by *s*timulated *e*mission of *r*adiation. Without doubt, lasers produce the best kind of light for optical communications. The laser is the preferred method of light generation for higher-speed communications systems and is used extensively in long-haul telecommunications networks. Table 2-6 summarizes the benefits and operating characteristics of the laser.

Table 2-6

Summary of Laser Characteristics

Characteristic	Description
Single wavelength	This is related to the materials used in the manufacturing process to produce the laser. The light is created in parallel beams and sent along the transmission path.
Better control over output	Lasers can be modulated (controlled) very precisely.
Lenses not required	The light source is designed for single-mode fiber and focuses better into the core of the actual glass.
Higher output power	Lasers can produce relatively high power. They have out put capabilities that are as much as 20+ times that of LEDs.
More light source	The light is created in parallel beams, so a stronger light can be introduced into the fiber. As much as 50 to 80 percent of the created light will make it into the fiber. This is much greater than with LEDs.
Heat	Lasers get hot, so they require additional equipment to keep them cool; otherwise, they will burn out.
Regulation	Rules for using and producing lasers are much more tightly controlled. Specifications also state the minimum distances and operations where lasers are allowed.
Higher cost	The cost of lasers is significantly higher than the cost of LEDs, and therefore, lasers are not suitable for localized communications networks in a corporate environment. Instead, they are better suited for long-distance networks.
Digital modulation	The on and off function is a more direct way to use the fiber in single-mode and laser combinations.

Fiber Cable Conditions

Fibers themselves are very small, with an outside diameter of 125 microns due to the cladding. Although they are also very strong under tension (greater tensile strength than steel), they break very easily when subjected to lateral pressure or any kind of rough handling. Therefore, to use fiber in "hostile" communications environments, the fiber needs to be enclosed in a cable. Depending on the location and type of installation, fiber cables vary widely in their characteristics. They are made to satisfy a specific need. The goal of using a cable is to protect the fiber from things that can harm it. Several risks pose problems for the installers and operators of fiber-based networks, including the following:

Tensile stress Fiber itself is very strong under tension. Stress causes a significant increase in light attenuation and creates a number of other problems. One has to be careful not to stress the cable too much. The fibers also can stretch, causing a change in the reflective and refractive indices and creating major problems.

Bends Tight bends in the fiber cause signal loss because the light escapes through the cladding material. Crimping the cable also causes signal loss because the microbends create the wrong angle of incidence for the light to bounce down the fiber. By placing the fibers in a cable, the bending radius is better maintained because of the additional materials inside the cable (strengthening members and other cladding components).

Physical damage The type of protection used in cables varies with the risks posed. Indoor conditions include the risk of rodent damage. The cables are a food supply that rodents cannot resist. They will chew through the outer cladding (and then some), causing damage and loss of reflective materials (the light will escape from inside the fibers). Rodent damage is not limited to indoor installations. Gophers, rabbits, termites, and fire ants all may eat through cables.

Backhoe fade This risk comes from heavy earth-moving equipment such as backhoes and plows. A major hazard for outdoor cables is cable-laying machines. In most countries, the cables are laid along rights-of-way. The contractors used by all the major telecommunications providers cut the cables they are hired to install. Many of the cable cuts are from the same contractors that initially laid them in the first place.

Damage during installation Cable also must withstand the stresses of being installed. The installation crews have a job to do, and they do it. They have little regard for the stresses, tugs, and snags they put in the cable. Their job is to install x amount of cable per day, and they do just that. Consequently, they bend, stretch, and snag/cut the cabling in the process of installing it.

Water Water is the worst enemy of an optical fiber system. Waterproofing the cable is often more important than worrying about some of the other risks. Over time, the fibers begin to degrade because of a chemical reaction between the glass and water. The glass can change its absorption rate, and this can cause significant loss of signal strength. The change in the composition of the glass causes it to cloud and changes the refractive and reflective characteristics. Basically, this means that water is a big problem. As access holes flood, the water can permeate through the outer jacket of fiber cables and cause these problems. Water also causes microcracking in the glass fibers, producing light scatter.

Getting Fiber to Carry the Signal

We always try to define the bandwidth of a cable or a radio transmission system. This is so because we relate everything to our telecommunications discussions. We try to determine the bandwidth of the optical signal.

- When transmitting light on a multimode fiber, capacity is quoted as an analog bandwidth measure.
- On single-mode fiber, a modulating signal broadens the spectral width (bandwidth) of the carrier signal.

In wavelength-division multiplexing systems, the modulating signal also broadens the spectral width. The bandwidth determination is not straightforward. A squarewave signal has a fundamental frequency of half the bit rate. A 1-Gbps digital signal has a fundamental frequency of 500 MHz operating as a simple sine wave. A squarewave contains many higher-frequency harmonics at several times the basic frequency. From there, the types of modulation techniques used in the telecommunications arena can be analyzed.

***Amplitude Modulation* (AM)** Lasers traditionally have been very difficult to modulate with standard amplitude-modulation techniques because of the nonlinear response typical of lasers. The major use of AM is in CATV and hybrid fiber and coax (HFC) distribution systems. An analog signal is prepared the same as for the coaxial cable (CATV). Instead of putting it straight onto the cable, it is used to modulate a laser. At the receiver, the signal is amplified electronically and placed onto a section of coaxial cable.

***Frequency-Shift Keying* (FSK) or *Frequency Modulation* (FM)** It is difficult to modulate the frequency of a laser, and this is one of the reasons that FM optical systems are not yet in general use. Some lasers are being introduced that will use an FSK technique. For this to work, the laser spectral line width has to be considerably narrower than the bandwidth of the signal. FSK promises much higher data rates than the pulse systems currently in use.

***Phase-Shift Keying* (PSK) or *Phase Modulation* (PM)** The phase of a laser's output signal cannot be controlled directly. Therefore, a laser will not produce phase-modulated light. However, a signal can be modulated in phase by placing a modulation device in the light path between the laser and the fiber. PM has similar advantages to FSK.

Polarity Modulation or *Polarity-Inversion-Shift Keying* (PISK) Lasers produce linearly polarized light. A modulation technique might work by changing the light's polarity. Unfortunately, current fiber changes the polarization of light during transit. Therefore, this may result in a conflict, producing a reversal of the pulse being transmitted. This is not available commercially yet.

Directional Transmission Fiber typically is a one-way transmission system. Two fibers are used for two-way transmission. The size of a single fiber and the number of fibers that can be packed into a cable make this attractive and the predominant mode of operation. However, a single fiber can carry light in both directions simultaneously. Devices doing this today use different wavelengths in different directions.

Many new techniques emerge as fast as the existing ones are installed. The market today is ripe for innovation in the use of fiber-based networks and capitalizes on the huge amount of bandwidth available.

Current fiberoptic systems produce a single bit per pulse. In the future, however, researchers probably will achieve 2, 3, or even 5 bits per pulse. This, of course, will expand the bandwidth of the fiber by orders of magnitude. With a single bit per pulse, the theoretical bandwidth (throughput in bits per second) is approximately 3×10^{13} bps (30 Tbps). Even if no improvements are made in the current technology, we can get a 10,000-fold increase using a single fiber over what we get today.

This is where the action is taking the industry. The industry is looking toward the following goals:

- To find a way to increase the modulation techniques to get 4, 5, or 6 bits per hertz
- To achieve a higher number of wavelengths on a single fiber
- To optically switch the light instead of having to convert it back to an electrical signal and then into photonic again
- To increase the distances between repeaters so that fiber is less expensive to deploy on long-haul circuits

CHAPTER 3

SONET

Once upon a time, standards were set in North America by the Bell System, in particular, by AT&T. As the prime carrier for network services, AT&T set the rules on how the network operated. In 1958, the designers at AT&T developed the North American Digital Hierarchy as a means of delivering high-speed digital communications. This worked throughout the network because at the time, only one provider existed. Because there was no competition, AT&T needed only to satisfy itself on the operation of the network. Although the North American Digital Hierarchy worked, many limitations also existed that curtailed the overall operation of the network. One such problem was in the asynchronous nature of many of the transmission systems. The industry needed some critical changes in the network to accommodate growth and competition. Moreover, other changes were underway. In the late 1960s, competition began to appear in the long-distance network. This competition began to bring additional constraints inside the network to the surface.

Until recently, signal transmission consisted of voice communications, dial-up data communications, and leased lines. These variations all depended on the voice concept of analog communications. However, modern networks must go beyond just a voice networking standard and support many different types of signals. These demands required the development of new standards that used synchronous transmission capabilities throughout. The services also required openness, including

- Multivendor support
- Multivendor compatibility
- Ease of adding new services when they develop
- Enhancements to operation, administration, maintenance, and provisioning
- Midspan meeting capabilities

These needs were not being met at the time because no competitors shared the services and the backbone networks other than Bell. The changes appeared when the emergence of competition changed the way the network worked. These requirements led to the development of the *Synchronous Optical Networking* (SONET) standard in 1984 and ratification in 1988. SONET is a standard developed by the *Exchange Carriers Standards Association* (ECSA) for the *American National Standards Institute* (ANSI). This standard defines an optical telecommunications transport for U.S. telecommunications. The SONET standard provides an extensive set of operational parameters for optical transmission systems throughout the industry. The North American industry uses the SONET specifications, whereas the rest of the world uses a close "cousin" called the *Synchronous Digital Hierarchy* (SDH), covered in Chapter 4, "Synchronous Digital Hierarchy." Between the two sets of standards, the industry attempted to define the roles of transport for the telecommunications providers using optical fibers as the transport medium.

SONET provides more, though. It defines a means to increase throughput and bandwidth through a set of multiplexing parameters. These roles provide certain advantages to the industry, such as

- Reduced equipment requirements in the carriers' networks
- Enhanced network reliability and availability
- Conditions to define the overhead necessary to facilitate managing a network better
- Definitions of multiplexing functions and formats to carry lower-level digital signals (such as DS-1, DS-2, and DS-3)
- Generic standards encouraging interoperability between different vendors' products
- A flexible means of addressing current as well as future applications and bandwidth usage

SONET defines the *optical carrier* (OC) levels and electrical equivalent rates in *synchronous transport signals* (STS) for the fiber-based transmission hierarchy.

Background Leading to SONET Development

Prior to the development of SONET, the initial fiber-based systems used in the *public switched telephone network* (PSTN) were all highly proprietary. The proprietary items included

- Equipment
- Line coding
- Maintenance
- Provisioning
- Multiplexing
- Administration

The carriers (local and long-distance providers) were frustrated with the proprietary nature of the industry because of interoperability problems, sole-source vendor solutions (which held the carriers hostage to one vendor), and cost issues. These carriers approached the standards committees and demanded that a set of operational standards be developed that would allow them to mix and match products from various vendors. In 1984, a task force was established to develop such a standard. The resulting standard became SONET.

The North American Digital Hierarchy

The North American Digital Hierarchy is a set of standards established for the telecommunications industry in North America. Three countries supported this set of standards initially—the United States, Canada, and Japan. These three counties adopted sets of multiplexing and operating speeds that satisfied the communications networks at the time. The digital signals accepted and adopted included DS-0, DS-1, DS-2,[1] and DS-3.

DS-0

When a user makes a call on the PSTN, his or her voice is filtered down to a 4-*kilohertz* (kHz) analog signal. It is then sampled at 8,000 times per second (the clock rate). The sampling technique creates a

[1]DS-2 is defined but not widely used anymore.

quantification of the voice in a digital pattern (1s and 0s) using 8 bits per sample. The result is a 64,000 bits per second (8,000 samples/s ×8 bits/sample) stream. This is called DS-0 and is the basis of the North American Digital Hierarchy. If higher rates of communication are needed, a multiplexer is used to merge signals together at the desired rate.

DS-1

The DS-1 signal is created by multiplexing 24 individual DS-0 digital signals together. Thus, a DS-1 signal is 24 DS-0 signals plus some extra bits for overhead (that is, 8,000), producing the 1.544-*megabit per second* (Mbps) signal. Each DS-0 signal is assigned its own timeslot on the DS-1. Conceptually, DS-1 is shown in Figure 3-1 (DS-0s).

DS-3

Once the DS-1 is created, 28 DS-1 signals are multiplexed together to create a DS-3. This higher-speed communications channel combines to create a 44.736-Mbps capacity. Therefore, 672 individual DS-0 signals can be multiplexed together to create a DS-3. A framing format is used to carry the DS-1 signals on this high-speed channel, as shown in Figure 3-2.

DS-3 is an M13 (pronounced M-one-three) asynchronous transmission that uses the M13 Asynchronous Protocol. This means that

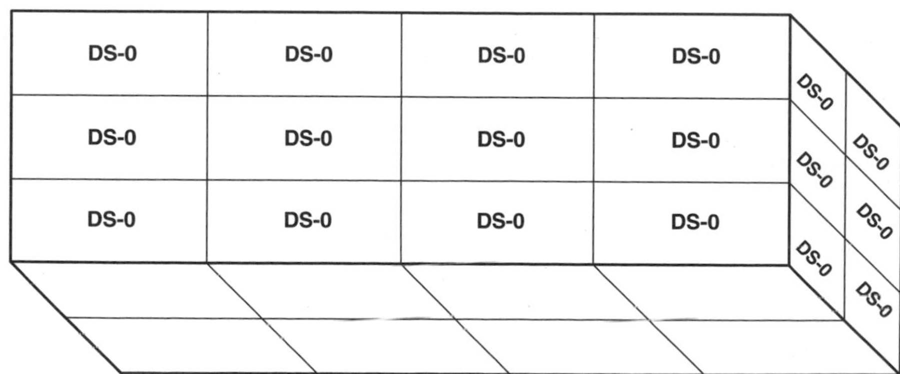

Figure 3-1 A multiplexing overview of DS-1

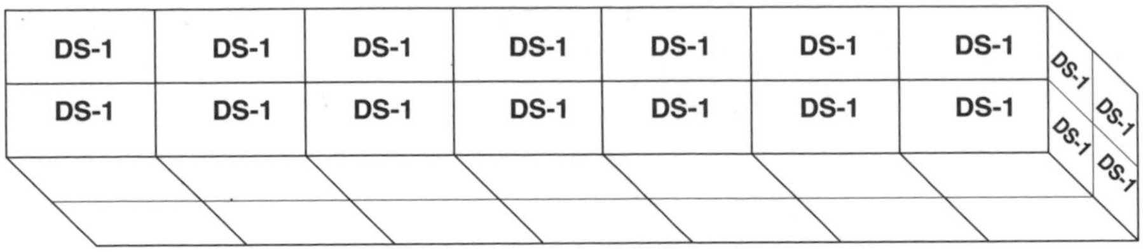

DS-1	DS-1	DS-1	DS-1	DS-1	DS-1	DS-1	DS-1	DS-1
DS-1	DS-1	DS-1	DS-1	DS-1	DS-1	DS-1	DS-1	DS-1

Figure 3-2 DS-3 mapping and multiplexing uses 28 DS-1 signals inside.

the information, although using synchronous DS-1 signals inside, is transmitted in an asynchronous manner. *Asynchronous* means that the timing of signals carried on the network is random.

Asynchronous Transmission

Just what does it mean to say that a signal is asynchronously transmitted, especially that DS-1 signals are synchronous? SONET is synchronous. DS-1 is also synchronous. However, DS-3 is asynchronous! Are you confused?

When using a copper- , radio- , or fiber-based network, *asynchronous* refers to digital signals generated on equipment that operates in one of two conditions—using its own internal clock (timing source) or using separate timing sources (master clocks). Conceptually, again, we have to understand what is happening. DS-1 signals are synchronous unto themselves but not unto others. This means that a DS-1 signal is internally timed and operated synchronously.

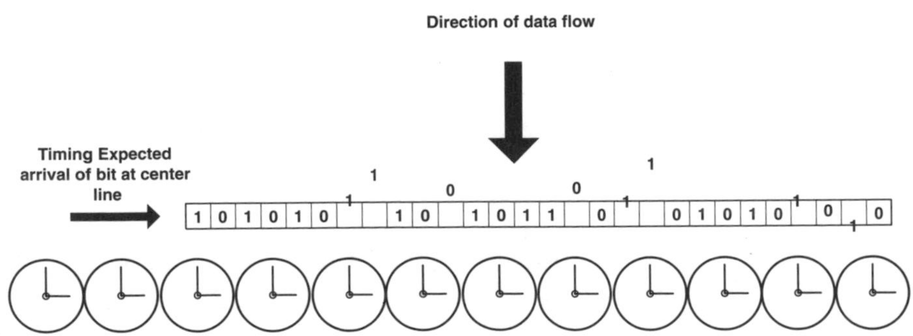

Figure 3-3 Because some data bits arrive later than other bits, timing can be a problem.

However, the signals are multiplexed one bit at a time into a DS-3 signal using a DS-3 multiplexer (the M13). Because each DS-1 signal operates with its own clock, phase and frequency deviations may exist among the individual bit streams. This means that the bits can arrive early or late, in contrast to the other inputs. This is shown in Figure 3-3, which presents a conceptual view of the arrival sequence.

Bit Stuffing

To compensate for the potential problems and delays in the data arrival, the equipment must be capable of inserting a bit into an empty slot. This is called *bit stuffing.* The bits will be inserted into blank slots so that if a DS-1 line is slow to deliver the necessary bits, substitutes will be put in their place. This creates a scenario where the data can be aligned properly. Unfortunately, when we stuff these bits into a DS-3 data stream, the equipment at the receiving end cannot tell the difference between real data and fake data placed there to keep the slot occupied. Thus, the multiplexer does not know where to look for its reference point to find the DS-1 signals inside the DS-3 stream. To get back to the DS-1 signals, the entire DS-3 stream (all 28 DS-1 signals) must be demultiplexed. This is time-consuming and expensive. Figure 3-4 illustrates the bit-stuffing process.

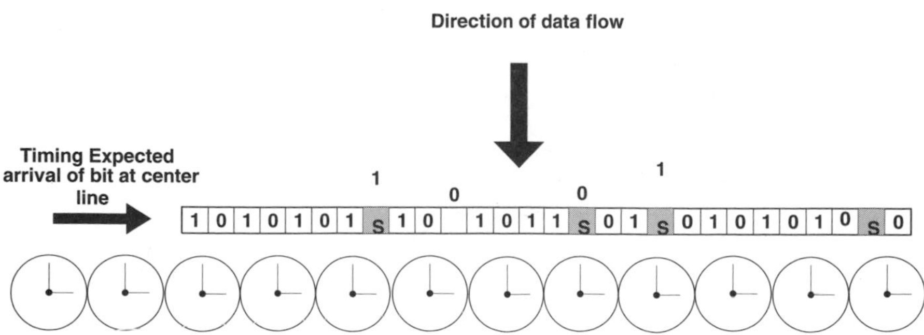

Figure 3-4 Bits are "stuffed" because the time slots were empty.

SONET: A Means of Synchronizing Digital Signals

SONET involves synchronization of the digital signals arriving at the equipment. Keep in mind that the signals may be introduced in one of three ways. Therefore, it is important to attempt to get everything on a common set of clocking mechanisms. In digital transmission, the normal way of synchronizing traffic is to draw a common clocking reference. In the hierarchy of clocking, systems use a stratum clocking architecture. The stratum references in North America come in a four-level architecture. These are shown in Table 3-1.

In a set of synchronous signals, the digital transitions in the signals occur at the same rate. A phase difference may occur between the transitions in the two signals, but this would be in specified ranges and limits. The phase differences can be the result of delay in systems, jitter across the link, or other transmission impairments. In a synchronous environment, all the clocks are traceable to a common reference clock (the primary reference clock). Figure 3-5 is a representation of the various clocks used in the network and the need to compensate for different transmission paths. This figure assumes that the different switching systems at the various locations can buffer the data to overcome jitter or phase problems. Buffers are used to compensate for the different transmission media, the various path lengths that can be taken, and the operation of the switching and multiplexing systems.

Table 3-1

Summary of Clocking Systems

Stratum Reference	Location Used	Accuracy
1	Primary reference drawn from GPS or the national reference atomic clock	±1 pulse in 10^{-11}
2	Toll offices (long distance COs)	±1.6 pulses in 10^{-8}
3	End offices (local COs)	±4.6 pulses in 10^{-6}
4	Customer equipment (multiplexer, channel bank, and so on)	±32 pulses in 10^{-6}

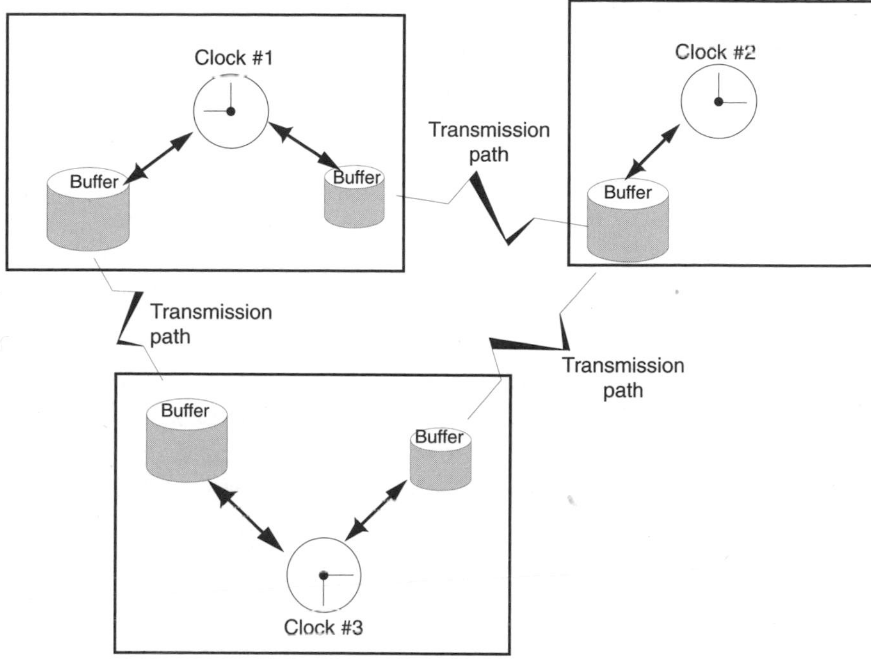

Figure 3-5 Buffers compensate for timing problems that occur in the network.

If two signals are almost the same, they are said to be *plesiochronous.* Their transitions are close (or almost the same), and variations are contained within strict limits. The clocking between the two different sources, although accurate, may be operating at different rates.

Finally, if two signals are arbitrary in their generation and do not occur at the same rate, they are said to be *asynchronous.* The difference between the two clocks is much greater, possibly running from a free-running clock source.

Any one of these signals—synchronous, plesiochronous, or asynchronous—may arrive at a SONET multiplexer to be formulated and transmitted across the network. SONET defines the means of synchronizing the traffic for transmission.

SONET Line Rates

SONET defines a technique to carry many signals from different sources and at different capacities through a synchronous optical hierarchy. The flexibility and robustness of SONET are two of its strongest selling points. Additionally, in the past, many of the high-speed multiplexing arrangements (DS-2 and DS-3) used bit interleaving to multiplex the data streams through the multiplexers. SONET uses a byte-interleaved multiplexing format. This is a strong point because it keeps the basic DS-0 signal intact throughout the network, making it easier to perform diagnostics and troubleshooting. Byte interleaving simplifies the process and provides better end-to-end management.

The base level of a SONET signal is called the *synchronous transport signal level 1* (STS-1), operating at 51.84 Mbps. The first step in using the SONET architecture is to create the STS-1. Other levels exist in multiples of STS-*n* to create a full family of transmission speeds. The SONET hierarchy is shown in Table 3-2. In SONET, the higher-level line rates are direct multiples of the OC-1 rate (51.84 Mbps), which means that additional stuffing is not necessary in the multiplexing procedures.

Table 3-2

Summary of Electrical and Optical Rates for SONET

Electrical Signal	Optical Value	Speed	Capacity
STS-1	OC-1	51.84 Mbps	28 DS-1 or 1 DS-3
STS-3	OC-3	155.520 Mbps	84 DS-1 or 3 DS-3
STS-12	OC-12	622.08 Mbps	336 DS-1 or 12 DS-3
STS-24	OC-24	1.244 Gbps	672 DS-1 or 24 DS-3
STS-48	OC-48	2.488 Gbps	1,344 DS-1 or 48 DS-3
STS-192	OC-192	9.953 Gbps	5,376 DS-1 or 192 DS-3
STS-768*	OC-768	40 Gbps	21,504 DS-1 or 768 DS-3

Note: Other rates exist, but these are the most popularly implemented.

*The OC-768 and STS-768 rates are newly defined. As the capacities are increased, the rates will follow.

Why Bother Synchronizing?

In the past, transmission systems have been primarily asynchronous. Each terminal device in the network was timed independently. In a digital synchronous transmission system, clocking is all-important. Clocking uses a series of pulses to keep the bit rate constant and to help recover the 1s and 0s from the data stream. Because these past clocks were timed independently, large variations occurred in the clock rate, making it extremely difficult (if not impossible) to extract and recover the data. A DS-1 stream operates at 1.544 Mbps ± 150 *pulses per second* (pps), whereas a DS-3 stream operates at 44.736 Mbps ± 1789 pps. This difference means that one DS-1 stream may be transmitting at up to 300 pps more or less than another (assuming that one DS-1 signal is at -150 pps and the other is at +150 pps). The differences can make it difficult to determine the actual data across a common receiver.

Earlier we discussed the asynchronous method of multiplexing a DS-3 stream. We saw that bit stuffing was used. Therefore, the method of synchronously multiplexing in the SONET architecture provides for better efficiency and problem resolution. Using SONET, the average frequency of all the clocks will be the same. Every clock can be traced to a common reference, which is highly reliable and stable. Bit stuffing can be eliminated in the preparation of the STS-1 signal, and therefore, the lower speed signals are more readily accessible. The benefits outweigh the possible overhead associated with the SONET multiplexing scheme. In SONET, the hierarchy of clocking follows the master-slave clocking architecture. Higher-level (stratum 1) clocks will feed the timing across the network to lower-level devices. Any jitter, phase shifts, or drifting by the clocks can be accommodated through the use of pointers in the SONET overhead. The internal clock in a SONET multiplexer also may draw its timing from a *building-integrated timing system* (BITS) used by switching systems and other devices. This terminal will then serve as the master for other SONET nodes downstream, providing timing on its outgoing signal. The receiving SONET equipment will act in a slave mode (loop timing) with their internal clocks timed by the incoming signal. The standard specifies that SONET equipment must be able to derive its timing at stratum 3 or higher. Figure 3-6 is a reference drawing of the clocking hierarchy used for the network and SONET showing the way the timing is passed across the network.

The SONET Frame

SONET also defines a frame format in which to produce the basic rate of 51.84 Mbps (STS-1). Each addition to the multiplexing rates is a multiple of STS-1. The basic format consists of a frame that is 80 bytes (columns) wide and 9 bytes high (rows). The basic STS-1 signal is then applied into this 810-byte frame. The frame is shown in Figure 3-7. The frame will occur 8,000 times per second. If we do the math on this, we have

$$810 \text{ bytes} \times 8 \text{ bits/byte} \times 8000 \text{ frames/s} = 51.84 \text{ Mbps}$$

Overhead

From the 810-byte frame, overhead is enabled in several ways to facilitate *operations, administration, maintenance, and provisioning* (OAM&P) services. The first part of the overhead is defined as the *transport overhead.* The transport overhead uses the first three

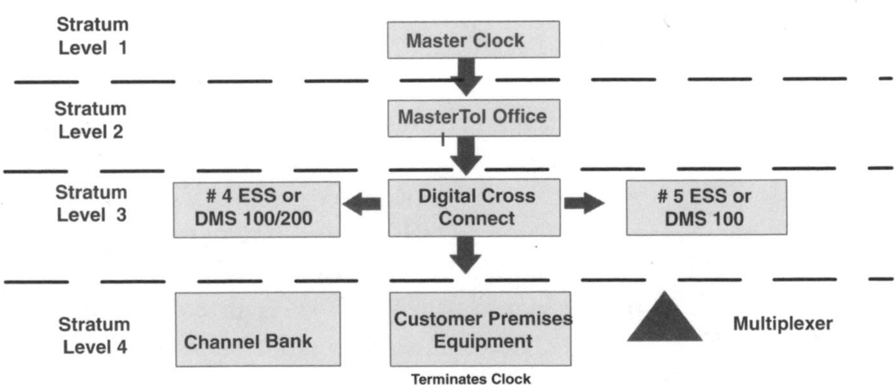

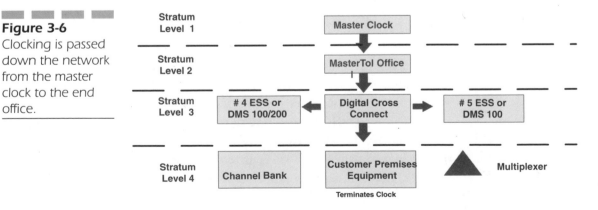

Figure 3-6 Clocking is passed down the network from the master clock to the end office.

columns and all nine rows. This creates 27 bytes of transport overhead. As shown in Figure 3-8, the transport overhead is divided into two pieces. The first three columns and the first three rows (9 bytes) are used for section overhead. The remaining six rows in the first three columns (18 bytes) are used for line overhead.

Figure 3-7 The SONET frame

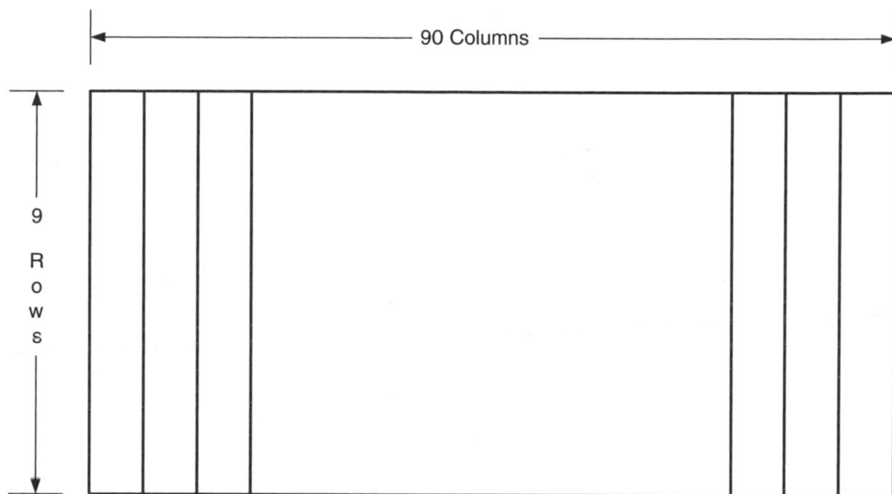

Figure 3-8 The transport overhead is divided into section and line overhead.

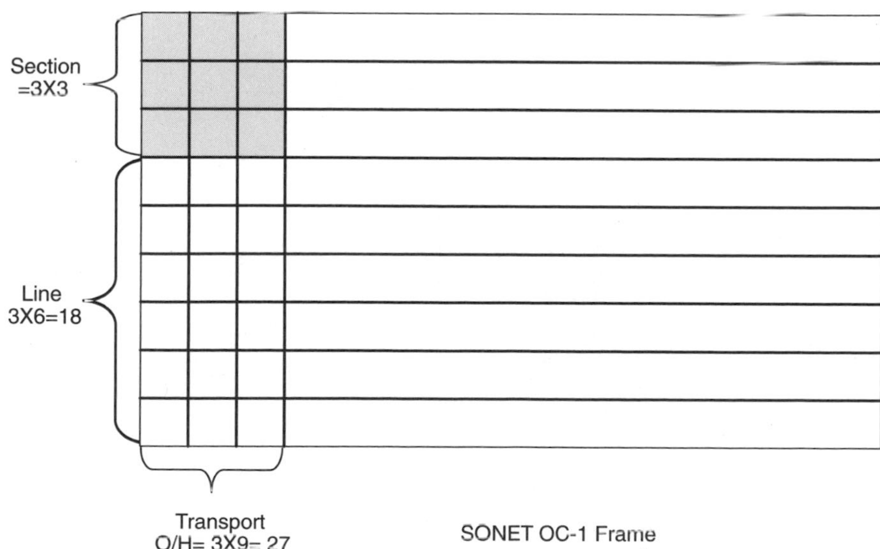

The remaining 87 columns and 9 rows (783 bytes) are designated as the *synchronous payload envelope* (SPE). Inside the SPE, an additional one column nine rows high (9 bytes) is set aside for *path overhead.* This is shown in Figure 3-9. After the path overhead is set aside, the resulting payload is 774 bytes. In these 774 bytes, the services are then mapped into the frame. The STS-1 payload can carry the following:

- 1 DS-3
- 7 DS-2s
- 21 E-1s
- 28 DS-1s

Combinations of these payloads are also allowable. Two columns are reserved as fixed stuff columns; these are columns 30 and 59. The remaining 756 bytes carry the actual payload.

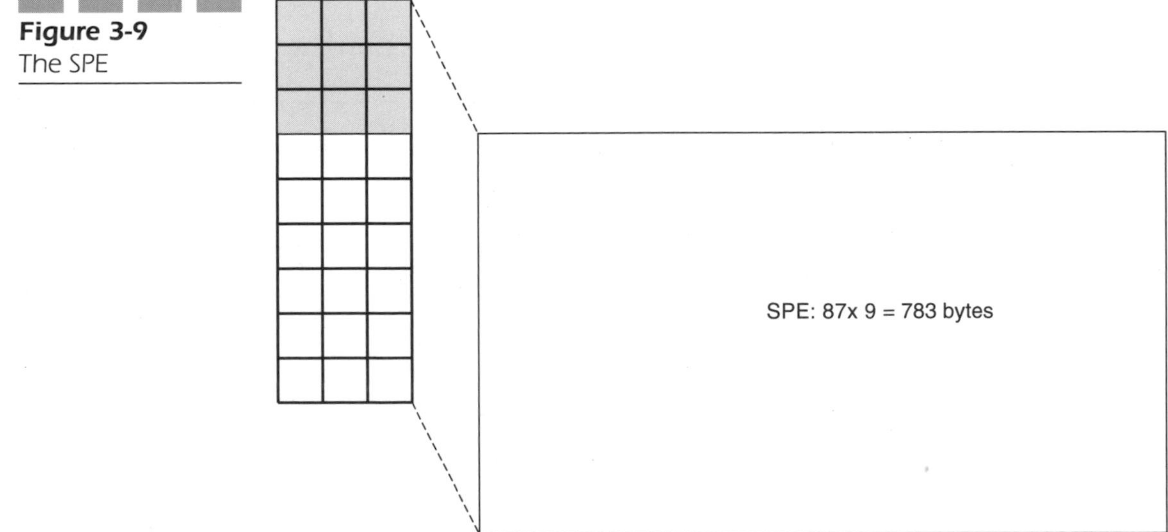

Figure 3-9
The SPE

Inside the STS-1 Frame

The SPE can begin anywhere inside the STS-1 envelope. Normally, it begins in one STS-1 frame and ends there. However, it may begin in one STS-1 frame and end in another. The STS payload pointer contained inside the transport overhead points to the beginning byte of the SPE. The possibilities, then, are that the frame can carry a locked payload or a floating payload. *Floating* in this regard refers to the payload floating between two frames. The overhead associated with SONET is designed to let the receiver know where to look for its payload and extract the information at a starting point. A floating frame is shown in Figure 3-10.

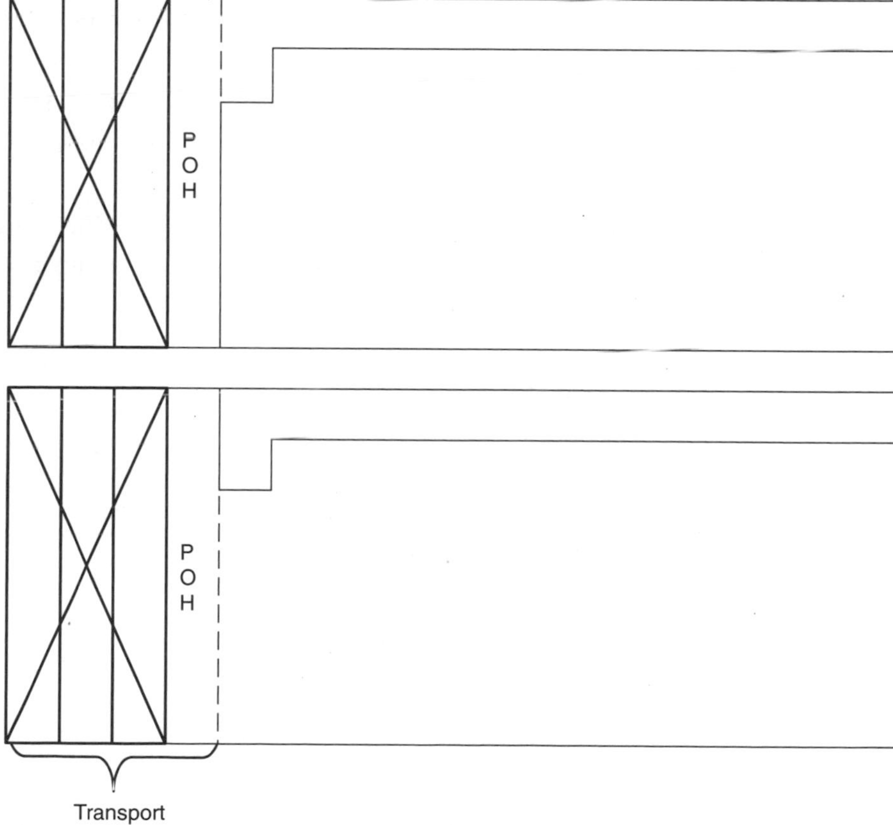

Figure 3-10
A floating payload inside two frames

SONET Overhead

SONET provides significant overhead, enabling simpler multiplexing techniques and improved OAM&P operations. The next section examines overhead in greater detail so as to provide a better understanding of why so much time and energy is dedicated to overhead functions.

Figure 3-11 shows the architecture of the SONET link as defined by ECSA and ANSI. In this reference, the link architecture is broken down into three parts:

Section The section is defined as the portion of the link between two repeater functions or between a repeater and a piece of line-terminating equipment. Sufficient overhead is allowed to detect and troubleshoot errors on the link between these two points (STE).

Line The line overhead provides sufficient information to detect and troubleshoot problems between two pieces of *line-terminating equipment* (LTE).

Path The path overhead provides sufficient overhead to detect and troubleshoot problems between the end-to-end pieces of *path-terminating equipment* (PTE).

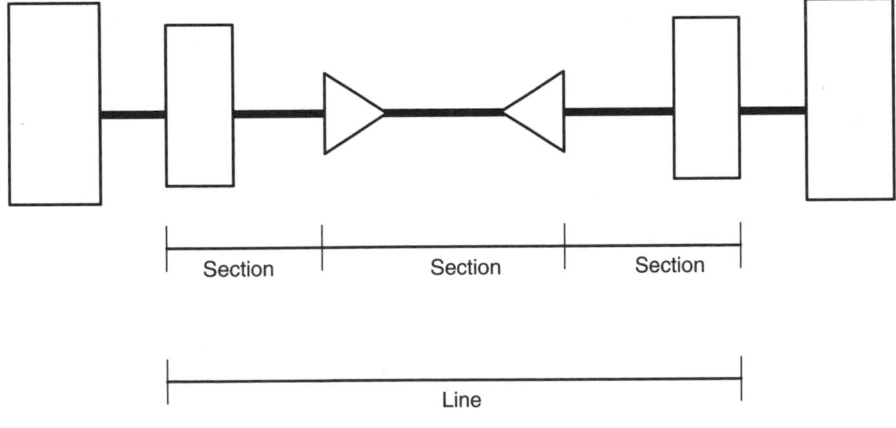

Figure 3-11 SONET link architecture

Overhead

The overhead is shown in Figure 3-12. This overhead contains 9 bytes of information that is accessed, generated, and processed by the section-terminating equipment. It supports functions such as

- Performance monitoring
- A local orderwire
- Data communications channels for OAM&P messages
- Framing information

Line Overhead

The line overhead used between two pieces of LTE provides for OAM&P functions. This is more extensive than the section overhead.

Figure 3-12 SONET overhead

A_1	A_2	J_0/Z_0	J_1
B_1	E_1	F_1	B_3
D_1	D_2	D_3	C_2
H_1	H_2	H_3	G_1
B_2	K_1	K_2	F_2
D_4	D_5	D_6	H_4
D_7	D_8	D_9	Z_3
D_{10}	D_{11}	D_{12}	Z_4
S_1	Z_2	E_2	Z_5

Path Overhead

The final piece of overhead is the path overhead contained inside the SPE. Path overhead contains 9 bytes of information starting at the first byte of the STS SPE. The path overhead provides for communication between two pieces of PTE. The PTE is where the actual multiplexing and demultiplexing functions take place as the services are mapped into the SONET frame. The functions supported by the path overhead are as follows:

- Performance monitoring of the STS SPE
- Signal labeling of the individually mapped payloads
- Path status
- Path trace

Virtual Tributaries

SONET is more than the STS frame. It also defines the sub-STS levels of payload that can be carried. The STS-1 payload can be subdivided into *virtual tributaries* (VTs), synchronous signals to transport lower-speed signals. The normal sizes defined by SONET are shown Table 3-3.

Table 3-3

The Values of the Virtual Tributaries (VTs) Defined for SONET

VT	Bit Rate	Equivalent DS-*n* Level	Required Bytes (rows × columns)
1.5	1.728 Mbps	DS-1	27 (9 × 3)
2	2.304 Mbps	E-1	36 (9 × 4)
3	3.456 Mbps	DS-1C	54 (9 × 6)
6	6.912 Mbps	DS-2	108 (9 × 12)

The SONET VT1.5 signal carries a 1.544-Mbps DS-1 signal plus path overhead. This forms a 1.728-Mbps digital signal. In Figure 3-13, the VT1.5 signals are inserted into the STS payload area. It is easy to see that the VT1.5 signals are still visible within the STS-1 payload area.

SONET Multiplexing Functions

SONET can accommodate several different signal sizes within the STS-1 (49.536 Mbps) payload. SONET then multiplexes together the individual STS-1 signals to form larger signals for transport across a fiber medium. SONET also has the ability to carry larger signals than the STS-1 payload through a process called *concatenation.*

The primary principles of the SONET multiplexers are as follows:

- Mapping the tributaries into the STS-*n* frame
- Aligning the information by using the pointer information to determine where the first byte of the tributary is located

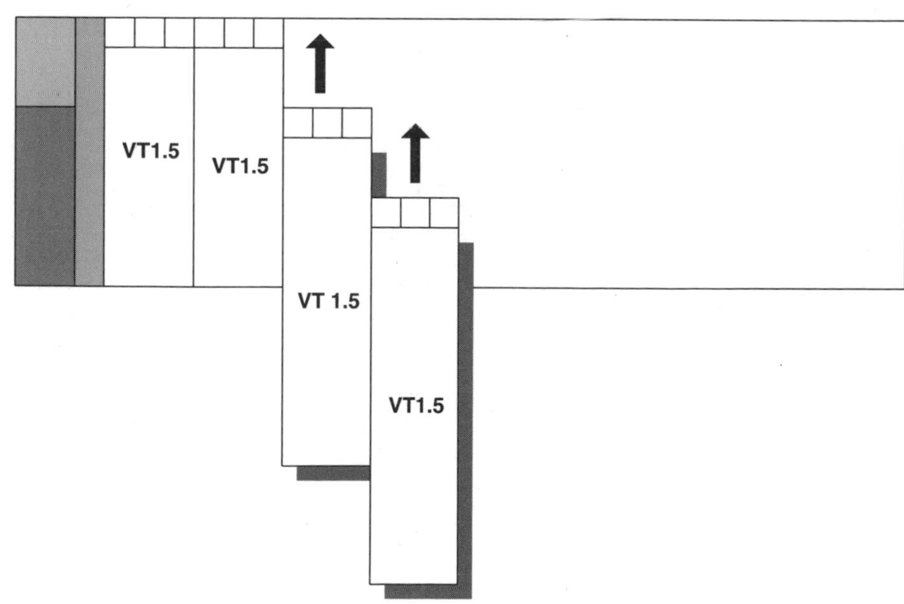

Figure 3-13 VT1.5s are still visible in the payload of a SONET STS-1 signal.

- Multiplexing lower-order signals to higher-order signals
- Stuffing of bits necessary to handle the various lower-speed asynchronous channels and filling up the spare bits to keep everything in alignment.

The SONET equipment provides these functions. SONET can carry very large payloads, as we have seen in the hierarchy of the data speeds. Up to now, we have seen the primary mapping and layout of an STS-1 (OC-1). SONET equipment can add the value necessary to protect investments by either lower- or higher-rate multiplexing. If one looks at an OC 3, for example, the multiplexer will produce a larger STS frame. In this case, as shown in Figure 3-14, the frame is three times larger, or 270 bytes (columns) wide and 9 rows high, for a total of 2,430 bytes. Note from this figure that the overhead for the STS-*n* is located in the beginning of the frame, whereas the *path overhead* (POH) is located at the start of each payload.

When multiplexing the data rates together, there may be a multistage multiplexing function from the individual OC-1 to an OC-3 and OC-12, and so on. Figure 3-15 is a graphic representation of the

Figure 3-14 The STS-3 (OC-3) frame

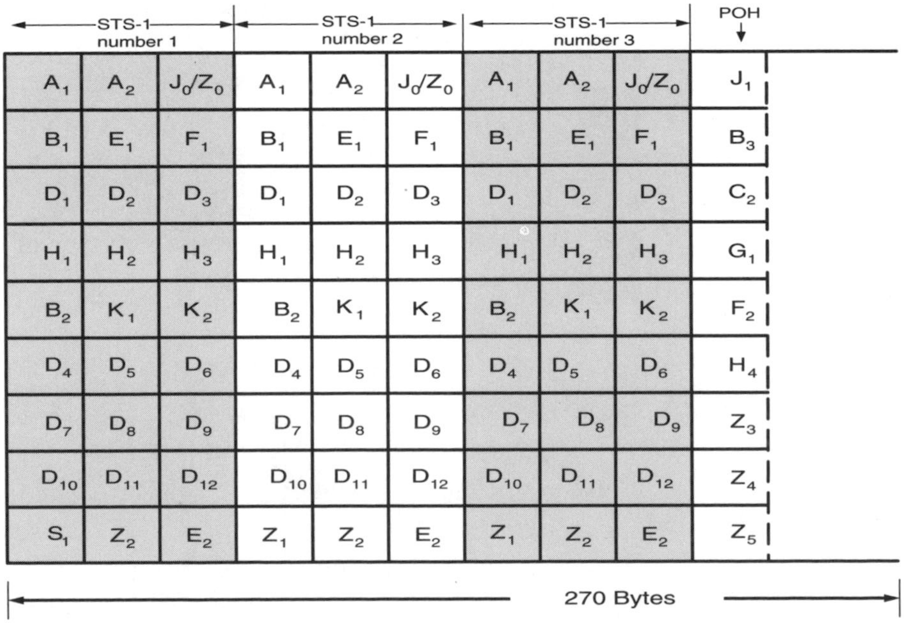

STS-1 number 1			STS-1 number 2			STS-1 number 3			POH
A_1	A_2	J_0/Z_0	A_1	A_2	J_0/Z_0	A_1	A_2	J_0/Z_0	J_1
B_1	E_1	F_1	B_1	E_1	F_1	B_1	E_1	F_1	B_3
D_1	D_2	D_3	D_1	D_2	D_3	D_1	D_2	D_3	C_2
H_1	H_2	H_3	H_1	H_2	H_3	H_1	H_2	H_3	G_1
B_2	K_1	K_2	B_2	K_1	K_2	B_2	K_1	K_2	F_2
D_4	D_5	D_6	D_4	D_5	D_6	D_4	D_5	D_6	H_4
D_7	D_8	D_9	D_7	D_8	D_9	D_7	D_8	D_9	Z_3
D_{10}	D_{11}	D_{12}	D_{10}	D_{11}	D_{12}	D_{10}	D_{11}	D_{12}	Z_4
S_1	Z_2	E_2	Z_1	Z_2	E_2	Z_1	Z_2	E_2	Z_5

270 Bytes

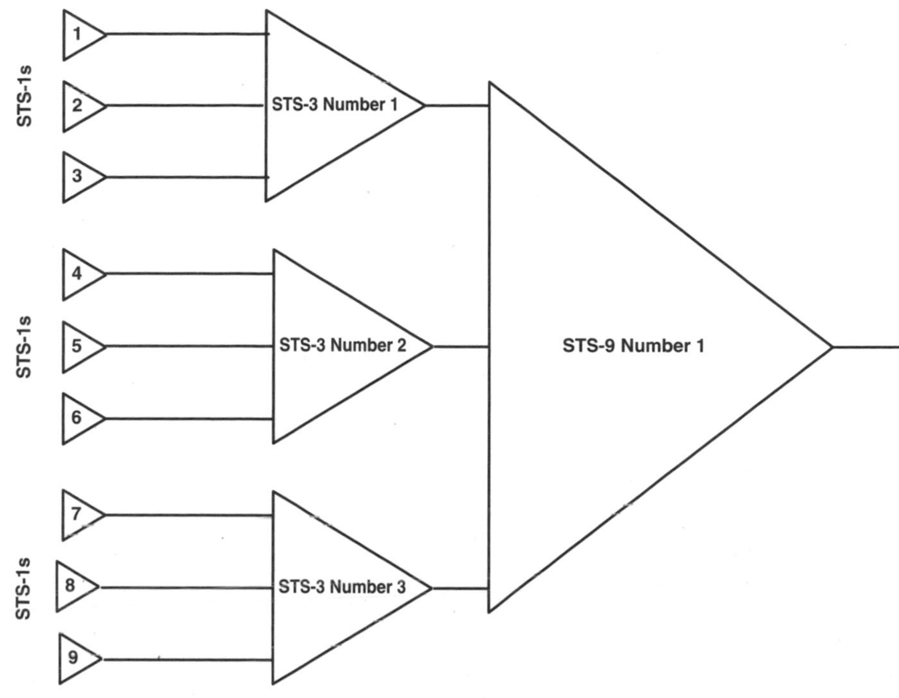

Figure 3-15 The multiplexing function of SONET

multiplexing function from an STS-1 to an STS-3 and then to an STS-9. This interleaving is what SONET is designed to perform.

Another alternative to this multistep process is to use a single multiplexer to handle an STS-12 output with 12 individual STS-1 signals inserted directly into it, as shown in Figure 3-16. This single-stage interleaving process directly byte-interleaves the *n* STS-1 signals into the STS-12 signal shown. However, the numbers can vary, but the outcome is the same; it is a matter of equipment selection and processing.

Concatenation

Concatenation provides SONET with the flexibility to carry digital signals that are larger than the payload described earlier (49.536 Mbps). A designator of a concatenated signal occurs when a small *c* appears after the number of the STS-*n* (that is, STS-3c). The *c* indi-

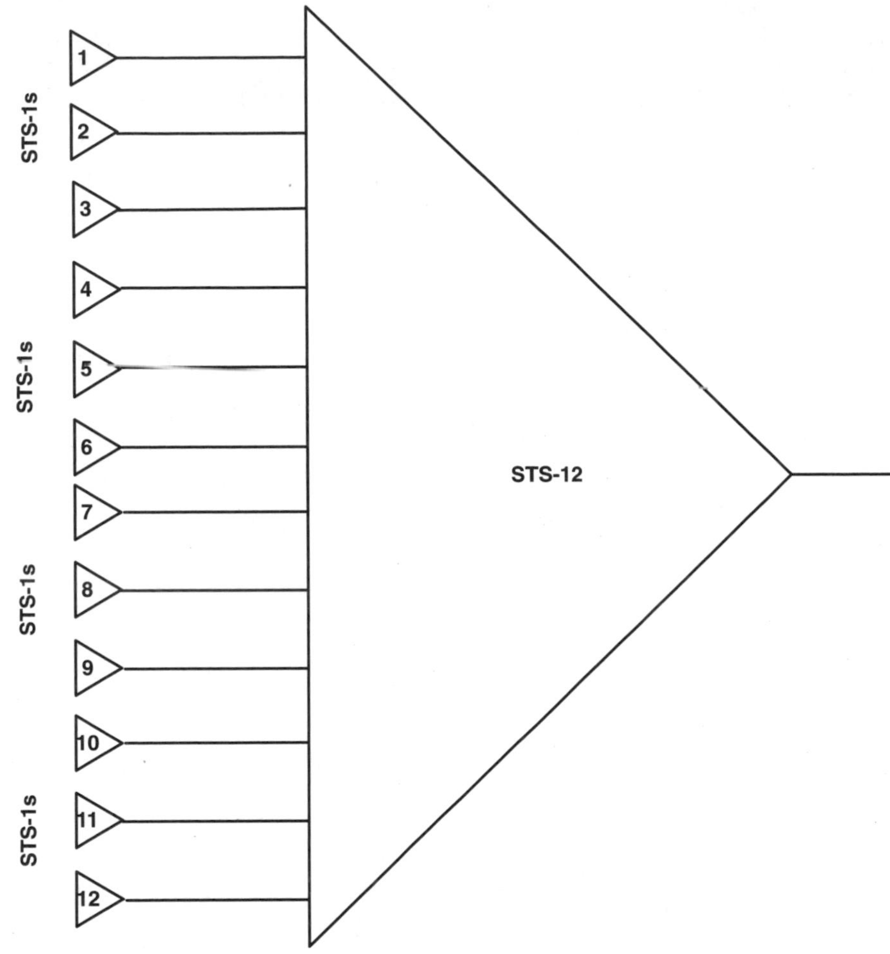

Figure 3-16 Single-step interleaving into a higher-speed multiplexer.

cates that the payload is concatenated, not multiplexed, into three different payloads. This means that a normal STS-3 carries three separate STS-1 signals inside, as shown in Figure 3-14. However, in a concatenated state, the total payload is one super rate multiplexed signal at 155.52 Mbps instead of three smaller ones at 51.84 Mbps each. This is shown in Figure 3-17.

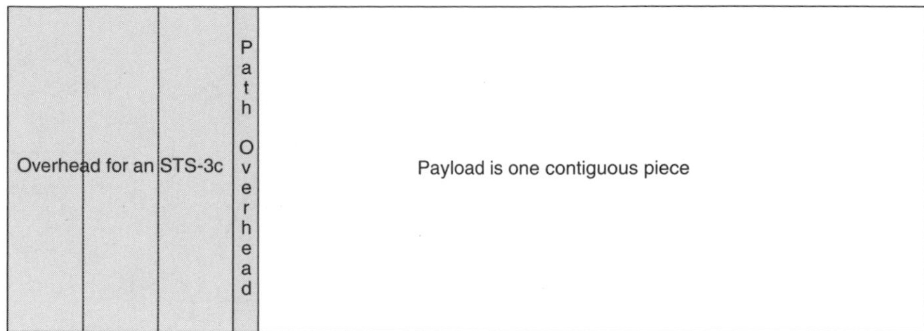

Figure 3-17 An OC-3c concatenated

Add-Drop Multiplexing: A SONET Benefit

Another major benefit of the SONET specification is the ability to perform add-drop multiplexing. Even though network elements are compatible at the OC-*n* level, they may still differ from vendor to vendor. SONET does not attempt to restrict all vendors to providing a single product, nor does it require that they produce one of every type out there. One vendor may offer an add-drop multiplexer with access to the DS-1 level only, whereas another may offer access to DS-1 and DS-3 rates. The benefit of an add-drop multiplexer on a *wide-area network* (WAN) is to drop (demultiplex) only those portions of the optical stream required for a location and let the rest pass through without the demultiplexing process. It would be extremely inefficient to have to demultiplex an entire OC-12 stream, for example, only to drop out one DS-1. The ability to extract only what is necessary helps to prevent errors, loss of data, and other delays inherent to older technologies. The add-drop multiplexer makes this attractive for carriers to use in rural areas, where they may bundle many lower-speed communications channels onto a single OC-1 or OC-3 to carry the information back to the central metropolitan area. Moreover, beyond just dropping a digital signal out of a higher-speed OC-*n,* the carrier can fill in what has been vacated (for example, if a DS-1 is dropped off along the optical path, a new DS-1 can be multiplexed back into the OC-3 in its place). This enables the carriers considerable flexibility. Figure 3-18 shows an add-drop multiplexer. Here, portions of the bandwidth can be dropped off and

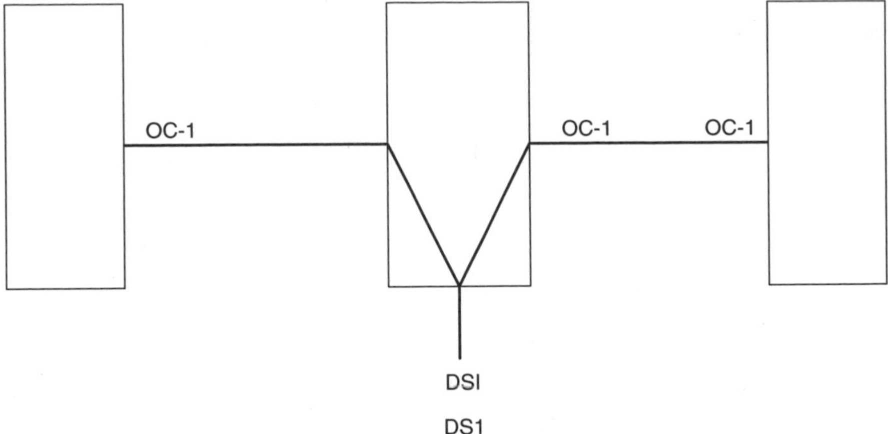

Figure 3-18 Add-drop multiplexing with SONET

additional new signals can be added in place of the data stream dropped out of the higher-speed signal. A single-stage add-drop multiplexing function can multiplex various inputs into an OC-*n* signal. At an add-drop site, only those signals which need to be accessed are dropped and inserted. The remaining traffic continues through the network switching system without requiring special processing.

SONET Topologies

Several different topologies can be used in a SONET network employing various multiplexers. These include the normal topologies most networks have become accustomed to over the years, such as

- Point-to-point
- Point-to-multipoint
- Hub and spoke
- Ring

The variations enable more flexibility for SONET in the WANs built by the carriers and now becoming the method of choice at many large organizations. With each of the topologies, larger organizations are finding the benefits of installing highly reliable interoperable equipment at private network interfaces and access points to public networks.

Point-to-Point

The SONET multiplexer, the entry-level PTE for an organization [or the equipment installed by the *local exchange carrier* (LEC) at the customer's premises to access the network], acts as a concentrator device for the multiple lower-speed communications channels such as DS-1 and DS-3. In its simplest form, two devices are connected with an optical fiber (with any repeaters as necessary) as a point-to-point circuit. As the entry-level point into SONET architecture, the inputs and outputs are identical. In this environment, the network can act as a stand-alone environment and not have to interface with the public switched networks. Figure 3-19 illustrates the point-to-point multiplexing arrangement.

Point-to-Multipoint

The next step is to consider the point-to-multipoint arrangement. This will use a form of add-drop multiplexing to drop circuits off along the way. In a large corporate network spanning the country (or any subset), a single high-speed link may be employed. The SONET *add-drop multiplexer* (ADM) is used for the task, dropping circuits out without demultiplexing the entire high-speed signal. In Figure 3-20, the ADM is installed between two far-end locations so that signals can be added or dropped off as necessary. This is a better solution than renting three different circuits between points *AB, AC,* and *BC,* which adds to the complexity and cost. By using a circuit from *A* to *B* to *C* with ADMs, the service usually can be accommodated more efficiently.

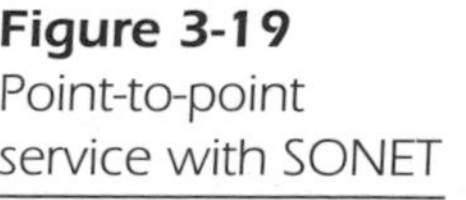

Figure 3-19 Point-to-point service with SONET

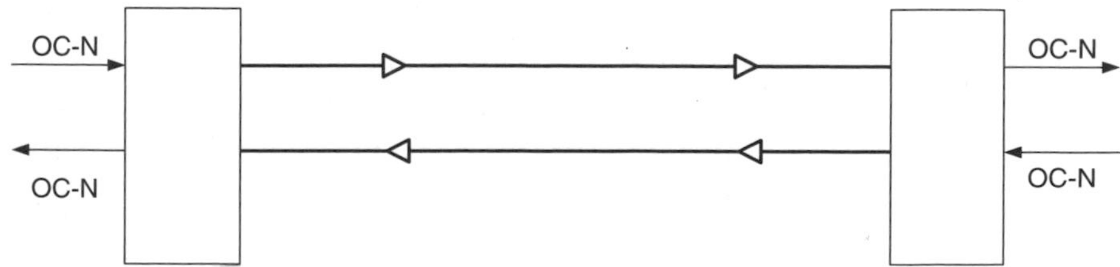

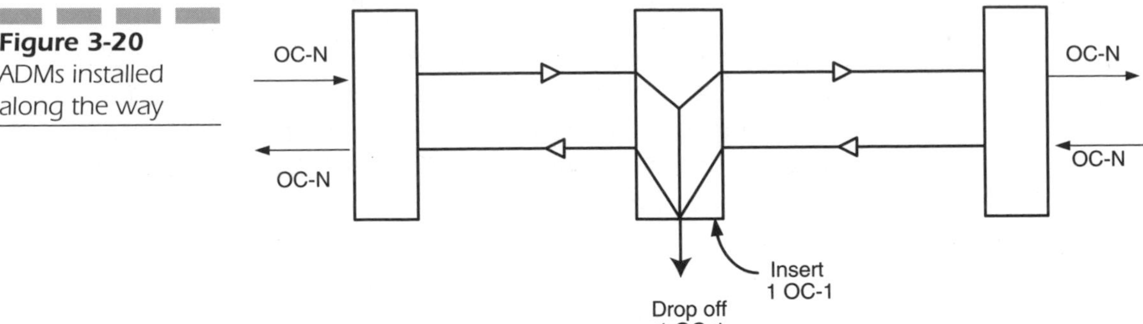

Figure 3-20 ADMs installed along the way

Hub and Spoke

The hub and spoke method (sometimes referred to the *star network*) enables some added flexibility in the event of unpredicted growth or constant change in the architecture of the network. SONET multiplexers can be hubbed into a digital cross-connect, where the signal is concentrated and then forwarded on to the next node. This is used in many larger organizations where regional offices are located at some distance, and district or branch offices are tied into the network through the hub. Once again, the flexibility is available if a major change occurs in the network architecture or in the event of major campaigns in the organization. Hubs will act as the cross-connect points to link the various echelons in the network together. These may be developed in a blocking or nonblocking manner. Typically, some blocking may be allowed. The hub and spoke arrangement is shown in Figure 3-21.

Ring

Next comes the real glory of SONET. In a ring architecture, where SONET automatic protection switching is employed, the best of all worlds comes to fruition. In this topology, ADMs are used throughout the network, and a series of point-to-point links is installed between adjoining neighbors. The bidirectional capability provides the most robustness for the network; however, unidirectional services also can be installed. The primary advantage of the ring architecture is survivability in the event of a cable cut or a failure in a network node. The multiplexers have sufficient intelligence to reroute or reverse direction in the event of a failure. If more than one fiber link is installed, the systems could use alternate paths, but they must recover in milliseconds (which APS on SONET is designed to do). Figure 3-22 shows the ring topology with dual fibers running (bidirectional service) between the ADMs.

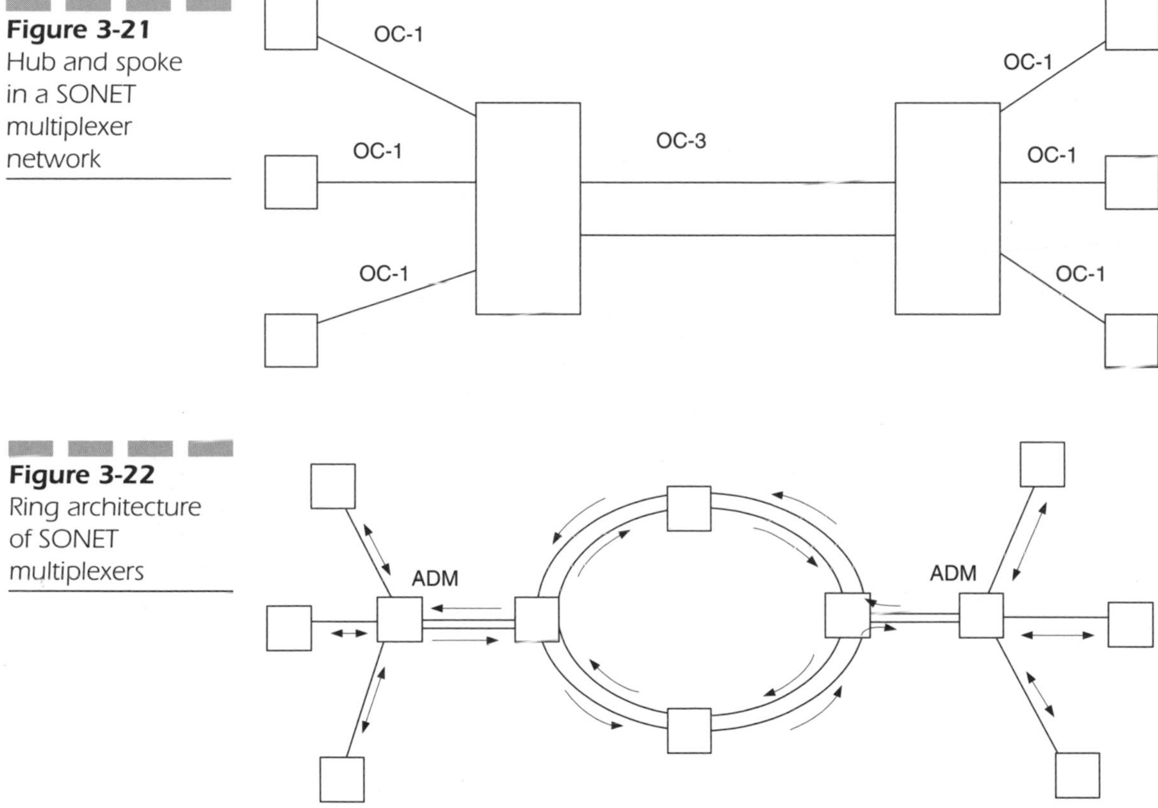

Figure 3-21 Hub and spoke in a SONET multiplexer network

Figure 3-22 Ring architecture of SONET multiplexers

CHAPTER 4

Synchronous Digital Hierarchy

As discussed in Chapter 3, *Synchronous Optical Networking* (SONET) is the high-speed optical-based architecture for carriers and users alike. This optical-based networking strategy was developed in North America by the *American National Standards Institute* (ANSI). While the ANSI committees were working on SONET, though, another movement was underway. In Europe, the standards committees also were wrestling with the logical replacement to the *Plesiochronous Digital Hierarchy* (PDH), which is an asynchronous multiplexing plan to create high-speed communications channels. The Europeans came up with a separate multiplexing hierarchy called *Synchronous Digital Hierarchy* (SDH) in support of the SONET standards.

Ever since the standards bodies approved the recommendations for the SDH (and SONET), the services have been used effectively to improve and revolutionize the industry. Significant cost efficiencies and performance improvements have been shown. SDH provides a means for the rest of the world to use the capabilities of fiber-based transport systems and multiplexing architectures to improve on the older PDH, which was inefficient and expensive. The PDH evolved in response to the demand for *plain old telephone services* (POTS) and was not ideally suited to promote the efficient use of bandwidth and high-speed services.

Digital networks continue to expand in complexity and penetration within the carriers' networks, now moving closer to the consumers' premises. High-speed communications prior to the formulation of SDH in 1990 operated at speeds of up to 139.364 *megabits per second* (Mbps). However, the carriers implemented coaxial and radio-based systems operating at 140 to 565 Mbps. The networks were severely constrained due to the high cost of the transmission medium (coaxial cable especially). The multiplexing rates used plesiochronous rates, which led to the European PDH.

After the development of fiber and the enhancements of integrated circuitry, the newer transmission speeds and complex networking architectures became realistic. In Europe, the evolution and deployment of *Integrated Services Digital Networks* (ISDN) also led to proliferation of the *Broad Band ISDN* (B-ISDN) standards, which enable a simple multiplexing technique. In the United States, the breakup of Bell Telephone prompted the local carriers to look for interoperability and improvements in network management because of proliferation of the number of carriers providing long-distance services.

The *International Telecommunications Union-Telecommunications Standardization Sector* (ITU-TS) agreed that something had to be done to improve and standardize the multiplexing and interoperability while at the same time taking advantage of the higher capacity of optical fiber. The older bit interleaving of multiplexers should be replaced by byte interleaving to provide for better network management. The new standard appeared as SONET in the North Americas, drafted by BellCore.[1] Later this same standard developed into the SDH/SONET standard as approved by the ITU. Although SONET and SDH were drafted initially in support of fiber, radio-based systems supporting the same multiplexing rates also became available.

Why SDH/SONET

Many reasons explain why SONET and SDH were necessary. The primary reason was that previous technology (PDH) was limited in many ways, such as

- U.S. and European systems had little in common in their mapping and multiplexing systems. Therefore, expensive translators were required for trans-Atlantic traffic on leased lines.
- "Standard" equipment from different vendors in the same country was incompatible. Everyone produced a proprietary solution that worked with his or her own equipment.
- Systems did not offer self-checking of equipment and network components. Expensive manual checks were required, and extraordinary repair systems were the norm.
- No standard for high-bandwidth links existed. Everything maintained the proprietary approach. This created havoc in the industry and needed to be improved.

[1]The BellCore name has since been changed to TelCordia Technologies.

- Not all the multiplexing systems were synchronous. In the United States, anything above DS-1 bandwidth was asynchronously multiplexed, timed, and mapped.

Synchronous Communications

What does synchronous mean anyway? Why is it so important to the telecommunications industry? The easiest way to describe the need for synchronization is that the "bits" from one telephone call are always in the same location inside a digital transmission frame such as a DS-1. In the United States, telephone calls using digital transmission systems create a DS-0. The DS-0 signals are multiplexed 24 per DS-1 channel. DS-1 lines are synchronously timed and mapped; therefore, it is easy to remove or insert a call. Finding the location creates an easy add-drop multiplexing arrangement.

Plesiochronous

Plesiochronous means "almost synchronous." Variations occur on the timing of the line, so bits are stuffed into the frames as padding. The digital bits (1s and 0s) vary slightly in their specific location within the frame, creating jitter. This occurs on a frame-to-frame basis, creating ill timing and requiring some other actions to make everything bear some semblance of timing. An example seen in the preceding chapter with the multiplexing of a DS-3 stream occurred when

- Four DS-1 lines were bit-interleaved and multiplexed together to create a DS-2.
- Seven DS-2 lines were bit-interleaved and multiplexed to create a DS-3.
- We needed to isolate a particular call from a DS-3 stream, and the entire DS-3 stream had to be demultiplexed to the DS-1 level, where we could then extract the individual DS-0 signals.

- It became apparent that very expensive equipment was needed at every central office to demultiplex and multiplex high-speed lines across the backbone networks.

Consequently, the standards committees (both ANSI and the ITU) began working on solutions to these multiplexing problems. The ultimate attempt was to develop a synchronous transmission system that could replace the plesiochronous transmission systems.

Table 4-1 presents a summary and comparison of worldwide speeds and hierarchical arrangements. This table brings the differences to light when you compare the speeds and multiplexed channels combined.

In 1986, the *Consultative Committee of International Telegraphy and Telephony* (CCITT)[2] published a standard set of transmission rates for SDH. The SDH standards finally emerged in 1992. These are filed under the following standards:

- G.707
- G.708
- G.709

Table 4-1

Comparing the Speed Rates for Various Levels of the Digital Hierarchy [in kilobits per second, (kbps)]

Hierarchical Level	North American DS-n	European CEPT-n	Japanese Level	International Rules
0	64	64	64	64
1	1,544	2,048	1,544	2,048
2	6,312	8,448	6,312	6,312
3	44,736	34,368	32,064	44,736
4	274,176	139,264	97,728	139,264
5	564,992	397,200	564,992	

[2]CCITT is now called the ITU-TS

Using the same fiber, a synchronous network is able to increase the available bandwidth while reducing the amount of equipment in the network. Moreover, the provisioning of SDH for sophisticated network management introduces much more flexibility into the overall networking strategies for the carriers.

Synchronous Digital Hierarchy

As synchronous equipment was rolled into the network, the full benefits became more apparent. The carriers experienced significant cost reductions and avoidances, less hardware, and increased efficiencies in multiplexing of the various rates established by the ITU. However, other benefits required less spares to be maintained in the network. Additional benefits were had by the use of the SDH standard multiplexing formats, which could encapsulate the PDH multiplexed signals inside the SDH transport. This protects the carriers' investments and prevents the use of forklift technology. In fact, SDH offered the network operators the ability to future-proof their networks, allowing them to offer *metropolitan area network* (MAN), *wide-area network* (WAN), and B-ISDN services on a single platform.

The SDH forms a multiplexing rate based on the STM-n frame format. STM stands for synchronous transmission module. The STM-n general frame format works as follows: Similar to the SONET OC-1 (albeit larger), the basic STM-1 frame consists of

$$270 \text{ columns} \times 9 \text{ rows} = 2430 \text{ octets}$$

$$9 \text{ columns} \times 9 \text{ rows} = 81 \text{ octets section overhead}$$

The remaining 2349 octets create the payload. Higher-rate frames are derived from multiples of STM-1 according to the value of n. The standard STM-1 frame is shown in Figure 4-1. This is similar but different from the frame in an OC-3 stream.

Figure 4-1
The STM-1 frame formats

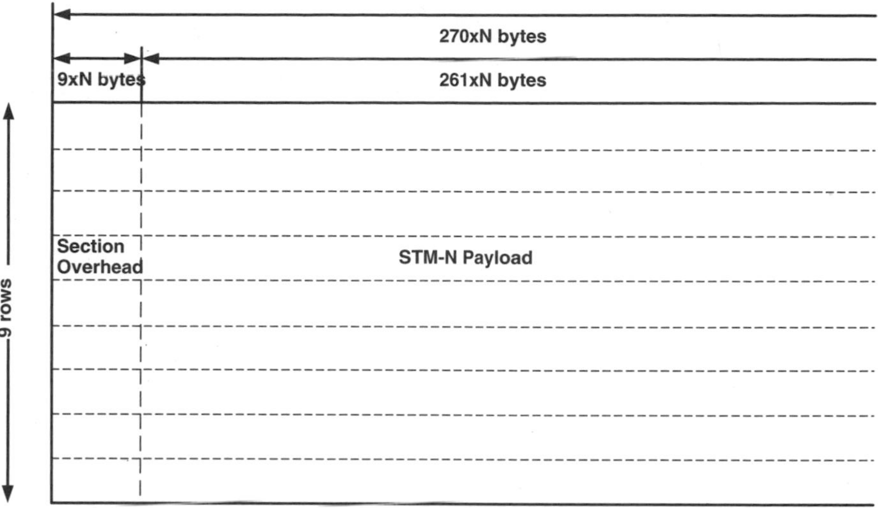

Data Transmission Rates

In the standards, a number of transmission rates are defined or possibly based on multiplexing rates. Not all rates are available commercially; however, the rates are there in case a new rate is needed. Similar to the SONET standards, SDH defines the synchronous transport signal level n (STS-n) and the SDH level n (SDH-n). These define the electrical rate of multiplexing and the optical rate of multiplexing, both working at the appropriate rate of speed necessary to map and multiplex the higher rates of speed. The typical rates of speed and the appropriate STS and STM rates are shown in Table 4-2.

Only three of the hierarchical levels are actually defined in the standard and are available commercially: STM-1, STM-4, and STM-16. Other rates will become available as needed. As the multiplexing occurs and the overhead is subtracted from the payload, the actual throughput is shown in Table 4-3. This table reflects the aggregates of throughput in the three commercially available STM payloads.

Table 4-2

Comparison of STS and STM Rates

Electrical Rate	Optical Rate	Speed
STS-1	STM-0	51.84 Mbps
STS-3	STM-1	155.52 Mbps
STS-9	STM-3	466.56 Mbps
STS-12	STM-4	622.08 Mbps
STS-18	STM-6	933.12 Mbps
STS-24	STM-8	1.244 Gbps
STS-36	STM-12	1.866 Gbps
STS-48	STM-16	2.488 Gbps

Table 4-3

SDH Payload Compositions for Hierarchical Rates

STM Level	Data Rate	Actual Payload
1	155.52 Mbps	150.112 Mbps
4	622.08 Mbps	601.344 Mbps
16	2.4883 Gbps	2.40537 Gbps

Some Differences to Note

Many of the actual rates in use are defined under the initial capacities of SONET in the CCITT standards. The original SDH standard defined the transport of 1.5, 2, 6, 34, 45, and 140 Mbps within the transmission rate of 155.52 Mbps (STM-1). SDH was intended to carry the SONET rates; however, the European manufacturers and carriers carry only the *European Telecommunication Standards Institute* (ETSI)-defined PDH rates of 2, 34, and 140 Mbps (the E-2 specification was deleted in the specification). SDH really turns out to be more than just a set of multiplexing speeds and transport rates. It is also a *network node interface* (NNI) defined by the ITU-TSS for worldwide use that is partially compatible with the ANSI SONET specification. Further, it is one of two options for the *user-to-network interface* (UNI) to support the B-ISDN.

The Multiplexing Scheme

When trying to understand the SDH architecture, it is important to remember that the North Americans have always done things one way and the Europeans (actually the rest of the world) have done things a different way. The two entities never seem to become harmonized. As a result, the way the mapping and multiplexing were arranged differs from the way the standards and multiplexing techniques work in the North American communities (ANSI and SONET). The language differs from what is used in SONET specifications.

As the framing and formatting begins with the STM-1 frame, using the equivalent of the OC-3 specifications, the language begins to shift in a simple yet confusing manner. The STM-1 frame is shown in Figure 4-2 again, but with a few differences. First, the frame does consist of 270 columns and 9 rows, creating a frame of 2430 bytes. Second, there will be 8,000 frames per second (the frame time is 125 μ = micro(s). This creates an overall throughput of 155.52 Mbps, the same as SONET.

Figure 4-2 Size of the STM-1 frame

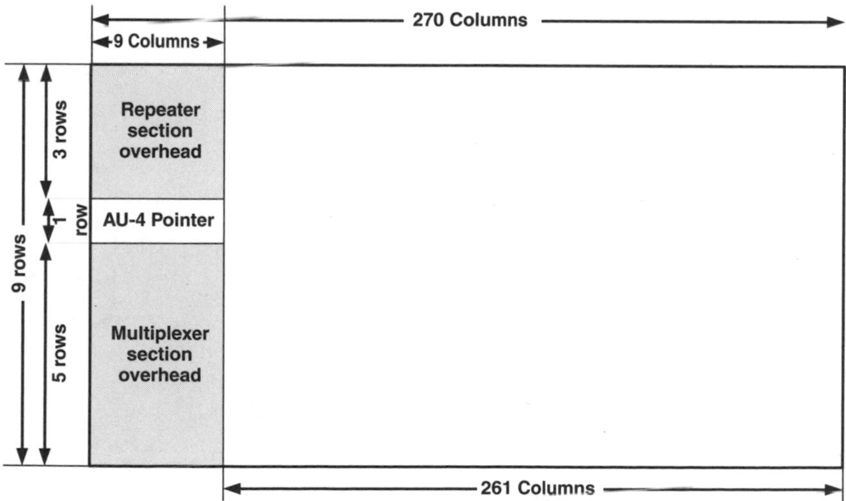

As the data are prepared for placement in the frame, several different modes of transport are available. At the input, the data flow into a container with a size designation. For example, C11 is the equivalent of a T-1 transport mechanism at 1.544 Mbps. C12 will carry the E-1 transport mechanism at 2.048 Mbps. Another transport is C2, which is the equivalent of a DS-2 operating at 6.312 Mbps.

Each of these container levels is then input into a virtual container (VC level n). In Figure 4-3, the inputs flow into the basic container and then are mapped into the VC. This may sound very similar to the SONET *virtual tributary* (VT). SDH defines a number of containers, each corresponding to an existing plesiochronous rate. The information from a PDH signal is mapped into the relevant container. This is done in a manner similarly to the bit-stuffing procedure used in conventional PDH multiplexers. Each container has some overhead and control information contained in it, called *path overhead* (POH). The bytes associated with the POH enable the car-

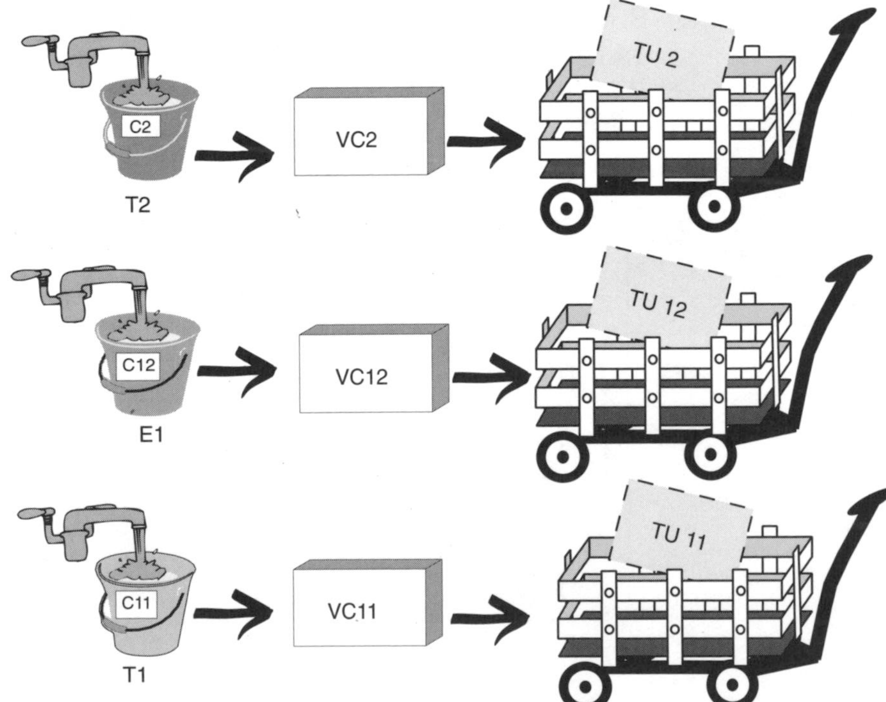

Figure 4-3 The VCs are created.

Table 4-4

Levels of Input as They Map into Tributary Units

Equivalent	Rate	Input	Mapping	Aligning
DS-1	1.544 Mbps	C11	VC11	TU11
E-1	2.048 Mbps	C12	VC12	TU12
DS-2	6.312 Mbps	C2	VC2	TU2
E-3/T-3	34-368/44 .736 Mbps	C3	VC3	TU3
E-3/T-3	34.368/44 .736 Mbps	C3	VC3	AU3
E-4	139.264 Mbps	C4	VC4	AU4

riers to perform end-to-end monitoring and provisioning for performance rates. The container and the POH combined together form the VC.

Next, the VCs are mapped and multiplexed within the frame into a tributary unit level n. Our example will now complete the input from a container to a VC to a tributary unit. The levels are basically the same designation as shown in Table 4-4. The T-1, E-1, and T-2 lines can be mapped and multiplexed into VCs that provide the format needed within SDH. The containers are then aligned with the timing of the system to create a *tributary unit* (TU).

Four T-1s (TU11), three E-1s (TU12), or one T-2 (TU2) can be multiplexed into a TU group 2, as shown in Figure 4-4. The architecture begins this way at the entry levels of the SDH.

The next step in the process is to develop a higher level of multiplexing. Here, the TUs or TU groups are multiplexed into a higher level. Let's think of this as the T-1/T-2 and T-3 architecture in North America. Seven TU group 2s are multiplexed into a TU group 3. This is a T-3 operating at the ±45-Mbps rate of speed. The alternative to this is to take one T-3 and place that into a TU group 3. This is shown in Figure 4-5, where seven of the *TU group 2s* (TUG2) or one TU group 3 is multiplexed into a *TU group 3* (TUG3) and then carried into the system as an *administrative unit* (AU) group 3.

To make this even larger, the next step is to continue the multiplexing process. Therefore, three of the TUG3s or one E-4 mapped into a C4 are then multiplexed into the next higher level in the hierarchy called a *virtual container 4* (VC4). This is shown in Figure 4-6.

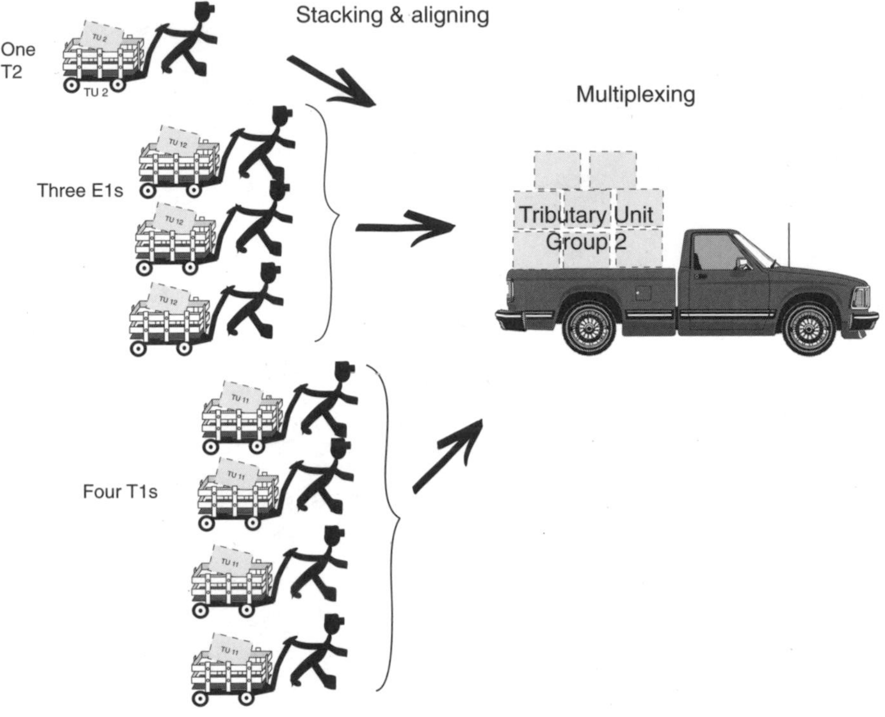

Figure 4-4 Mapping and aligning into TU group 2

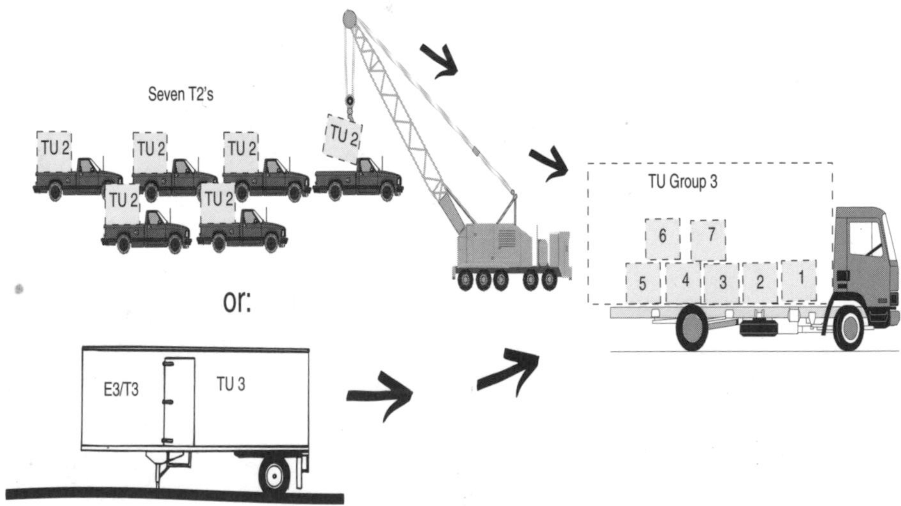

Figure 4-5 The process of creating a TU group 3

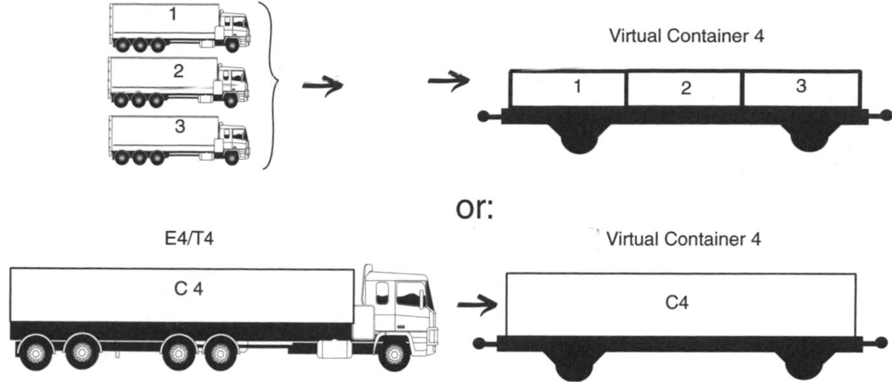

Figure 4-6
Creating a VC4

When VC4 is aligned into an SDH frame, it becomes *AU group 4* (AUG4) and is carried through the system. Figure 4-7 show this unit aligned to the SDH framing format of an E-4 rate of 139.364 Mbps inside a 155.52-Mbps framed SDH transport (STM-1).

One can see that the rates of multiplexing are very similar to the SONET specification; however, differences in bit stuffing and clocking still exist inside this framing and formatting. The comparison now turns to the look and feel of SONET tributary multiplexing and SDH multiplexing in the overall scheme of this transport system.

Figure 4-8 is a representation of a SONET multiplexing arrangement used to produce AUG3 (which by all stretches of the imagination is T-3 or the seven T-2s). Here, the AUG is the equivalent of three AU3s. One can now derive the fact that the three AUs creating the AUG is an OC-3 operating at 155.52 Mbps.

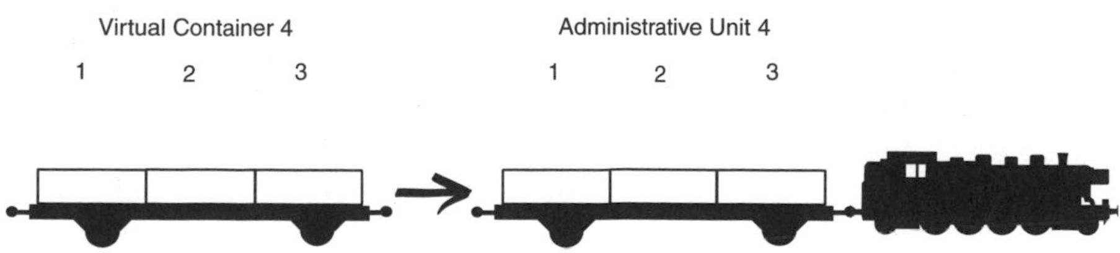

Figure 4-7
The E-4 is created inside an STM-1.

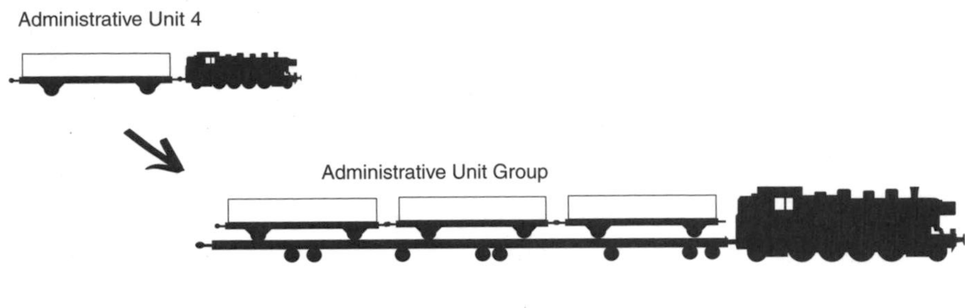

Figure 4-8 The SONET tributary multiplexing scheme

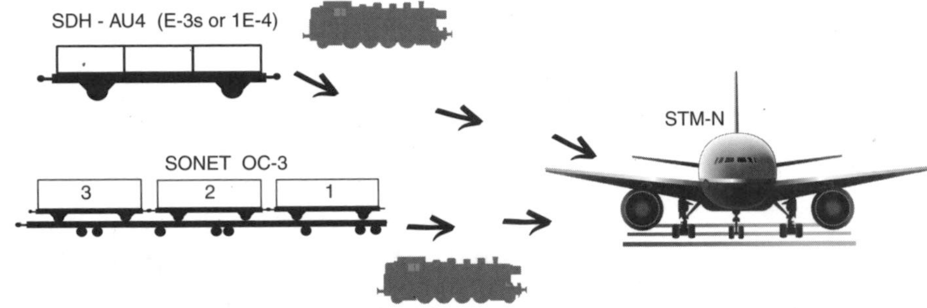

Figure 4-9 The final outcome of SDH or SONET framing

Finally, comparing the multiplexed rates into these AUGs in both SDH and SONET, the outcome is STM-n, as shown in Figure 4-9. We can add the services as necessary to get to STM-4, which is the 622.08-Mbps transport, or STM-16, which is the 2.488-Gbps transport system. One can see that the two systems are very closely aligned to each other; just different multiplexing and formatting arrangements are used in defining the overall platforms.

Table 4-5 is a comparison of the combined services just described, including the two systems: the electrical rates and the payloads. This comparison also includes information regarding the overall frame size. Looking at the table shows that industry standardization was somewhat successful in getting the systems to align with each other and prevent some of the age-old problems of the past.

Figure 4-10 shows the overall structure of VC multiplexing as a graph in the flow of channels inside the overall STM-n as depicted by ITU Standard G.707. This is a simple way to view the overall structure of the SDH multiplexing scheme.

Table 4-5

Comparing SDH and SONET Frame Sizes and Nomenclature

SDH	SONET	Fiber	Mbps	Frame Size	Rows/Frame	Payload Bytes	Payload Bytes/Row*
STM-0	STS-1	OC-1	51.84	810	90	774	86
	STS-3	OC-3	155.52	2,430	270	2,322	258
STM-1	STS-3c	OC-3c	155.52	2,430	270	2,340	260
	STS-12	OC-12	622.08	9,720	1,080	9,288	1,032
STM-4	STS-12c	OC-12c	622.08	9,720	1,080	9,387	1043
	STS-48	OC-48	2,488.32	38,880	4,320	37,152	4,128
STM-16	STS-48c	OC-48c	2,488.32	38,880	4,320	37,575	4,175
STM-64	STS-192	OC-192	9,953.28	155,520	17,280	148,608	16,152
STM-256	STS-768	OC-768	39.81312	622,080	69,120	594,432	64,608

*In some cases, the concatenated payloads will produce more bytes because the payloads are all in one set of path overhead. For example, if we eliminate the path overhead of two OC-1s when using an OC-3c, then the payload increases to 2,340 and the payload bytes per row increases by two.

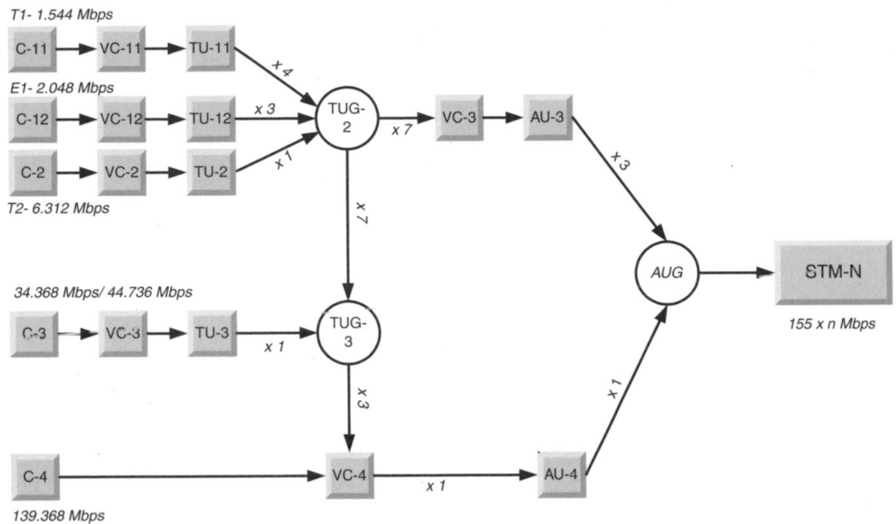

Figure 4-10 Multiplexing structure based on G.707

As the end user (that is, business user) becomes more dependent on the communications infrastructure and the efficiencies that are possible, use of this bandwidth is becoming explosive. At one time, a gigabit of capacity was considered an enormous amount. Now, gigabit to the desk is more the norm. Therefore, use of this bandwidth constitutes one of the fastest-growing segments of the industry. No longer will we be satisfied with just a basic voice call. Instead, we are looking for the necessary bandwidth, on a global basis, to handle voice, data, video, and multimedia. Moreover, we require a network that is close to 100 percent available. PDH networks could not provide this level of service and flexibility. However, SDH networks can and will continue to offer virtually unlimited bandwidth.

In a synchronous network, all the equipment is timed (synchronized) to an overall network clock, as we saw in Chapter 3. The delay associated with transmission links may vary slightly from link to link. Consequently, the location of the virtual containers within an STM-1 frame may not be fixed. The variations are handled using pointers associated with each VC. The pointer "points" to the beginning position of the VC in relation to the STM-1 frame. This pointer can be increased or decreased as necessary to handle variations in the position of the VC.

ITU G.709 defines different combinations of VCs that can fill the payload of an STM-1 frame. The process of data filling in the containers and the addition of overhead is repeated many times at different levels in the SDH. This results in the nesting of smaller VCs within larger ones. The nesting process is repeated until the largest bundle (VC4) is filled. After this, the filled VC4 is loaded into the payload of the STM-1 frame, as shown in Figure 4-11. The pointer processing is different here in the TSM-1 frame than in an STS-3 frame in SONET.

After the payload envelope of the STM-1 frame, additional control information is added to the frame to form the section overhead. This overhead stays with the payload as it propagates along the fiber route between two multiplexers. The reasons this overhead is used include the following:

- It aids in the provisioning for *operations, administration, and maintenance* (OA&M).
- It creates user channels for diagnostics.

Figure 4-11 The data fill based on G.709

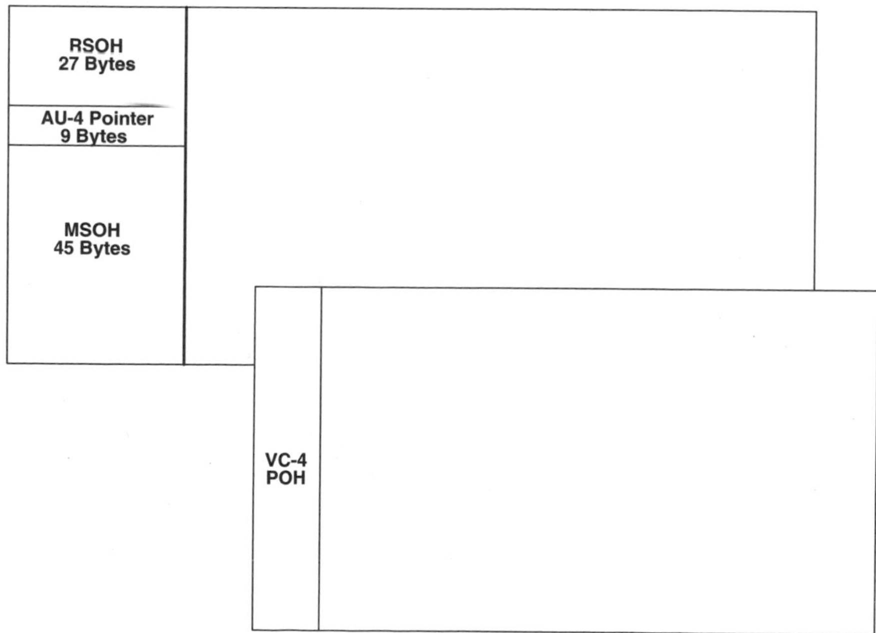

- It provides protection switching.
- It aligns on frame boundaries.
- It determines performance at the section level.
- It performs other associated chores.

Table 4-6 reviews the common rates and interfaces we use in our daily communications lives. These rates include the common interfaces used in an organization for various connectivity solutions.

In Figure 4-12 we see that the use of SONET and SDH equipment became prevalent in the early 1990s. However, the movement is away from the older PDH technologies and more toward the installation of newer SONET and SDH equipment. Within the carrier communities, the movement is dramatic, with virtually no older PDH equipment remaining in the pipeline for installation in the future. This market (PDH) is just about completely gone, with the synchronous marketplace exploding at a rate that exceeds anyone's wildest expectations.

Figure 4-12 Market for SONET/SDH equipment

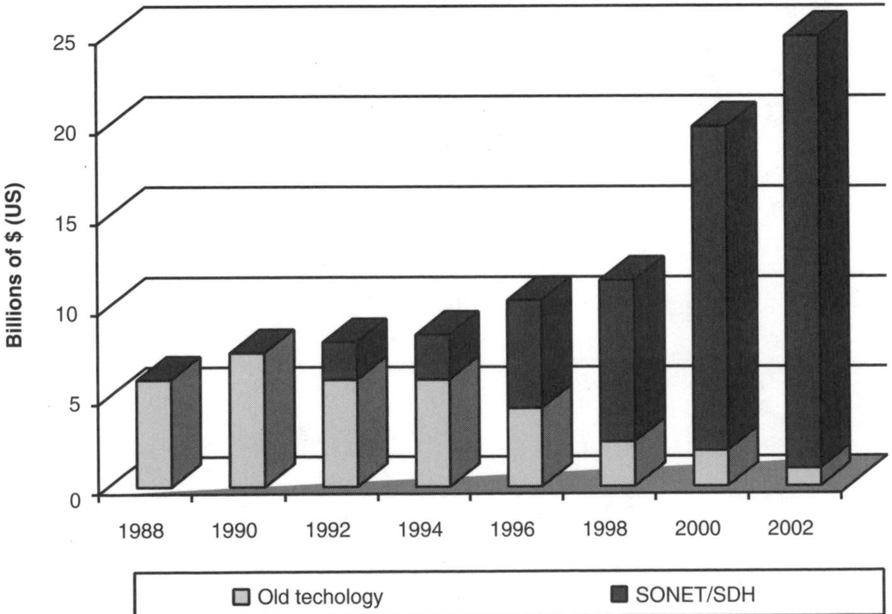

Table 4-6

Comparison of Common Interfaces

Interface	Medium Used	Data Rate, Mbps	Capacity in DS-0s	VT/VC Designator
DS-0	Twisted pair	0.064	1	
ISDN BRI	Twisted pair	0.144	2B+D (2)	
DS-1/ISDN PRI	Twisted pairs (1 or 2)	1.544	24	VT1.5/VC-11
E-1	Twisted pairs (2 or 3)	2.048	32	VT2/VC-12
ADSL	Twisted pair	1.5 up 6.384 down		
Ethernet	Coaxial/twisted Pair (4)	10		
E-3	Coaxial/fiber	34.368	512	VC-31
T-3	Coaxial/fiber/MW	44.736	672	VC-32
STS-1	Coaxial	51.84	672	
Fast Ethernet	Twisted pairs	100		
FDDI	Fiber	100		
Gigabit Ethernet	Fiber	1000		
STS-3	Coaxial	155.52	2016	
E-4	Coaxial/fiber	139.368	2048	VC-4
OC-1	Fiber	51.84	672	
OC-3/STM-1	Fiber	155.52	2,016	
OC-12/STM-4	Fiber	622.08	8,064	
OC-48/STM-16	Fiber	2,483.32	32,256	
OC-192/STM-64	Fiber	9,953.28	129,024	

Why the Hype?

The use of SDH affords significant benefits to the carrier, as well as to the end user. Clearly, any technology that is used in the infrastructure of the network must offer benefit to the end user and carrier alike. Otherwise, the user will not take advantage of the potential share of the services. When we first introduced digital networking to the network, many users wanted to access the digital circuits. Bear in mind that the carriers installed digital services in the 1960s. Yet 1984 was the first time they tariffed use of the digital architecture to the customer's door. Mind you, certain exceptions existed. I personally installed a special assembly in the mid-1970s using a T-1 from Boston to California. This special arrangement was both expensive and difficult to work with because of its newness to end users. However, the carriers had the services in place and converted the backbone networks (wide-area) to all-digital standards-based infrastructures. They needed to operate in this fashion to meet the demand for higher-speed communications, reliability expectations, and cost ratios.

Unfortunately, with the introduction of their networks and standards, problems still existed. The North American carriers installed standards-based equipment in their networks, whereas the European carriers installed their own standards-based equipment. The major problem was that the two did not "speak" with each other. To solve the problem, gateways were required to interface between the different pieces of equipment. However, when the SDH and SONET standards were completed, a new beginning was possible. The intention of both standards was to enable interoperability and transparency between systems. SDH brings the following advantages:

- High-speed transmission rates of up to 10 Gbps in today's backbone. SDH is suitable for the overall carrier networks, which are the information superhighways of today.
- Simplified process for add-drop multiplexing. When compared with the older systems, the PDH networks were extremely complicated. PDH required that we demultiplex an entire DS-3, for example, in order to get at an individual DS-0. It is now much

easier to extract and insert low-bit-rate services into or from the higher-speed services.

- High reliability means high availability. With the SDH networks, providers can meet the demands of their customers faster, better, and cheaper. The providers now can use a standard set of equipment to meet the need, eliminating the need for multiple spares and different operations systems. Moreover, with the *automatic protection switching* (APS) services of the SDH, the network can heal itself when a component fails. This means that the customer never realizes that a network error or failure has occurred.
- Future networking equipment will be based on multiples of the SDH and SONET equipment. The perfect platform for the carriers is one that satisfies the demand without changes en masse. SDH can satisfy the basic telephony needs, low- and high-speed data communications demands, and the newer demands of the Internet, specifically for streaming audio and video capabilities. This also meets the need for video or multimedia on-demand services, only recently becoming more popular.

Three words are crucial to network operators and end users alike: bandwidth, bandwidth, bandwidth. The need for bandwidth cannot be overstated in the network today. There is never too much, only enough to satisfy the current need. As we see use of the networks increasing, the carriers and manufacturers are continually developing new SDH speeds and multiplexing rates to meet that demand. Recently, OC-768 in SONET and SDH-256 were developed to support up to 40 Gbps on a multiplexed circuit. Add to this the ability to perform multiple wavelength multiplexing on a single piece of fiber, and we have the potential for terabits per second. That will hold us for a short term; however, telecommunications services are like water, and water seeks its own level. Thus telecommunications services will increase when we have more bandwidth until we consume it all. Then it is back to the drawing board to develop a new technique to increase the capacities again. This is a vicious circle, but one that is also extremely exciting as the thresholds are pushed to new levels and limits.

The Model as It Pertains to SDH

Everything we do usually ties back to a reference to the international standards. For this we use the *Open Systems Interconnect* (OSI) as a reference model. In general, SDH operates at the bottom layer (layer 1, physical) of the OSI. This physical layer is subdivided into three separate components. When we deal with this mapping on the OSI, we usually refer to four sublayer components.

Similar to the SONET architecture, SDH networks are divided into various layers that are directly related to the network topology. The lowest layer is the physical transmission section, the medium in the form of glass (fiber), but it also can represent radio systems such as microwave or satellite. Actually, the photonic layer is below the physical layer, where we turn the pulses into light (photons) and propagate them on the fibers. In many cases, the photonic and the physical layers are combined. The regenerator section is a path between repeaters. This is also at the physical layer because it involves that length of fiber between two repeaters. The overhead is called the *repeater* (or regenerator) *section overhead* (RSOH). Signaling across the medium also occurs at this level. Following the repeater portion, we have the *multiplexer overhead* (MSOH) used by the multiplexers for the necessary overhead to track operation of the circuits and OAM&P. The multiplex section deals with the part of the SDH link between two multiplexers where we map and multiplex our services (DS-1) into the SDH transport. Sitting on top of the MSOH are two VC layers. These two layers are a part of the mapping process whereby the individual tributary signals are placed inside the SDH payload. VC4 is the mapping for the 139-Mbps payload, whereas VC12 contains the individual E-1 signals mapped into the SDH.

An overall picture of this (the SDH layer model) is shown in Figure 4-13. The lowest layer is the physical transmission section, the medium in the form of glass (fiber), but it also can represent radio systems such as microwave or satellite. In the figure, the photonic layer is shown as a subset to the physical interface. Note that the ATM, POTS, and *Internet Protocol* (IP) networks are also shown in this figure in as much as they fit into the overall scheme of the model.

Figure 4-13 SDH layer model contrasted with OSI

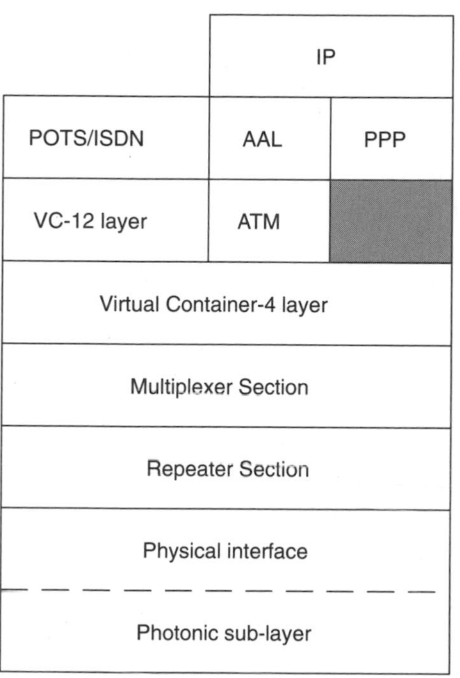

Figure 4-14 Path mapping of SDH

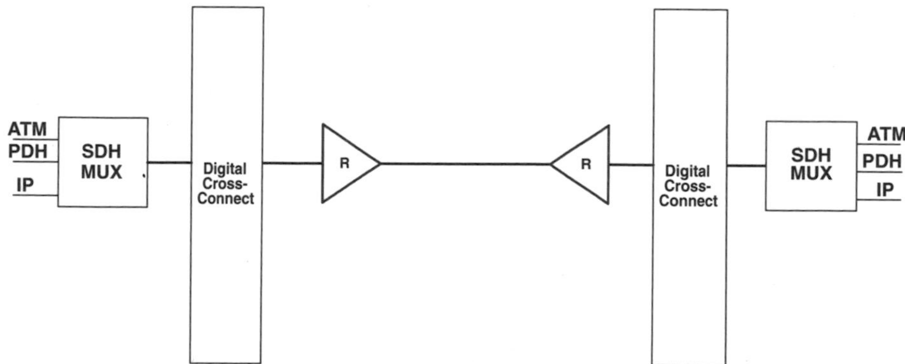

Figure 4-14 shows the mapping of the payloads at the SDH multiplexer, whereby the next portions of the circuit are added. This is shown in the path description.

SDH brings harmony to the overall multiplexing of the various signals and transport rates. It also acts as the gateway between SONET and SDH structure. It has been over a decade since actual ratification of the standards, and now more than ever, the benefits are visible. Transcontinental links are now in heavy use around the world on fiber-based architectures. The costs of circuits between and among countries are at an all-time low due to the bandwidth. As more equipment and carriers are deployed across the world, the World Wide Web of carriers and Internet access will definitely become the norm.

CHAPTER 5

Wave-Division Multiplexing and Dense-Wave-Division Multiplexing

In the past few years, several major improvements have been made in the use of optical fiber communications. In earlier discussions regarding the use of SONET (see Chapter 3) and SDH (see Chapter 4), the issue of bandwidth surfaced. Not only does the issue of bandwidth keep coming up, but more significant is the problem of just how quickly we consume all the bandwidth that is made available. No matter how much or how fast we improve our spectrum availability, newer applications crop up that literally "eat up" all the capacity available to us. The carriers have installed fiberoptic cables as the backbone to link their interoffice networks. This creates a mainstay in their communications infrastructure. Using standard *time-division multiplexing* (TDM), their standard is to carry between 2.488 and 9.953 *gigabits per second* (Gbps) on a single fiber. The revolution to high-bandwidth applications and the explosive use of the Internet have created capacity demands that exceeded the traditional TDM limits. TDM only can operate within the spectrum of the silicon that drives current technologies. What was once considered an inexhaustible amount of capacity when fiberoptics was first introduced has literally vaporized. The depletion of the excess capacity we once had drove a new demand for more bandwidth. To meet this demand, the use of *wave-division multiplexing* (WDM) surfaced.

To solve the problem, the use of *frequency-division multiplexing* (FDM) with our light-based systems became a topic of research. What ensued was the ability to introduce various wavelengths (frequencies) of light on the same fiber cable and the resulting increase in possible throughput. We have seen increases approximate between 16 and 30 times the original capacities of a single fiber. These capacities are now being pushed to the limit, with variations being promised of up to 128 times the capacity of existing fiber technologies. We also hear of 1000 wavelengths being possible. This means that the old days of having to replace the in-place fibers with new technology have been supplanted by newer technology that uses the in-place fiber, necessitating only a change in the electronics on the line. We can expect to see these advances provide virtually unlimited bandwidth without en masse changes in the infrastructure. The future holds the promise of reduced costs, increased bandwidth use, and ease of implementation that meets the demands of our higher-speed communications.

Growing Demands

Clearly, as we begin the new century, the revolution from a voice-centric network to a data- and video-centric network has permeated throughout our industries. Communications, once a narrowband service dominated by narrowband voice services, now demands the bandwidth capable of supporting broadband communications, video, and multimedia. Just about every aspect of our lives has changed. Business, government, medicine, academia, and entertainment activities all depend on high-speed communication networking. Indeed, since commercialization of the Internet, hundreds of millions of users are now engaged in "surfing" activities, music downloads, and video conferencing for the first time. The industry has been struggling to keep up with the explosive pace since 1995. Every prediction that the current fiber technology would hold us for decades was exaggerated tremendously. Figure 5-1 is a graph that shows the dramatic changes in the use of telecommunications capacities since the era began.

What Is Driving the Demand for Bandwidth?

Over the past decade, the world has been deregulating its telephone companies, many of which were owned and operated by governments. These *post, telephone, and telegraph companies* (PTTs) generally were monopolies in their respective country. Users had to accept whatever was offered as part of the regulated entity. New communications services were introduced when the deregulation began. As a result, the opportunity to increase communications interconnectivity and reduce costs was driven by competition.

In the United States, this deregulation began in 1984 with the AT&T divestiture agreement. Since that event, the cost of communications has plummeted, whereas the demand for access has skyrocketed. The growth in revenues due to access and usage has been approximately 40 to 45 percent, whereas the costs per minute (or

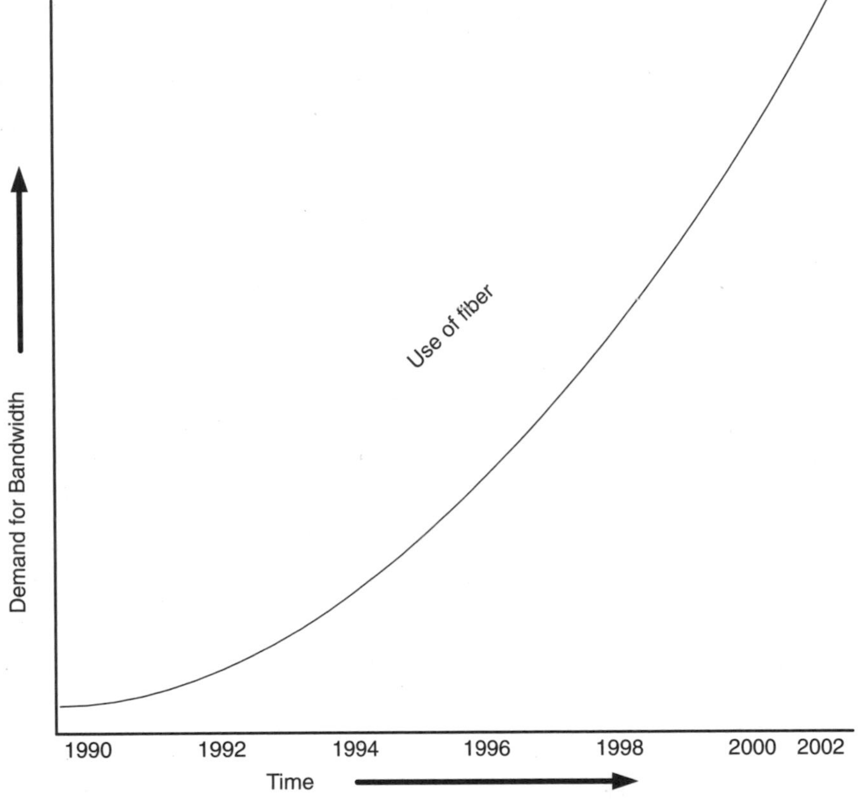

Figure 5-1 Demand represented over time

whatever other measure is used) have decreased by as much as 60 to 80 percent. This is shown in Figure 5-2. As an example, the cost for a long-distance call across the United States in 1984 was approximately $0.40 per minute. However, the cost per minute had declined in 2000 to approximately $0.10 to $0.05 per minute, representing as much as an 80 percent decline. This, of course, is matched by an annualized growth value of approximately 4 percent for voice communications and 30 percent for data communications. The combination of declining costs and greater availability has been dramatic. This has driven the investment in capital for the infrastructure (outside plant) to increase as much as 60 percent. Some of the driving factors in the industry have been the new applications that were introduced over the same period. Applications and network services such as the use of Frame Relay were introduced at speeds of 56 *kilo-*

bits per second (kbps) to 2.048 *megabits per second* (Mbps). However, as the popularity grew, faster services were needed. Frame Relay was bumped up a notch to run at speeds of up to 50 Mbps. At the same time, *Asynchronous Transfer Mode* (ATM) was introduced to operate at speeds of 50, 155, and 622 Mbps. The future will offer speeds of 2.488 Gbps. Add to these network services the growth of the Internet, the exponential growth of wireless connectivity (cellular and PCS), and the increased speeds of silicon chipsets and one can see where the bandwidth is being demanded more in the applications but also in the networks to sustain the throughput.

Wave-Division Multiplexing

Ten years ago, implementation of the OC-48 SONET specification had the industry believing that limitless bandwidth was available. One can just imagine that a mere decade ago the ±2.5-Gbps capacity of the optical fiber networks was innovative and exceeded our wildest imaginations about how we would ever fill these communi-

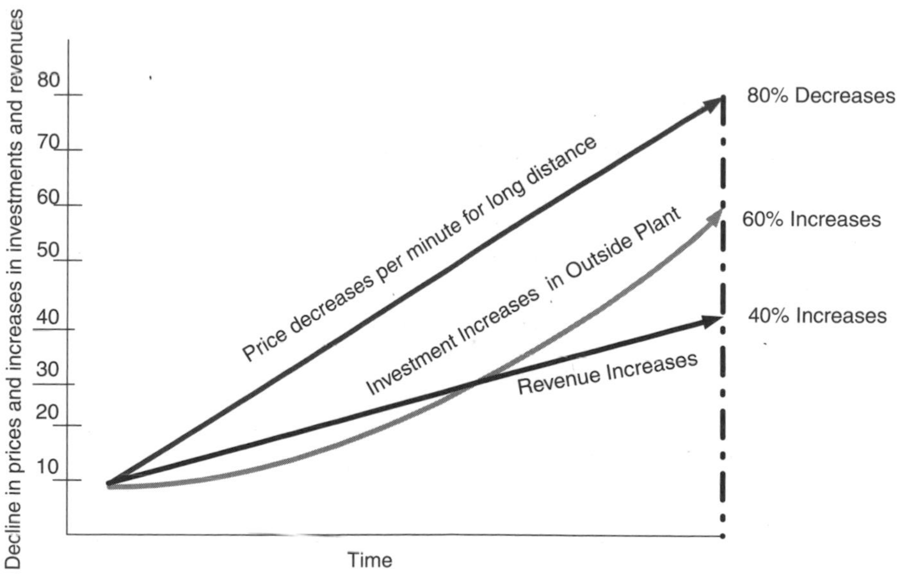

Figure 5-2 Chart of value over time

cations channels. Yet the industry began to recognize the changes in consumption patterns. The demand for multimedia communications, video, and *wide-area networks* (WANs) started to erode even the highest capacities available.

To solve this problem, researchers began to experiment with the use of more than one light beam on the same cable. Light operates in the frequency spectrum similar to the older cable TV systems employing *frequency-division multiplexing* (FDM), as shown in Figure 5-3. By using different radio frequencies on a cable TV system, the carriers were able to expand the number of TV channels available to them on the same coaxial systems. Why not do the same thing with the various frequencies of light?

Wave-division multiplexing (WDM), in contrast, can carry multiple bit rates, enabling multiple channels to be carried on a single fiber. The technique quite literally uses different colors of light down the same fiber to carry different channels of information, which are then separated out at the distant end by a diffraction grating that identifies each color. All optical networks employing WDM with add-drop multiplexers and cross-connects permit this. *Dense WDM* (DWDM) systems multiplex up to 8, 16, 32, or more wavelengths in the 1,550-*nanometer* (nm) window, increase capacity on existing fiber, and are data-rate-transparent.

WDM was first developed to increase the distance that signals could be transported in long-distance networks, from 35 to 50 km to as many as 970 km or more with optical amplifiers. Subsequently, companies discovered that DWDM would work in metropolitan networks just as well. These DWDM ring systems can be connected with

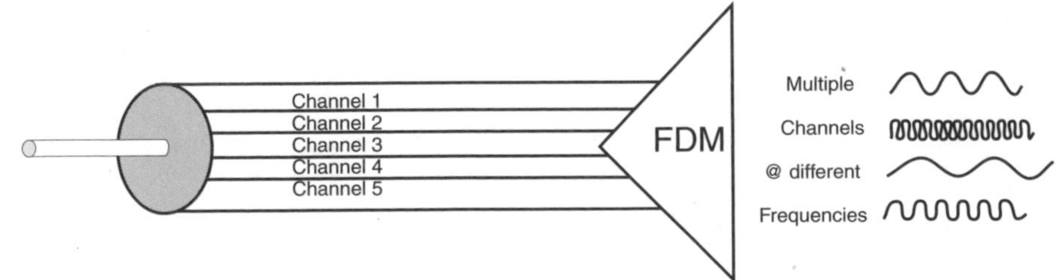

Figure 5-3
Frequency-division multiplexing has been used by cable TV operators to carry more information on their coaxial cables.

ATM switches and *Internet Protocol* (IP) routers. ATM networks are expected to use SONET/SDH physical layer interfaces with OC-12 add-drop multiplexers. ATM can carry voice, video, and data communications in the same transport and switching equipment.

WDM systems require nonzero-dispersion fiber. This type of fiber introduces a small amount of dispersion that decreases nonlinear component effects. Originally, SONET equipment makers expected to be forced to make reliable OC-192 (10-Gbps) systems or face stiff competition from DWDM manufacturers.

Thus a new era was born in the use of WDM. By adding a tightly separated wavelength of light on the same cable, more capacity could be obtained. In normal fiber transmission, the use of two standard wavelengths was originally deployed, as shown in Figure 5-4. First, a red band of light was used to transmit the signal from the originating end. A blue band was used at the opposite end. Therefore, the same cable can carry both send and receive traffic using different color bands. The original OC-48 transmission (operating at ±2.5 Gbps) was exciting, using a single wavelength of light and driving the signal over 20 to 30 miles of fiber. However, the carriers soon recognized that the skyrocketing demand for bandwidth would outpace the throughput of this single-wavelength transmission.

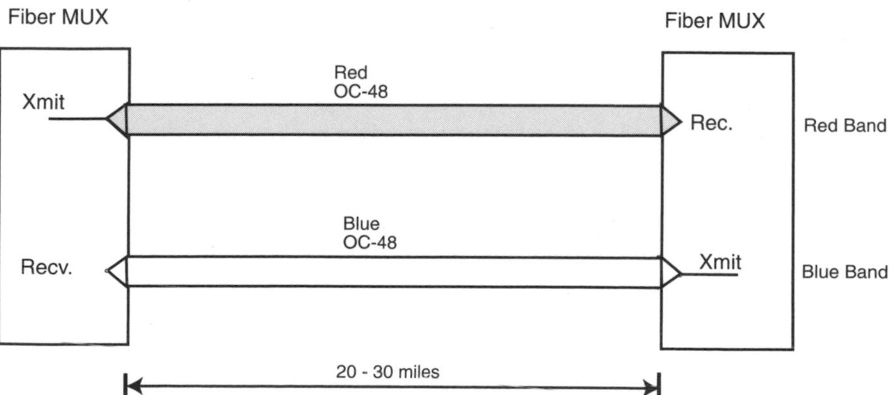

Figure 5-4
The colors of light separate the bands carried on the cable.

Depending on usage of various types, the life cycle of OC-48 was anticipated to be approximately two years. Clearly, the rapid increase in Internet access, cellular communications, high-speed data, and the multimedia improvements were on a collision course with the capacity of this OC-48 architecture. Choosing to move to a higher-capacity multiplexing technique in TDM was a definite consideration. This led to the higher-rate multiplexing of the OC-192 level (±9.953 Gbps), a fourfold increase in the speed and throughput of SONET networks. Yet, even though such increases were achieved at the OC-192 level, the initial implementation was with one wavelength of light.

At the same time, OC-48, using two wavelengths, produced a 5-Gbps throughput on the same fibers, proving that the technology could work. Shortly after the introduction of OC-192, strides were taken to introduce OC-48 running four wavelengths (10 Gbps) or a single OC-192 using one wavelength.

Shortly after 10 Gbps were demonstrated, the designers began to experiment with 20-Gbps capacity using eight wavelengths of OC-48 and/or two wavelengths at the OC-192 rate. Now the stage was set to push the envelope as far as possible. It was only a matter of a few years before the developers began introducing quantum leaps in their multiplexing ability. Now, with multiples of OC-48 and OC-192, the capabilities of fiber-based transmission exceed the wildest imagination. Capacities for the DWDM service are now ranging from 160 Gbps to as much as 400 Gbps. This is the first of many steps we can expect to see in the near future. Some rumors indicate 128 wavelengths of OC-192 (that is, 1.2 Tbps) being possible shortly.

Figure 5-5 shows a variable number of wavelengths being selected in a WDM system that can carry many different wavelengths, exponentially increasing the throughput.

Table 5-1 summarizes the capacities of DWDM today and what the future may hold. The table shows the level of multiplexing as well as the possible throughput one can expect for the future. The table also shows the number of wavelengths on the single-mode fiber.

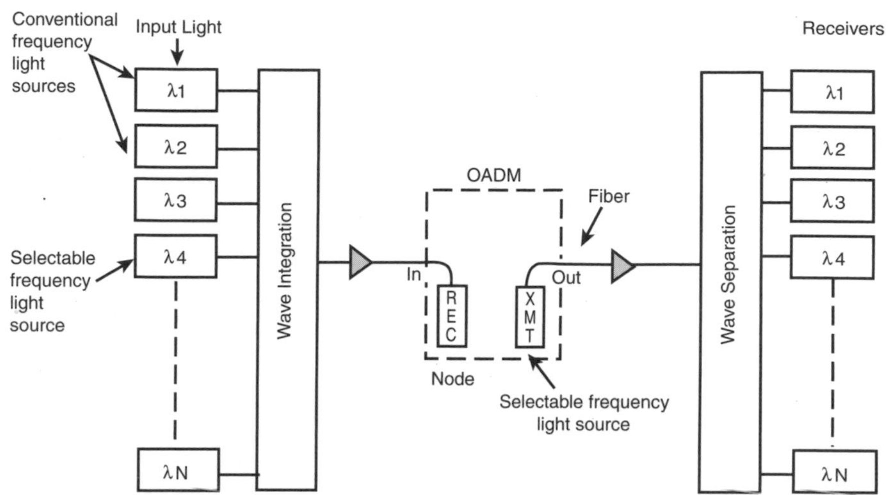

Figure 5-5 WDM systems

Table 5-1 Summary of the Current Capacity of DWDM Services

DWDM Level	Number λ	Number OC-48	Number OC-192	Total Throughput
1	1	1	-	2.5 Gbps
	2	2		5.0 Gbps
2	4	4		10 Gbps
	1		1	
3	8	8		20 Gbps
	2		2	
4	4 Hybrid	1	2	25 Gbps
5	16	16		40 Gbps
	4		4	
6	8 Hybrid	4	4	50 Gbps
7	32 Hybrid	32	8	80 Gbps
8	16	12	4	100 Gbps
9	16	-	16	160 Gbps
10	32 Hybrid	16	16	200 Gbps
11	32	-	32	320 Gbps

Benefits of Fiber over Other Media

The benefits of fiber over other media are shown in Table 5-2. However, it is important to note that fiber has been used extensively in the long-distance telecommunications networks and the local telephone company networks. It is more recent that a single-mode fiber has worked its way into end-user networks (LANs and *Campus Area Networks* [CANs]). With single-mode fiber, the speeds are constantly being upped, while the error performances are continually being improved. This table concentrates on the *bit error rates* (BERs) and the speed of the cabling systems.

Wave-Division Multiplexing

Now back to the wave division-multiplexing concept. There is no mistake; demands and needs for telecommunications services are growing. The combination of voice, data, and multimedia applications that are constantly putting pressure on the infrastructure adds to the growing problem, where normal digital transmission systems use TDM and *cable TV* (CATV) analog technologies use FDM. WDM is a combination of the two schemes. Use of a TDM multiplexer breaks the bandwidth down to specific timeslots such as those found in SONET-based networks. However, by using the combination of frequency (different wavelengths) and time (timeslots), the fiber can be used to carry orders of magnitude more than traditional fiber-based systems. Figure 5-6 shows the combination of the two multiplexing arrangements in a single format. Furthermore, several different wavelengths and colors of light can be used to produce far more capacity.

No one can mistake the fact that telecommunications capacity needs are growing rapidly. *Dense WDM* (DWDM) was developed to produce even better results on a single fiber pair than the original techniques deployed on the backbone networks. Expanding capacity

Table 5-2

Advantages of Fiber over Other Media

Lower errors	BER approximates 10^{-15} for fiber, whereas copper will be in the 10^{-4} to 10^{-8} range.
Attractive cost per foot	Cost per foot for fiber is now approximately $0.20 compared with $0.13 for copper.
Performance	Immune from RFI and EMI without extra cost of shielding on copper.
Ease of installation	Ease of installation due to lower weight and thickness.
Distances	Greater distance with fewer repeaters. Now can achieve 30 to 200 miles without repeaters. Copper and radio limited to less than 30 miles.
Bandwidth improvements	Fiber nearing 1 Tbps, copper 100 Mbps, and coax 1 Gbps
Capable of carrying analog and digital	Using TDM and WDM, the fiber is both digital and frequency multiplexed, increasing capacity.

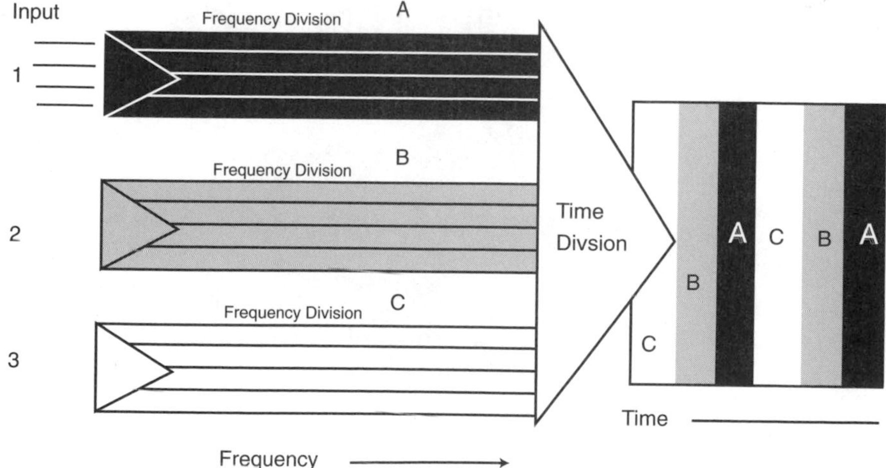

Figure 5-6 Combinations of frequency and time multiplexing produce the results in WDM.

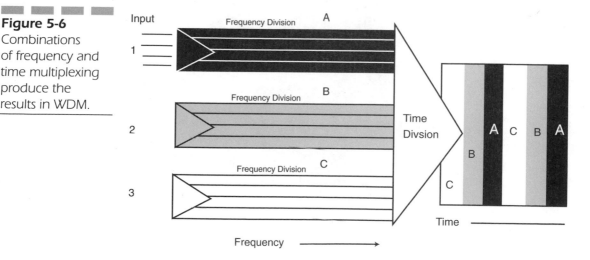

with DWDM can produce some significant improvements for today's technology. An example of this is the fact that some DWDM multiplexers can produce up to 240 Gbps on each pair of fibers. This equates to a call-carrying capacity of up to 3.1 million simultaneous calls on a single fiber pair. Now many of the carriers have installed at least 12 pairs of fibers in their backbone networks. Performing the math yields 37.2 million calls simultaneously on the fiber using current technology before more fibers are required. This is obviously very attractive to the carriers, who would prefer to get more service on their existing infrastructure rather than installing more glass in the ground. WDM is particularly useful when congestion begins to build up on the existing carrier networks. Surely, the equipment is expensive, but the cost of adding multiplexing equipment or changing it out is far less than digging up the ground to lay more fibers. The electronics of DWDM multiplexers are rapidly becoming very cost-efficient.

Using different light wavelengths, DWDM simultaneously transmits densely packed data streams on a single fiber. By combining DWDM with special amplifiers and filtering equipment on the links, the carriers can achieve unprecedented throughput on their existing single-mode fiber. Current technology supports approximately 16 different wavelengths on a single fiber (OC-192 is 10 Gbps; using 16 wavelength produces up to 160 Gbps in each direction). As stated in the beginning of this chapter, 128 wavelengths are targeted for early in the new millennium. Table 5.3 is a summary of some of the benefits of the DWDM usage.

Why DWDM?

Clearly, the use of fiber technologies has taken over the industry. However, the more information that can be generated over a single fiber, the better the carriers like it. To be specific, before digging up the ground to lay more fibers, it is far less expensive to use multiple wavelengths of light on a single fiber. Thus, as carriers seek more utilization on the existing fiber, the incentive is for manufacturers to continue proliferating this technology.

Table 5-3

Summary of Demand to Justify the Use of DWDM

Industry Demand	Cause
Need for bandwidth	Internet access, cellular and *personal communica tions* (PCS) and data/voice integration.
Need for reliable communications	In order to guarantee the reliability customers are demanding, the carriers have been committing alternate routes and spare fiber capacity to back up existing infrastructure.
More capacity	In order to get the *service-level agreements* (SLA) and maintain the network in a fashion expected by the consumer, the carriers have to install backup circuits and fibers in their highest-density routes.
Higher performance on the network	Network dependency has become the norm. All forms of traffic must run on the existing infrastructure, and the carriers must provision capacity to meet the ever-changing demands of the network.

The major manufacturers obviously have put all their resources into the development of DWDM techniques to meet the rising demand from carriers and end users alike. The use of multiple wavelengths enables the carriers to achieve 320-Gbps capabilities today, with terabit speeds being discussed at the beginning of the new millennium. Using a few different techniques, the major suppliers have developed keen interest in the ability to use DWDM. *Multiwavelength optical repeaters* (MOR) help in deploying this technology out to the carrier networks. An MOR (or MOR plus) is an amplifier used to support at least 16 wavelengths on the same fiber in each direction. Using 16 wavelengths (16λ) operating at the OC-192 rate yields 160 Gbps in each direction or 320 Gbps in one direction. Figure 5-7 shows a typical multiplexer used to generate a bidirectional flow of information through the fiber multiplexer. This figure shows the major components of the systems used by Nortel, but the components are the same as those used by others (for example, Lucent Technologies, Siemens, or Alcatel). In either case, the major point here is that use of a DWDM coupler aggregates the capacity of the fiber using two different light bands (red and blue) and multiple wavelengths to achieve the results we have grown to expect.

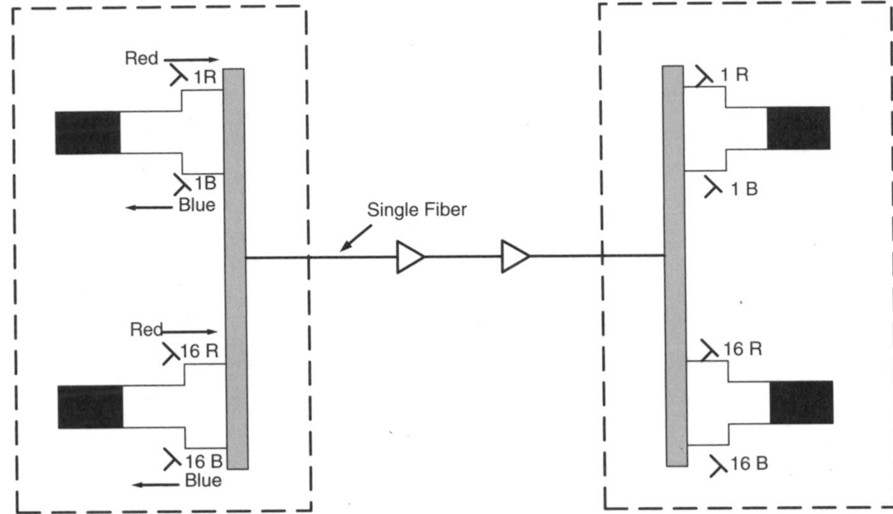

Figure 5-7 Bidirectional transmissions on a single piece of fiber

Increasing the capacity of the fiber through the use of DWDM appeals to many of the providers and carriers alike. Fiber-based multiplexing also adds some other enhancements that were not available in the past. Because the signal never terminates in the optical layer, the interfaces can be independent of bit rate and format. This enables the service providers the opportunity to integrate DWDM easily with their existing equipment and infrastructure while still gaining access to the untapped resources and capacities in their existing fiber.

DWDM combines multiple optical signals so that they can be amplified as a group and transported over a single fiber, increasing the capacity. Each signal carried on the DWDM architecture can operate at a different rate (for example, OC-3, OC-12, OC-48, and so on) and in a different format (for example, SONET, ATM cells, data). Using a mix-and-match approach enables the carriers to achieve different rates of speed and aggregated throughput, depending on the multiplexing equipment used. Future DWDM developments are touted as being able to carry up to 40 wavelengths of OC-192, or 400 Gbps. As a comparison, 400 Gbps will be 90,000 volumes of an encyclopedia in one second.

DWDM requires that the transmission lasers have a very tight wavelength tolerance so that the signals do not interfere with each other. After all, the systems carry 16 or 32 different wavelengths on a single fiber. It is imperative that the tolerances be held tightly to prevent mass destruction of the data signals being generated on the fibers. The *International Telecommunications Union* (ITU) has specified 100 GHz standard spacing between the wavelengths, and most of the vendors are now manufacturing lasers at the standards-based wavelengths for combination into DWDM.

The most advanced today, OC-192 lasers has a tolerance of 0.1 nm, which is small enough to preclude interference between two adjacent wavelengths. Designing OC-192 DWDM systems is ostensibly more difficult than the older OC-48 systems. OC-192 systems being deployed in the networks also use both unidirectional and bidirectional systems in support of the fiber and DWDM multiplexers. However, the future may change things very quickly. Where OC-192 offers a 10-Gbps operation, the future offers an OC-768, which will create a fourfold increase in the capacity of the network. At the OC-768 rate, a multiplexing scheme will produce 40 Gbps on a single fiber (SONET rate), which then can use the DWDM capabilities to create a throughput of up to four times the 320-Gbps rate currently available. This equals terabit speeds (1.28 Tbps). However, the use of spacing on the various wavelengths actually will allow up to 400 Gbps and offers future speeds of up to 1.68 Gbps. OC-768 will also bring to the table a capability to concatenate the OC-192 levels. Today's current technology can use a concatenated OC-48 but stops there in the bonding of higher speeds. In the future, as *Internet service providers* (ISPs) and traditional telephone carriers need to expand their capacities, the need to draw a 10-Gbps concatenated throughput will appear. Today, this is not a big concern, but in three to five years this will become a commonplace occurrence. Table 5-4 is a summary of some of the other things that we are expecting to occur over the next five to 10 years in the area of fiber transport systems. This table takes advantage of the work being done in many of the laboratories and research facilities around the world. The ability to push the envelope is what drives the communications industry.

Table 5-4

A Look at What DWDM and Fiber Rates Will Bring over the Next Decade

Technology and Capacities	Current versus Future Technology
DWDM at OC-192 and 40λ	Current technology capable of carrying 40 different wavelengths (using ITU 100-GHz spacing) at 10 Gbps each or 400 Gbps. Currently, the industry has achieved 320 Gbps, with the 400-Gbps rate available in the very near future.
DWDM at OC-192 and 80λ	The current spacing of 100 GHz as specified by the ITU is under attack. The near future holds the promise of doubling the number of wavelengths by using 50-GHz spacing, allowing up to twice as many wavelengths on the same fiber (80) each operating at 10 Gbps.
DWDM at OC-768 and 40λ	This is a turn-of-the-century technology with up to 40 Gbps per wavelength and 40 wavelengths or a total of approximately 1.6 Tbps.
DWDM at OC-768 and 80λ	By the year 2002, we can probably expect to see OC-768 plus the use of 80 wavelengths, or a 3.2-Tbps throughput on fiber.
DWDM at OC-192 and 160λ	By the year 2005, we can expect to see the decreased spacing of wavelengths and tighter tolerances on fiber lasers yielding a total of 160 different wavelengths at 10 Gbps each, or back to the 1.6-Tbps rate.
DWDM at OC-768 and 160λ	These 2008-2009 technologies will again double the capacity and yield 160 different wavelengths at the OC-768 rate (40 Gbps), or netting 6.4 Tbps on a single fiber.

These rates are all projected to be available in the next decade. However, because the technology seems to be doubling every 6 to 12 months, the rates shown in Table 5-4 could happen as soon as 2005. The issue is not how long it will take, but the ability to drive better and faster data and other communications needs on the same fibers. The future holds a lot of excitement with these speeds.

DWDM uses a composite optical signal inside, carrying multiple data streams, each sent on a different optical wavelength (different color of light). This has been around for years, but earlier versions were not as flexible as today's technologies. Earlier versions just used two different wavelengths and carried very wide band capacity on the same fiber. Recent developments finally have evolved to a point where it is practical and affordable to use multiple wavelengths and pack these different waves parallel in the same fiber. The signals now operate in the 192- to 200-*terahertz* (THz) frequency range. However, a new problem has reared its head. With signals as precise and dense as those employed with the cables now in use, we needed a way to provide accurate signal separation,that is, filtration, at the receiver. This had to be

- Easy to implement
- Maintenance-free
- Affordable

Early receivers were not very precise, so it was difficult to separate the signals back to the originating input. Moreover, cross-talk became a problem in handling the multiple wavelengths.

Another problem is the ability to regenerate the signals across the fibers. We needed something that would satisfy the fiber demands and yet enable the amplification of all wavelengths. The more we had to extract the signal to amplify it, the more the risk there was of failure. Moreover, this was expensive. The advent and implementation of *erbium-doped fiber amplifiers* (EDFAs) enabled the commercial development and implementation of DWDM systems by providing a way to amplify all the light waves at the same time. The way in which this is done is that when the fibers are created (pulled), erbium ions (a natural element and amplifier of light) are embedded in the core of the glass; this process is called *doping*. These dopants are fiber additives designed to produce the solution needed. Instead of using multiple electric regenerators, the providers now can use EDFAs to optically boost the signal, providing savings on the cost and maintenance of the electrical regenerators.

Installing More Fiber Just Does Not Do It!

In the past, the carriers have installed more fiber in their backbone networks, as well as more transmission equipment. With every new fiber installed, the carrier adds between 2.4 and 9.9 Gbps of capacity. Unfortunately, this is extremely costly, and in many cases, the installations are difficult and costly to maintain. Rights-of-way along major highways throughout the country are continually being dug up. Local communities are beginning to rebel at the continual digs that occur. Besides disrupting traffic patterns, frustrating drivers, and generally being unpleasant to view, the constant digging adds to the number of cable cuts, which disrupt existing network capacities. The cost of adding additional fiber cables can be estimated from \$70,000 to \$100,000 per mile depending on the dig. Moreover, as shown in Figure 5-8, this is escalating. To this we must add the support systems and electronics costs. As the cost of digging, establishing rights-of-way, and labor all escalate, overall costs continue to spiral upward.

The old joke about the "backhoe fade" problem is a reality. In fact, many of the carriers use the same construction crews. These crews should know where the lines have been installed from their last dig. However, record keeping is one of the least functional areas in this industry. Too often the construction crew must make in-field changes to overcome obstacles. This means that they dig in different places from where the drawings state. By using a WDM or DWDM arrangement, the carriers can get away from the constant digging and merely turn on new lights when necessary to satisfy the demands. This assumes that earlier installations included the correct equipment upfront.

Figure 5-8 Escalating costs per mile to add more fiber

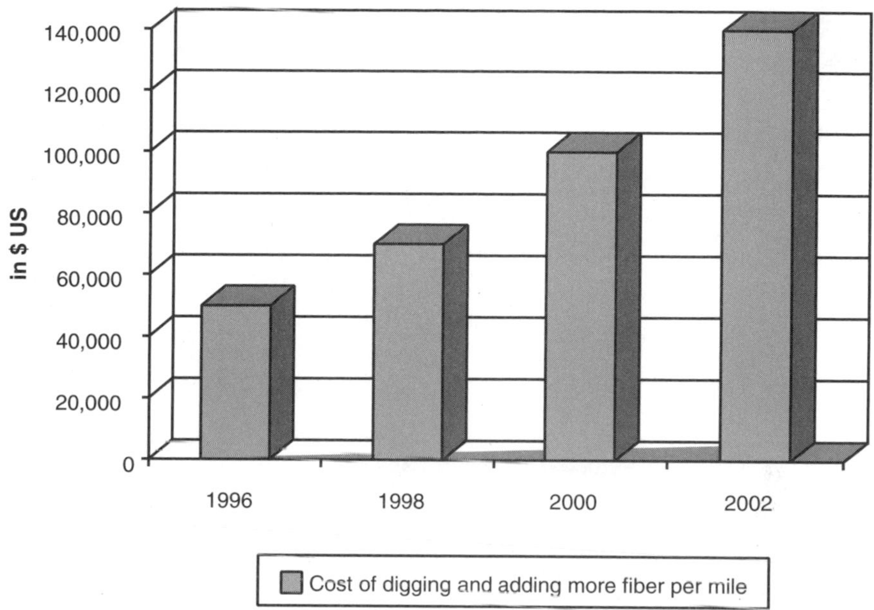

Getting There from Here

Assuming that the carriers have been providing due diligence in their efforts to meet and satisfy future demands, the following choices are available:

- **Installing new fiber**. As seen in the preceding section, this is too expensive and daunting a challenge.
- **Investing in new TDM technologies to get faster rates such as OC-192 and OC-768.** This again involves getting a fourfold increase for a large investment, but not the degree of growth that we are looking for.
- **Using a combination of the TDM and DWDM architectures to increase throughput by orders of magnitude.** This is the preferred method today. However, as early as 1998-1999, many of the carriers were making statements that they had sufficient fiber in the ground to enable them to just activate (light up) a new fiber rather than invest in new equipment. The old adage that "hindsight is better than

foresight" comes into play here. These same carriers are now feeling the lack of existing infrastructure on many of their routes. Consider backbone providers who have thousands of miles of interstate fiberoptics and who are now being placed into a position of having to rebuild their entire routing and infrastructure because of a short-sighted vision.

Figure 5-9 shows the overall demand outstripping the capacities over short periods. The carriers must now face this dilemma.

Figure 5-9 The shift from demand and capacity

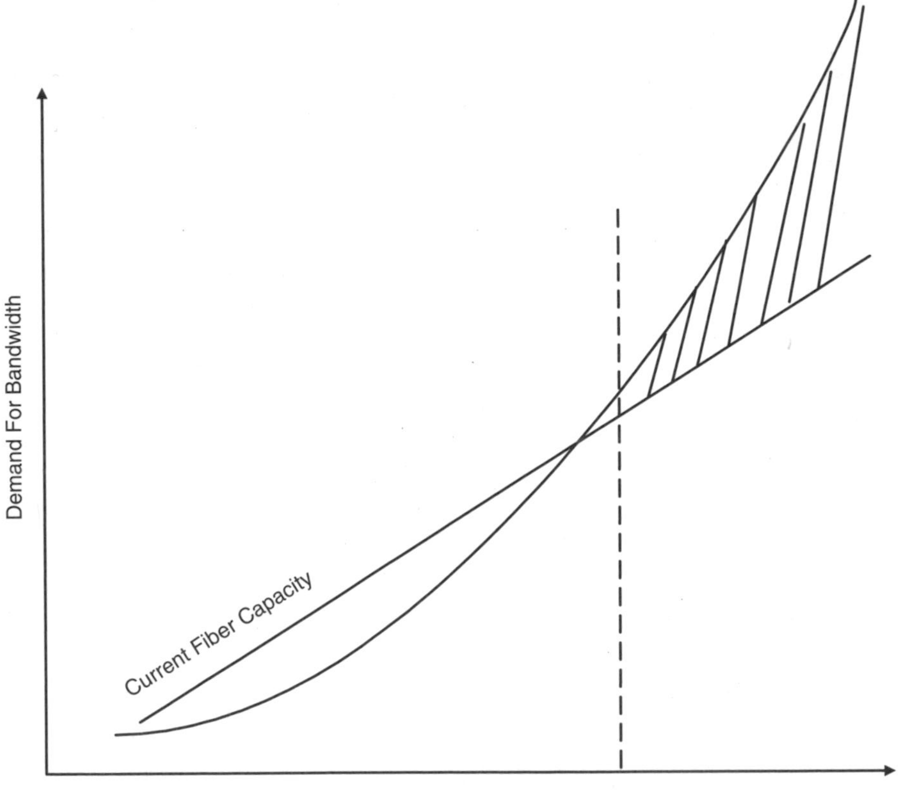

CHAPTER 6

Optical Switching Systems and Technologies

Up to now, our attention has been focused on the development of the protocols, multiplexing, and fiber characteristics. This chapter begins our focus on the use of optical switching technologies to move our light beams where they must go. Many different approaches have been used in trying to get to this end. This relatively infant business sector has spawned several startup companies and several different technologies to achieve the same result. The result, of course, is to do the following:

1. Switch the information as fast as we can
2. Increase the efficiency of the networks
3. Reduce the number of times we have to convert the information from electrical to optical, and vice versa

Advanced optical network solutions also have penetrated the metropolitan area networks, which offers the application services sector a chance to capitalize on potentially huge cost and performance improvements in the areas of transport and provisioning. The *application service providers* (ASPs), for example, see this opportunity to expand their offerings and services with unlimited users. The manufacturers also see a new market where the "older telco" market can be supplemented or totally revamped.

The ASPs, and now the facilities-based *integrated communications providers* (ICPs), must be cognizant of the fact that the choices they make today will have an impact on their longer-term viability and competitiveness. More than 60 manufacturers and value-added organizations are developing products that target the metropolitan areas. These companies are offering SONET-based solutions; others are offering *dense-wave-division multiplexing* (DWDM) with variations that span the spectrum. Functionally, the services providers have myriad offerings from which to select.

Optical Switching in the Metropolitan Network

Before we see the full deployment of metropolitan SONET and DWDM systems and before long-haul optical switches experience wide-scale deployment, the equipment vendors must introduce optical switches for metropolitan networks. This market ignited in a relatively short time. The abundance of options solidifies the fact that the metropolitan network is so different that new solutions are required to satisfy the escalating data demand regardless of the progress made with optical networking in the past. The metropolitan area is exploding. As much as 80 to 90 percent of corporate traffic is moving outward from corporate networks and must traverse the metropolitan networks to get to the wide-area long-distance market.

The typical features and functions that we incorporate into the long-haul network are significantly different from those of the metropolitan networks. Initially, the rather sluggish provisioning of metropolitan DWDM by carriers was perplexing. However, in the year 2000, a number of vendors announced optical cross-connects for the metropolitan market. Optical switches will manage the monstrous bandwidth needs to support new services in the metropolitan network. Several specialty consulting firms dealing with optical switching and networking predict that the market is growing exponentially from a mere $200 million in 1998 to an astounding $4 billion by 2004, as shown in Figure 6-1.

The metropolitan optical switch market as described by the various providers includes two main classifications of optical switching systems:

1. **Opaque** Systems that perform regeneration, reshaping, and resynchronization of the optical signal electronically.
2. **Transparent** Systems that perform all switching optically.

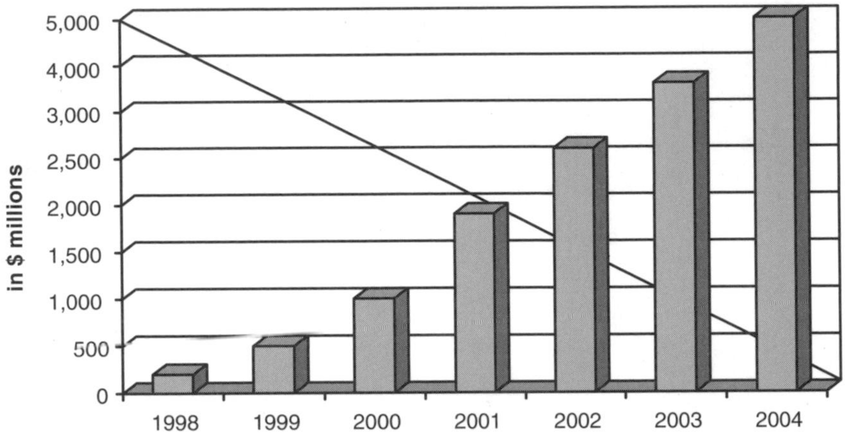

Figure 6-1 Growth of the metropolitan optical switching market

Wide-Area Networks

In *wide-area networks* (WANs), DWDM is driving the emerging optical switching systems market. As more DWDM systems are installed, managing many wavelengths becomes critical. Optical switching systems enable the carriers to support optical layer restoration while creating new optical layer services, such as *optical virtual private networks* (O-VPNs) and dynamic "designer" wavelength services. The carriers literally will be capable of designing the service provisioning and bandwidth for the user. This designer effect will create "ad hoc" service provisioning.

Opaque and transparent optical switches will have a role in the long-distance network. Many of the major network suppliers endorse the use of optical switching. These include Williams, Qwest, Extant, and others. Opaque optical switches are more common in the market (2000). However, transparent optical switching systems are nearing the final stages of delivery from the following companies: Lucent, Nortel/Xros, Chromisys, and Corvis.

Transparent systems are transparent to protocol and bit rate, meaning that they are highly scalable and useful for disaster recovery (backhoe fade, equipment failures, and so on) and network reconfiguration tasks. This transparency in protocols enables the carrier to literally move any type of data, such as *Internet Protocol* (IP)-centric networks, ATM, and SONET.

Metropolitan Migration

WAN changes and installations of the past offer logical steps to follow in the metropolitan area market. Very few *wave-division multiplexers* (WDMs) and DWDMs are installed in the metropolitan networks. Even at the SONET OC-192 rate, only limited installations have taken place. Therefore, it is difficult to imagine widespread requirements for optical switches. Nevertheless, the switches are coming. When the local providers begin offering customers (enterprise managers) newer gigabit and 10 Gigabit Ethernet transmission speeds across town or as an access method to the Internet through the ASP, then the higher-speed optical switches will become absolute requirements. Figure 6-2 shows a typical network that may be used to offer this type of service for DWDM end to end. As the carriers and ASPs begin their deployment, this model is one that may offer the advantages expected to meet the overall demand for the future. In this networking strategy, many suppliers are offering the equipment and managed services.

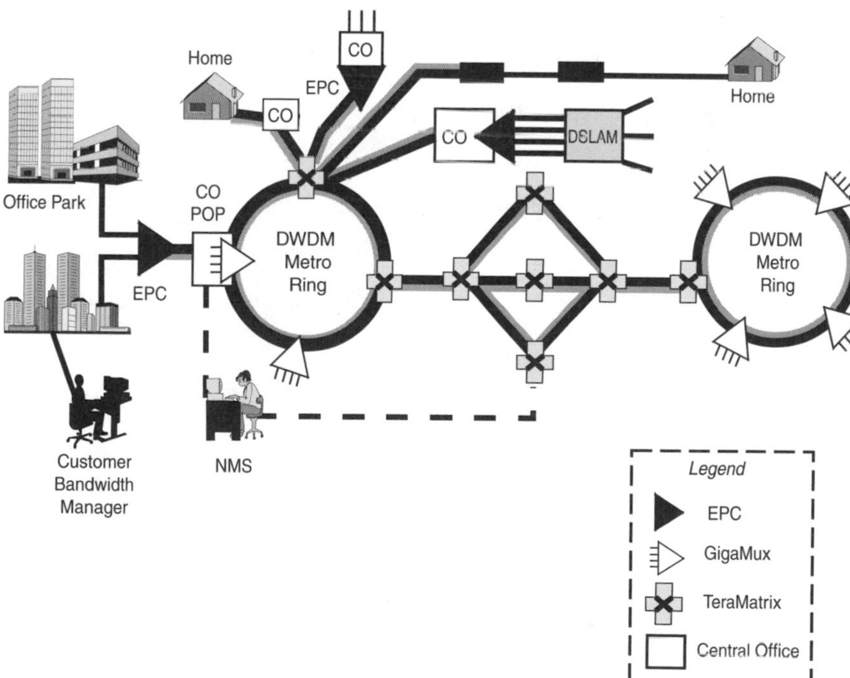

Figure 6-2 Metropolitan area end-to-end DWDM networks (Sorrento Networks)

One of the main concerns is the sizing of these switching systems. Each vendor has a specific configuration geared to the local providers in a metropolitan network, such as Sorrento Networks. Sorrento Networks announced its TeraMatrix photonic switch, which can be configured in a 4×4 to 512×512 configuration using two different types of switching matrices.

Network Photonics is a new company in this marketplace targeting the metropolitan market with an all-optical switch. More suppliers are soon to appear as the market heats up, and industry expectations of $4 billion make this more feasible. Newer players also may lend more credibility to the demands of the network rather than the assumption that the carriers and providers are trying to force the bandwidth on the enterprise user. One can safely assume that the bandwidth is desired; the delivery is the holdup today.

The services we are trying to satisfy include the following:

- Enterprise access
- Dynamic optical add-drop multiplexing
- Reconfiguration "on the fly"
- Ring interconnection
- "Designer" functions
- Enabling optical internetworking
- Reduced capital and operations costs
- Dynamic growth requirements
- Delivery of 99.999 percent availability
- Simplified network deployment and management
- Nonblocking, multipath switching
- Compelling metropolitan switching needs

It may be accepted that the metropolitan market is radically different from the long-haul market, so the need for optical cross-connects and switches also will differ radically. Whereas matrix size and line speeds are the important equipment attributes for long-haul networks, protocol transparency is the most important attribute in a metropolitan network.

The most critical and underappreciated aspect of the metropolitan WDM market is the enterprise access market. WDM systems link major corporate data centers with remote locations, offsite storage facilities, disaster recovery and alternate sites, or data warehouses. The main types of interconnection are as follows:

- **ESCON** For legacy mainframe data applications.
- **Fiber Channel** Legacy services benefit *metropolitan-area network* (MAN) services interconnecting FDDI networks and ATM services across town.
- **Gigabit Ethernet** (soon 10 Gigabit Ethernet) Applications for high-speed transparency across the environment are also crucial for *storage-area networking* (SAN) needs.
- **Storage-area networks** Enterprises increasingly need to interconnect SAN islands in different locations. SANs are being located in different sites for both operational and cost reasons, such as better alignment with distributed enterprise data, enhanced survivability, and lower costs for storage facilities located outside metropolitan centers.

Without interconnected SANs, enterprises are forced to perform data protection and data recovery using manual tape backup and vault storage. The interconnection of SAN islands with high bandwidth, high reliability, and low latency will enable a variety of storage applications across the extended SANs, including

- Remote backup/tape vaulting
- Batch replication
- Disaster recovery
- Synchronous replication

Without DWDM, each of these applications consumes a single fiber for each connection. This would be extremely expensive to provision and wasteful in the overall scheme of the providers' networks. Many organizations require at least one or more of these applications. Some require tens of these connections across an enterprise connection in a metropolitan area. Banks, health care facilities, manufacturing locations, insurance companies, and corporate headquarters fall into the basic category of organizations requiring this type of bandwidth.

One major supplier of enterprise WDM systems has several installations requiring more than 100 connections between two sites, making WDM essential to preserving fiber resources. Many major corporate users are asking for high-capacity private lines at OC-12 (622 Mbps) and OC-48 (2.5 Gbps) rates. To satisfy this need, WDM and DWDM are the preferred choices to deliver the speeds needed. The connections discussed are included in Figure 6-3 across the metropolitan area and Figure 6-4 for remote SAN access.

ONI has developed an optical switch for the metropolitan area to link the access to the metropolitan network, as shown in Figure 6-4. This high-end service offers the ability to interconnect from the customer door to the middle of the *incumbent local exchange carrier* (ILEC), for example the TELCO, networks or the *data local exchange carrier* (DLEC) networks.

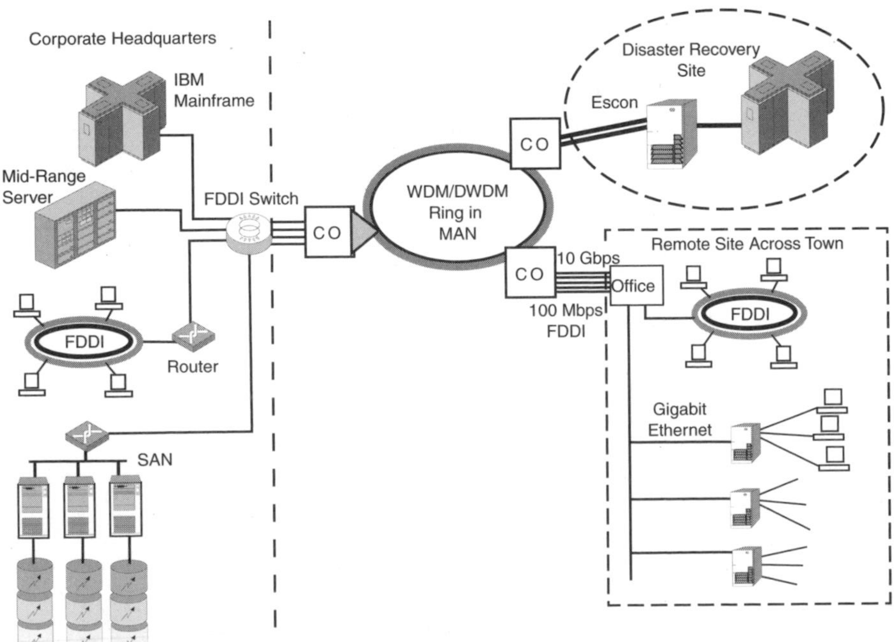

Figure 6-3 Applications requiring WDM/DWDM access in a metropolitan area (ONI Systems)

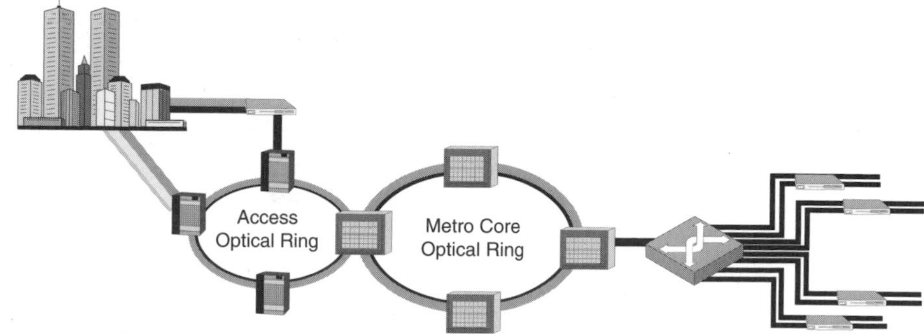

Figure 6-4 The ONI transport system (ONI Systems)

The Need for Metropolitan DWDM Networks

The task of interconnecting SAN islands is one that is naturally suited to optical networking. SONET/SDH-based network architectures were designed for voice and private-line services (for example, DS-1, DS-3) and cannot scale to support the gigabit channels required for storage transport. These networks also cannot transport storage data natively and in addition suffer from long provisioning times.

The solution lies in the next-generation metropolitan DWDM networks that are being built out rapidly today. These networks meet the requirements of metropolitan carriers for capacity, transparency, scalability, dynamic provisioning, manageability, and survivability for data-centric services at the lowest "first cost." Next-generation metropolitan DWDM networks, designed to offer wavelength services, will enable service providers to leverage the existing network infrastructure to offer SAN services and other user services (Figure 6-5).

Dynamic Optical Add-Drop Multiplexing

As the enterprise market evolves, Gigabit Ethernet and Fiber Channel will play increasingly important roles in all facets of metropolitan optical networks. Metropolitan optical cross-connects can provide dynamic reconfiguration of metropolitan enterprise networks, with optical layer survivability compatible with SONET recoverability. In the reconfiguration/survivability scenario, optical

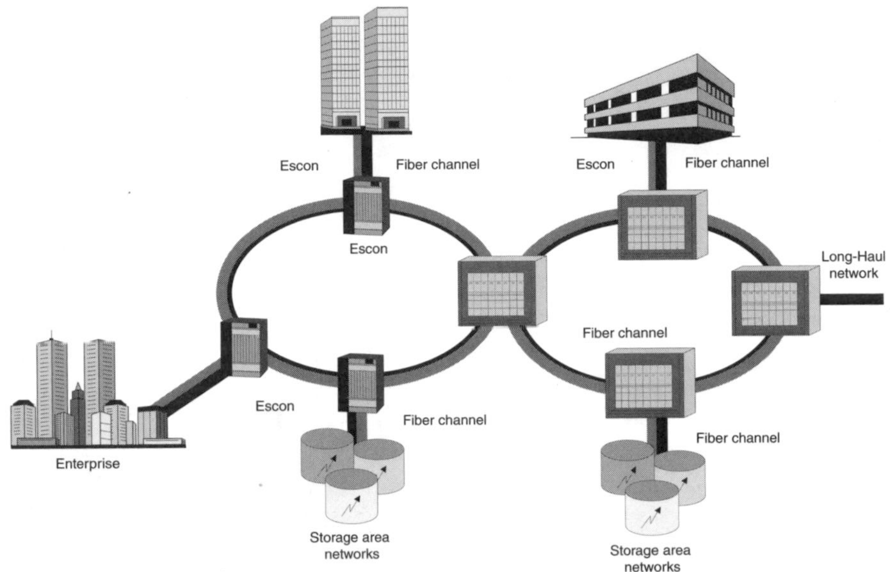

Figure 6-5 SAN access on metropolitan DWDM networks (ONI Systems)

switches are dynamic *optical add-drop multiplexers* (OADMs) with a greater degree of functionality. Dynamic OADM functionality is a key aspect of metropolitan optical switches. Agilent announced a low-cost "bubble" switch matrix suited for these applications that will be integrated into products starting in 2001.

These justifications for metropolitan optical switching enterprise access with dynamic OADM favor optical switch solutions. A third requirement, ring interconnection, is better suited for opaque optical switches.

Ring Interconnection

High-bandwidth private-line services and optical VPNs will make ring interconnection more important in metropolitan optical networks. Provisioning high-bandwidth circuits across multiple rings is a difficult process in many metropolitan networks today.

Manufacturers are responding to the need for ring interconnection with customized, scaled-down versions of their long-haul switching systems. Ciena, for example, announced a lower-priced, smaller-scale (64-port) version of its CoreDirector. This is optimized for ring interconnection and STS-1 level grooming at the network edge.

In ring interconnection, optical switching systems operate as SONET switches, providing integrated management of optical circuits spanning multiple rings. These switches will support the following:

- Automated provisioning of OC-n circuits in the metropolitan area
- Varying levels of restoration on SONET rings
- Diversely routed 1 + 1 protection
- Mesh-based protection using Datacomm routing protocols

Bottlenecks at the Switch

One potential technology bottleneck is that of telecom switches, the essential network elements that enable traffic to be routed from a source to a destination. An optical cross-connect switch may be thought of as a black box with multiple input and output fibers carrying network traffic. The basic function of the switch is to enable the signal on any one of the input fibers to be redirected to any one of the output fibers in the manner configured by the users.

The optical cross-connect switches used in today's networks rely on electronic cores. An optical signal arriving at a switch input port is converted to an electronic signal by a high-speed photo detector (receiver). Electronic circuits in the switch core then direct the signal to the desired output port. A final electrical-to-optical conversion is performed by a laser diode, transforming the signal back into light for onward transmission on the fiber network.

The fundamental problem with these electronic cores is that they do not scale well to large port counts (numbers of input and output channels) and are costly to replace for network upgrades to the higher data rates needed for the growing demand for bandwidth. Many workers in the industry now believe that electronic-core cross-connect switches cannot efficiently meet the needs of tomorrow's communication networks, so a major challenge is to develop new, all-optical switching technologies that can fill this gap. To gain acceptance, these new technologies must be able to demonstrate low-optical-loss switching with extremely high reliability.

Multiple Choices Available

Among the different choices competing to replace electronic cores are optical switches based on the following:

- Thermal bubble generation in planar waveguides (developed by Agilent Technologies)
- Electro-optic properties of liquid crystals (being developed by Chorum, Corning, and Spectra-Switch)
- The MEMS switches (developed by Nortel Networks, Xros, Lucent, and others)

Some of these products are ready commercially in low-port-count (2 to 32 channels) switch configurations. However, it remains uncertain whether they can be extended beyond their current forms. In addition to the relatively high optical throughput losses of these devices, the need for temperature control and uncertainties over long-term aging effects are common causes of concern.

Mirror-Mirror on the Wall . . .

In the swift-moving world of optical networking, long-distance operators are using new technologies to facilitate the rocketing demand for higher and higher levels of bandwidth. Included in the technological choices are *microelectromechanical systems* (MEMS). Based on MEMS technology, tiny mechanical structures can be made using processing techniques derived from the *integrated circuit* (IC) industry. Using micromirrors made of single-crystal silicon, input light beams are directed to the appropriate output ports to perform the switching function. MEMS consist of optical switch technology using microscopic mirrors to route signals from fiber to fiber in a network cross-connect or node. A typical mirror capability is shown in Figure 6-6. These mirrors are smaller than a pinhead.

Theoretically, the essentially all-optical switch bypasses the need to convert optical signals to electric signals, as is done with traditional switches. This was the overall goal to save time and prevent

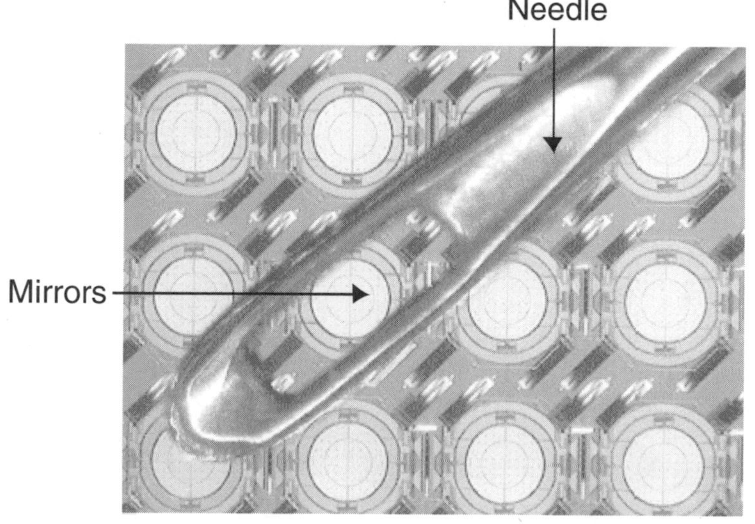

Figure 6-6 Using micromirrors, the light can be used as switches in the networks. (Lucent)

corruption during the conversion process. When looking at optical conversion, we see that the process follows the overall concept shown in Figure 6-7. Here, the electrical signal is converted into an optical signal at the left side of the figure. Next, the signal moves across the network; at a regenerator, the signal is then converted from light back into an electrical signal, regenerated, and reconverted back into a photonic signal (light). Now, at the far left side of the figure, we proceed through a cross-connect. Here, the signal is extracted from an add-drop multiplexer and converted back into an electrical signal to be switched into the next fiber network leg.

Nortel Networks (Xros) and Lucent Technologies have both chosen to use MEMS-based switches. With long-haul providers (including those with Internet backbones) faced with dramatic increases in bandwidth demand, the race to develop and bring to market optical switching technologies is on. MEMS is the first technology that looks like it meets the basic requirements, include scaling to large numbers of ports, relatively low loss and attenuation throughout the system, and support for a wide spectrum of bandwidth.

Xros's silicon-based micromirror technology will enable data to be switched through large-scale optical networks entirely in the form of

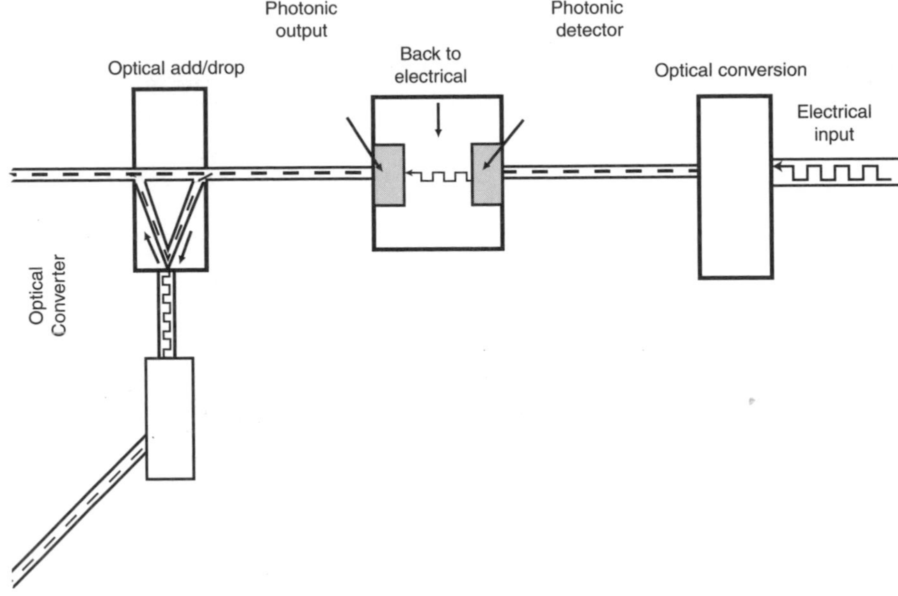

Figure 6-7 The multistage conversion

light, another key building block in Nortel's strategy to be the first mover in delivering the all-optical Internet. Combining the Xros technology with the ultra-long-reach solution, the Qtera ULTRA delivers high-performance with the speed, reliability, quality, and security that can meet the needs of the twenty-first century. The OPTera Packet Core is Nortel Networks' solution for converging optical and packet networks. The OPTera Packet Core transports IP, ATM, and SONET/SDH traffic with direct interfaces to the optical layer.

An all-optical Internet will deliver millions of instant Internet sessions, thousands of video channels, and vast amounts of e-business transactions on an unprecedented scale. More than 75 percent of North American Internet backbone traffic travels across Nortel Networks' systems. In 1999, Nortel Networks set the standards for speed with its 80-Gbps line rate OPTera technology and for bandwidth with the OPTera 1600G, which transmits 160 colors of light across a 10-Gbps system, for a total capacity of 1.6 *terabits per second* (Tbps). The OPTera switch, which is the core switch, is shown in Figure 6-8.

Figure 6-8
The OPTera core switch (Nortel Networks)

Source: Nortel Networks

Nortel Networks' (Xros's) system, on the other hand, handles up to 1,152 pairs of inputs and outputs with a transparent all-optical pathway. The cross-connects consist of two facing 6 × 6 inch arrays of 1,152 mirrors each. Incoming beams of light are directed to their destinations by these movable mirrors. Thus an entire incoming fiberoptic channel can be switched as a whole to any output port. This scheme also facilitates redundancy by allowing network planners to create an architecture where multiple alternate paths can be made available to protect each link. A sample of this system is shown in Figure 6-9.

Port-provisioning ease further enhances MEMS switches because of the inherent transparency of the system. In telecommunications networks of the past, it took months to get high-speed circuits provisioned and installed. Newer systems can perform this function on the same day.

Figure 6-9 The Nortel Networks (Xros) system (Nortel Networks)

Lucent Takes to the Waves

Lucent's WaveStar LambdaRouter is an all-optical device that switches light from one fiber to another without first converting the light to an electrical signal and then back to an optical one. This electrical detour slows the traffic down on today's fiberoptic networks. Lucent's product is targeted at service providers. However, enterprise networks could be the ultimate beneficiaries if carriers are able to offer higher-speed services more widely.

A single LambdaRouter can switch up to 40 *gigabits* (Gb) of traffic, the capacity of 256 separate optical fibers, each carrying a single wavelength. With WDM, each fiber can carry more than one wavelength, increasing the potential capacity of the device.

Lucent has yet to answer whether the devices will scale as large as carriers will need and whether the devices will be inexpensive enough to make them worthwhile. Lucent claims the LambdaRouter will cut carrier operating expenses by 25 percent.

Despite its name, the device is not actually a router. It is more akin to a cross-connect, a static switch in conventional telephone networks. Each LambdaRouter can take 256 fibers in and put 256 fibers out. The traffic is carried on waves of light that are switched through the LambdaRouter using two banks of adjustable circular mirrors that are each a half millimeter in diameter. This is shown in Figure 6-10.

Lucent uses a MEMS switch with its WaveStar LambdaRouter, an all-optical switch capable of routing 10 times more information than is traveling today across the worldwide Internet. It uses 256 micromirrors, on less than a square inch of silicon, to instantly direct and route optical signals from fiber to fiber in the network without first converting them to electrical form, as done today. This will save service providers up to 25 percent in operational costs and enable them to direct network traffic 16 times faster than with electrical switches. The Lucent micromirror is shown in Figure 6-11.

Figure 6-10
The two rows of arrays (Lucent)

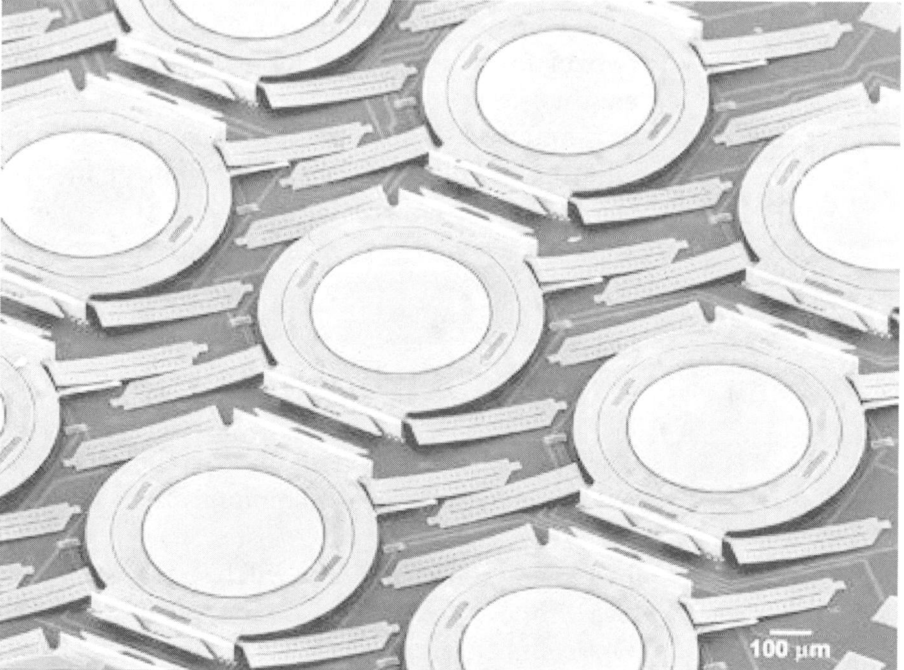

Source: Lucent

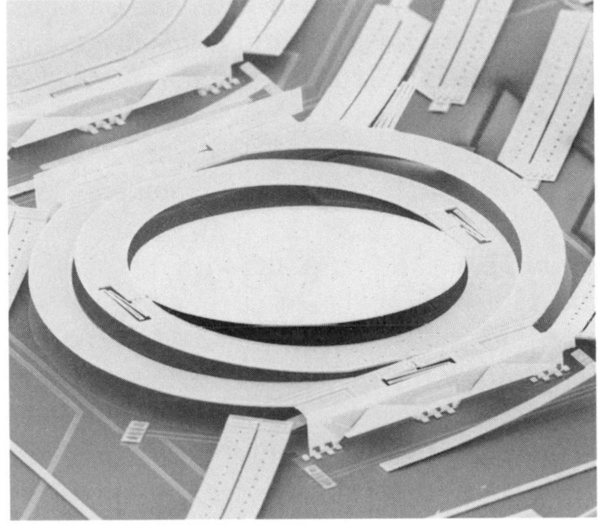

Figure 6-11 One of an array of 256 microscopic mirrors, each the size of the head of a pin, tilts to steer light-wave signals from one optical fiber to another (Lucent).

Source: Lucent

AT&T Labs' light-wave networks department is using MEMS-based switches in a cross-connect of 16 input and 16 output ports. AT&T may be experimenting with the switching technology in hybrid fiber-coax networks, particularly in the fiber-based return channels.

If and when cable operators turn to heavy-duty optical switching, whether to augment high traffic in large metropolitan systems or to route traffic from one large cluster to another, mature technologies should be available to meet the demand.

MEMS Enhance Optical Switching

Paralleling the exponential growth in computing muscle is an explosion in demand for communications bandwidth. Users and carriers alike are demanding faster, better, and cheaper access. Ever-increasing volumes of data will be a major force in shaping the way we use computer technology and the way in which that technology evolves. Optical fiber links are a key element of this bandwidth explosion.

Fiberoptics has enabled the adoption of telecommunications standards with bit rates far higher than were possible using copper cables. Advances in fibers, lasers, and photo detectors have enabled the introduction of telecom standards with data rates higher than 10 Gbps. The adoption of DWDM permits many independent data channels carried on different optical wavelengths to coexist on one fiber. This has further increased available network bandwidth. Meanwhile, an increase in the variety and volume of data traffic passing through these fiber links brings new challenges as service providers manage and expand their networks.

Economical MEMS

Often with integrated microactuators built into them, these MEMS devices typically are addressed using electrical signals to produce controlled motion of the micromechanical structures on the chip. The batch-processed nature of the fabrication procedure means that MEMS devices can be mass produced on a large scale, which reduces manufacturing costs. In addition, the extremely small physical size and mass of these silicon "machine parts" often make them more robust and capable of faster operation than conventional macroscopic mechanical devices.

Onix Microsystems is bringing optical MEMS to the market with a range of optical switching products based on patented micromirror technologies. The key element of its switching engines is a two-dimensional matrix of micromachined mirrors fabricated in single-crystal silicon. Control signals applied to the MEMS chip fix the position of each individual mirror to either pass or intersect the input light beams, directing each incoming light signal to the desired output port.

Because the intersecting micromirrors must direct the outgoing light beams into small-diameter fiber cores (typically fewer than 9 microns), tight control of the mirror angles is vital to minimizing power loss incurred from passing through the switch. Extremely low insertion loss and channel cross-talk are achieved by this architecture to produce compact, all-optical switch modules with up to 64 input-output ports. The concept is that as the light is reflected off mirrors in the switching system, the micromirror is sent a signal to move in a certain direction. As the mirror moves, the light is bounced across the mirror to an output fiber carrying the full capacity through the switch without conversion back to an electrical signal. This is shown in Figure 6-12.

Scalable Solutions

These relatively small-port-count switches are useful, for example, for network protection and restoration, to enable carriers to quickly reroute data traffic around fault locations in the event of fiber breaks or equipment failures. However, central offices often require larger switches with hundreds and up to thousands of input-output ports. To scale up channel counts beyond 32 × 32 ports, two solutions are available depending on the specific requirements of the end system.

One solution is to use the smaller switch modules as building blocks, cascading them to form a larger switch. A three-stage net-

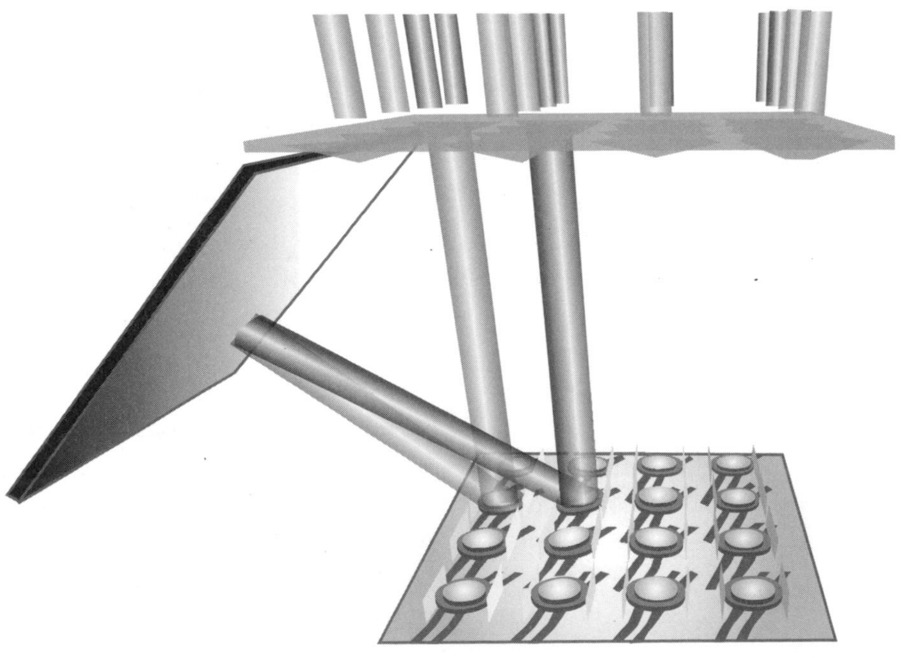

Figure 6-12
The MEMS switch in action (Lucent)

work configuration enables one to construct a fully nonblocking cross-connect with up to 1,024 × 1,024 channels by linking together 32 × 32 switch modules. Alternatively, instead of using n^2 mirrors, each with two-controlled positions, to form an $n \times n$ switch, one can use $2n$ mirrors each having n controllable positions to achieve the same functionality. This architecture, called the *steered beam configuration*, is used to construct large optical cross-connect switches within a single switch stage.

Switching is accomplished by manipulating the free-space propagation paths of the light beams directly. Consequently, MEMS switches are optically transparent. In other words, they can be used in networks with widely varying data rates, modulation formats, and signal wavelengths. Moreover, changes in the network properties have no effect on switch functions. Therefore, no hardware modification is needed when the communication service providers upgrade the other parts of their networks or systems.

Easy Upgrades

This last feature will increase in importance as high-bandwidth connections become more popular with consumers. With the large variety of data traffic passing through the ever more complicated communication links from local-area to global networks, the ability to work with existing equipment while accommodating future upgrades will be the key feature that makes all-optical switches the preferred choice of carriers. "Forklift" technological decisions are outdated with the carriers.

As high-speed data networks further penetrate the consumer market, network service providers are turning to technology solutions that will enable them to offer diverse services with varying bandwidth demands. The vision of a future all-optical network that can deliver these potentials seems less and less like a distant dream. All-optical switches and MEMS-based optical switches in particular are going to be the key enablers for the future of ultra-high-bandwidth, all-optical communication networks.

Not Everyone Is Convinced

Despite the momentum built by MEMS technology by Nortel and Lucent, MEMS has not won over everyone. MEMS is a viable technology and a good way to do a scalable switch solution. However, early implementations of MEMS-based switches were very lossy when passing a signal through a WDM system, through an optical switch, and through a DWDM system.

Agilent Does Optical Switching Differently

Optical cross-connects (OXCs) will be used to route wavelengths between inputs and outputs while adding and dropping local traffic. Many carriers expect to need nodes with several thousand input and output wavelengths within a few years. When considering this entire scenario, 25 fibers times 160 wavelengths per fiber implies a 4,000 × 4,000 OXC.

From an engineer's standpoint, the most flexible architecture is the opaque *wavelength interchange cross-connect* (WIXC) shown in Figure 6-13. In the WIXC, all wavelengths are received and retransmitted at the cross-connect by transponders at each port. In this architecture, any wavelength can be switched to any other wavelength on any fiber through transponder wavelength conversion. However, long-haul transmitter and receiver costs at these nodes for 10- and 40-Gbps data rates may be considerable.

Single Big Fabric or Multiple Smaller Fabrics?

Ultra-long-haul transmission systems will enable unregenerated transmission over very long distances and thus the possibility of transparent cross-connects that eliminate expensive OEO conversions. Eliminating transponders does away with wavelength conver-

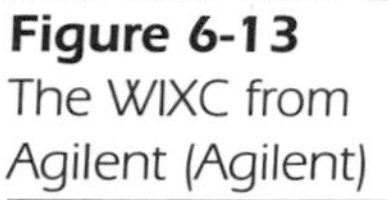

Figure 6-13 The WIXC from Agilent (Agilent)

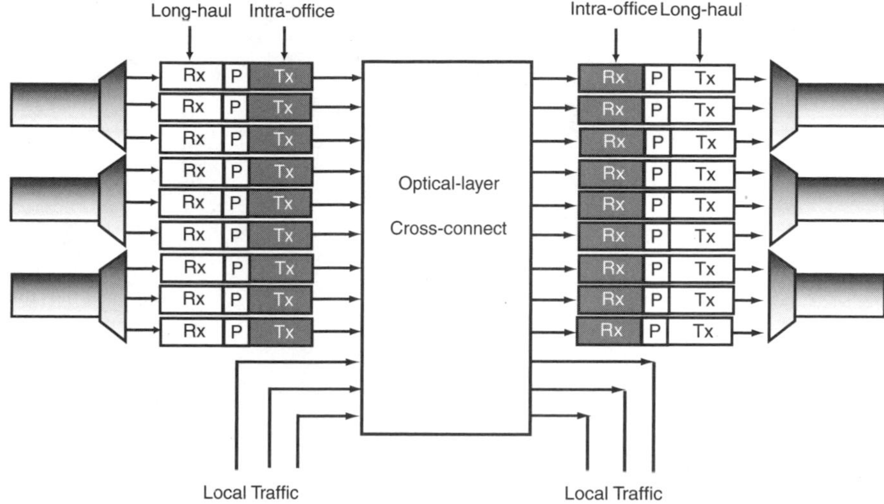

sion. Advances have been made in all-optical wavelength converters, but even if these devices materialize, they still will be expensive.

The most attractive transparent node architecture is the *wavelength-selective cross-connect* (WSXC), which can be constructed out of a single fabric or several smaller fabrics, as shown in Figure 6-14. The WSXC operates by switching all the "green" wavelengths between fibers on one plane, the "blue" wavelengths on another plane, and so on. A WSXC node with 25 fibers and 160 wavelengths per fiber requires 160 25 × 25 switches or a single 4,000 × 4,000 switch. Slightly larger switches enable dropping and adding of local traffic, enable some channels to be regenerated, and enable some channels to move between wavelength planes.

Agilent Technologies, Inc., introduced 32 × 32 and 32 × 16 port switches that use tiny bubbles to deflect light from one path to another at speeds faster than 10 ms. The technology competes with MEMS and has the advantage of having no moving parts to lock up or wear out. It also contains the light within the device, unlike some MEMS equipment, making it less prone to problems.

Figure 6-14
The WSXC from Agilent (Agilent)

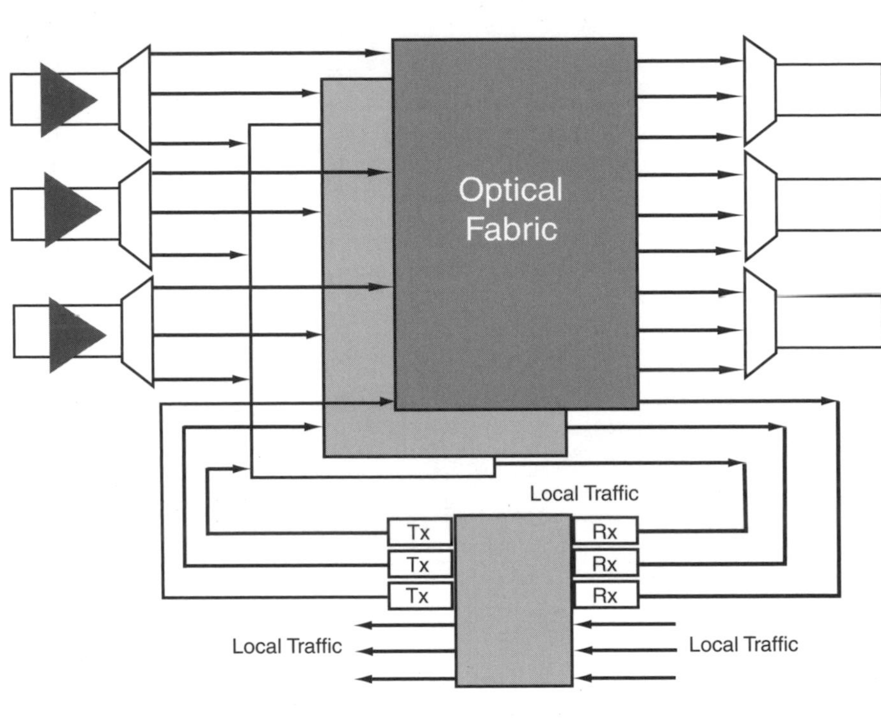

Agilent is packaging its Photonic Switching Platform devices so that it can be used by vendors to build switches. Large numbers of these devices can be connected together to offer carriers a "building block" approach to expanding the capacity of optical cross-connects.

It is unclear whether Agilent's products will scale to the 1,000+ port optical cross-connects required by carriers. The number of devices needed to build nonblocking cross-connects increases quickly as the port count goes up. A 512 × 512 port assembly would need 64 devices. The number of devices in larger assemblies could be reduced by making equipment partially nonblocking.

The light must pass through several devices, and each device takes its toll in reducing the strength of the signal by about 4.5 *decibels* (dB), which is a lot of loss. Therefore, the light signals need to be regenerated electrically when they exit the cross-connect.

Bubble Bubble, Who Has the Bubble?

Ink-pen technology, already used by *Hewlett-Packard* (HP) in its bubble-jet printers, has been reused to solve many of the intrinsic problems of mechanical devices employed to switch light. What was that? Agilent's switch is composed of a vertical and horizontal array of fixed, aligned waveguides. Light is transmitted across a horizontal path from the input to output port until a switch command is issued. When commanded, a bubble is created at the intersection of the appropriate waveguides, and the light is reflected down a vertical path to the switched port. This bubble is formed using the same technology used in ink-jet printers.

Agilent's Photonic Switching Platform consists of two layers:

1. A bottom layer of glass through which multiple streams of light travel
2. A top layer of silicon containing the ink-jet technology (technology from ink-jet printers that has been around for years)

In the bottom layer, 32 parallel microscopic trenches are carved into the silica. These intersect each other at 120-degree angles. The trenches are filled with a liquid with the same refractive index as the silica. Light passes straight through each of these trenches unless it runs into a bubble at one of the intersections. If a bubble is there, the light bounces off into the trench crossing its path. The bubble is created by tiny electrodes in the upper silicon ayer of the device. The electrodes heat up the liquid to form a gas in exactly the same way as in a bubble-jet printer.

The trenches (waveguides) traverse the whole device, which means that unlike other optical switching devices, it has ports on four sides. This has two big advantages: It makes it easy to link together devices to create higher-capacity switches, and it also makes it easy to create add-drop multiplexers-equipment that peels off some wavelengths for local use while enabling other wavelengths to pass straight through.

Reusing bubble-jet technology also promises big benefits for Agilent and its customers. The same production process can be used, which will cut cost and reduce development time. Reliability also promises to be good, because millions of ink pens have been manufactured. This is proven technology that everyone uses.

However, ink jets used in printing make temporary bubbles, not bubbles that might have to be maintained in place almost permanently with cross-connects. This may cause some heat-dissipation problems and demands. It also may mean using more electricity.

Alcatel Blows Bubbles

Alcatel SA announced plans for an all-optical cross-connect called Crosslight. The first release of the switch will scale up to 512 × 512 ports, each operating at speeds of 10 Gbps. According to Alcatel, by 2004 it may handle as many as 4,000 × 4,000 ports, each operating at 40 Gbps.

The real significance of the announcement, however, is that this is the first switch to be based on bubble technology. All the other developments of large-scale all-optical cross-connects have so far been based on MEMS.

However, Alcatel is working on MEMS developments. The company plans to use MEMS rather than bubbles for larger switches. Apparently, it is very hard to get to thousands of ports using the bubble technology. One must remember, however, that all these technologies are at a very early stage of development, and it is really too early to say which one, if any, will end up in widespread use.

The downside of this argument is that bubbles in printers only have to last a split second before they are allowed to collapse. In an all-optical switch, they may have to be maintained indefinitely. This implies that the pen would have to keep heating up the fluid. This also raises the question of whether this would increase the temperature of the fluid in adjoining channels and whether this might interfere with their light-carrying properties.

Agilent's technology was used by Alcatel for its photonic cross-connect system.

Alcatel initially chose Agilent's bubble technology over MEMS because of time-to-market issues and because it was scalable to larger numbers of ports. MEMS does have some advantages because of its ultimate scalability. Possibly the maximum size is 4,000 ports. As three-dimensional MEMS mirrors become available, more ports and enhancements will be the norm. MEMS technology is today geared to long-haul fiber networks. As operators drive fiber deeper and as high-bandwidth applications become omnipresent, MEMS may be adapted for both access and metropolitan networks.

Analysts forecast that the world market for optical bandwidth management systems will rise from an estimated US$543 million this year to US$15 billion by 2004. Figure 6-15 reflects the growth in this market.

Figure 6-15 Growth expectations for optical network management systems

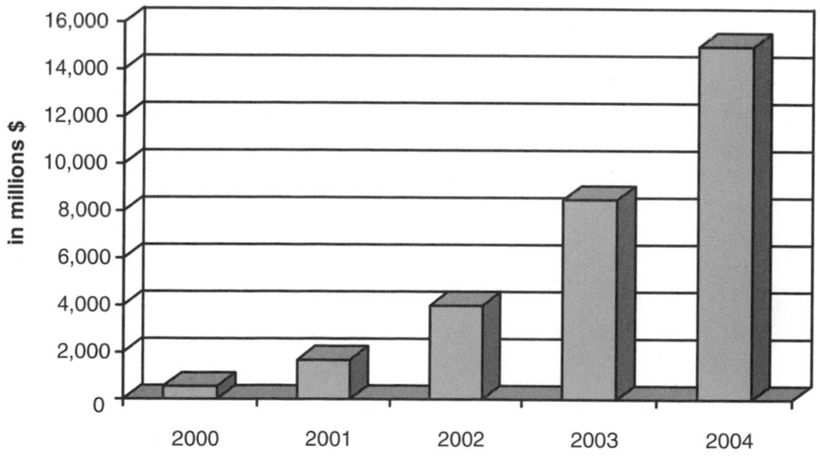

CHAPTER 7

Optical Networking and Switching Vendors

Starting in 1988 up through 1996, *Synchronous Optical Networking* (SONET) and *Synchronous Digital Hierarchy* (SDH) commanded all the investments from manufacturers and carriers alike. Both were touted as the backbone standards for future telecommunications. Therefore, there was no lack of manufacturers, research and development, or implementation schedules. As always, networks mature. Standards undergo changes, and many fall by the side of the road. SONET and SDH are no different. Recently, one manufacturer made a comment that SONET was dead.

In 1997, *wave-division multiplexing* (WDM) began its stellar rise in popularity. Manufacturers and technical wizards saw the benefit of using multiple wavelengths to dramatically increase the capacity of existing fibers without the problems created by *time-division multiplexing* (TDM) systems at these speeds. Both SONET and SDH standards were designed to carry TDM digital signals in the middle to late 1980s. Using TDM, a higher-speed signal is created by multiplexing many lower-speed channels. Problems surface when we plan to upgrade to OC-768 and above because TDM has trouble operating at these speeds. TDM on SONET or SDH still needs electrical signals and electronic switching systems. Conversion of these TDM signals may be too expensive at these higher speeds.

On the other hand, WDM carries multiple data speeds on a single fiber. *Dense WDM* (DWDM) is a fiberoptic transmission technique that employs light wavelengths to transmit data parallel-by-bit or serial-by-character. The all-optical networks using WDM with add-drop multiplexers and cross-connects permit this. DWDM systems multiplex up to 128 wavelengths in the 1,550-*nanometer* (nm) window. The money for research and development has shifted to WDM and DWDM because, as we have seen, this is where the action is. This addresses the importance of scalable DWDM systems in enabling service providers to accommodate consumer demand for ever-increasing amounts of bandwidth. DWDM is a crucial component of optical networks that enables the transmission of e-mail, video, multimedia, data, and voice-carried in *Internet Protocol* (IP), *Asynchronous Transfer Mode* (ATM), and SONET/SDH, respectively, over the optical layer.

The Growing Demand

It was clear as the new millennium began that a remarkable revolution in information services was overtaking our society. Communication, which was confined to narrowband voice signals, demanded a higher-quality visual, audio, and data content. Every aspect of interaction (whether business-to-business, entertainment and social demands, government, or academia) increasingly relies on rapid and reliable communications networks. The Internet alone thrust millions of individual users into a new world of information and technology. The telecommunications industry struggled to keep up with these demands. All predictions that current fiber capacities would be adequate for our needs into the new century have proven wrong. What was once a voice network growing at 4 percent per year is now a data-centric network growing at 30 percent (and more) per year. To meet the demands, the carriers sought help from the manufacturers and the standards committees. They were faced with obsolescence of their entire network infrastructure or a meltdown of the network. The committees went to work looking for a new way to handle this phenomenal growth and unrelenting demand.

Caution: Standards Committees at Work

The standards bodies were aggressively specifying and enhancing the various techniques, standards documents, and the implementations of the SONET and SDH architectures. These same bodies influence all the other networking standards, yet different committees are involved. The committees include representation from the list in Table 7-1.

Ciena and Cambrian were the first to include DWDM in metropolitan networks. These DWDM ring systems can be connected with ATM switches and IP routers. ATM networks will use SONET/SDH physical layer interfaces at 622 Mbps using add-drop multiplexers.

Table 7-1

Interested Committees and Standards Bodies

International Telecommunications Union (ITU) (www.itu.org)
American National Standards Institute (ANSI) (www.ansi.org)
Alliance for Telecommunications Industry Solutions (www.atis.org)
Telecommunications Industries Association (TIA) for *Fiber Optics* (FO) (www.tiaonline.org)
Bellcore/Telcordia Technologies (www.bellcore.com)
European Telecommunications Standards Institute (ETSI) (www.etsi.org)
Full-service access networks (FSAN) committees

The industry anticipated that the SONET equipment makers would make reliable OC-192 (10-Gbps) systems or face stiff competition from DWDM manufacturers, setting the stage for a new wave of competition. Actually, the SONET/SDH manufacturers jumped on the WDM bandwagon with their own products. The major SONET/SDH and WDM systems manufacturers include the vendors shown in Table 7-2.

Not everyone makes full systems; some make the components that go into a system. Still others create components and networking elements in their catalog of offerings. The networking elements include the following:

- DWDM
- Optical amplifiers
- Add-drop multiplexers
- Optical cross-connects
- Optical gateways
- Optical network units

The market has been in a feeding frenzy since the late 1990s and early 2000.

Table 7-2

Major SONET/SDH Manufacturers

ADC Telecommunications
Alcatel
Artel Video Systems, Inc.
Bosch Telecom, Inc.
Cambrian
Ciena Corporation
Ericsson
Fujitsu
Hitachi Telecom
Lucent Technologies, Inc.
NEC America, Inc.
Nortel Networks
Osicom Technologies Inc.
Pirelli Cable Corporation
Scientific Atlanta
Siemens Telecom Networks
Tellabs, Inc.
Tellium

Many component firms exist, including these shown in Table 7-3.

SONET and SDH ring networks will continue to be the backbone for high-speed networks using OC-48 and OC-192 add-drop multiplexers at network nodes. However, increased use of WDM technology will enable network capacity to grow exponentially. WDM also may be integrated into OC-12, OC-48, and OC-192 networks, so long as vendors provide standard wavelengths in the 1550-nm window. In some cases, WDM cannot be placed over the SONET layer. Instead, transponders that are more expensive are used. In general, though, WDM will be the most cost-effective option that provides the necessary bandwidth without installation of additional fiber. The market has been hot, as discussed in previous chapters, with industry predictions continuing to spiral upward, as shown in Figure 7-1. The market was approximately $4.4 billion in 1998 and is expected to

Table 7-3

List of Component Vendors

Advanced Optronics.
Akzo Nobel, USA
Alcatel Optronics SA
Alliance Fiber Optics
AMP
Amphenol Fiber Optic Products
Anritsu
APA Optics, Inc.
Applied Fiber Optics
Bosch Telecom
Bragg Photonics, Inc.
Canoga-Perkins
Corning
DiCon Fiberoptics, Inc.
Ditech Corporation
Eagle Opto-Electronics, LLC
EPITAXX
Ericsson Components
E-TEK Dynamics, Inc.
FITEL-PMX Inc.
Gould, Inc.
GPT Optical
Hewlett-Packard/Agilent
Instruments, SA, Inc.
Integrated Photonic Technology (IPITEK)
JDS Uniphase
Kaifa Technology, Inc.
LightPath Technologies, Inc.
Lightwave Microsystems
Mitel
Mitsubishi
MP Fiberoptics
Nortel Networks Optoelectronics

Optilas International

Optivision

Ortel Corporation

Photonic Integration Research, Inc. (PIRI)

Rockwell Semiconductor Systems

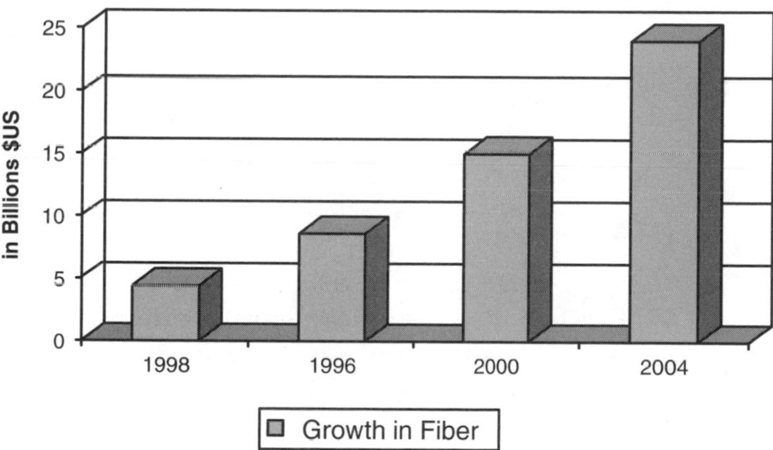

Figure 7-1 Expected growths in the North American fiber market

grow to $24 billion by 2004. This is a dramatic increase in the overall installation of fiber-based communications facilities over the next few years across North America.

The rest of the world also will see a dramatic increase in the use of the optical systems, with international growth rates approximating 20 percent or better per year over the next few years, as shown in Figure 7-2.

This growth leads to a feeding frenzy as the manufacturers and carriers begin to compete for market share and start gobbling up each other in the industry. Undoubtedly, many shifts will occur in ownership and penetration as this phenomenon takes place.

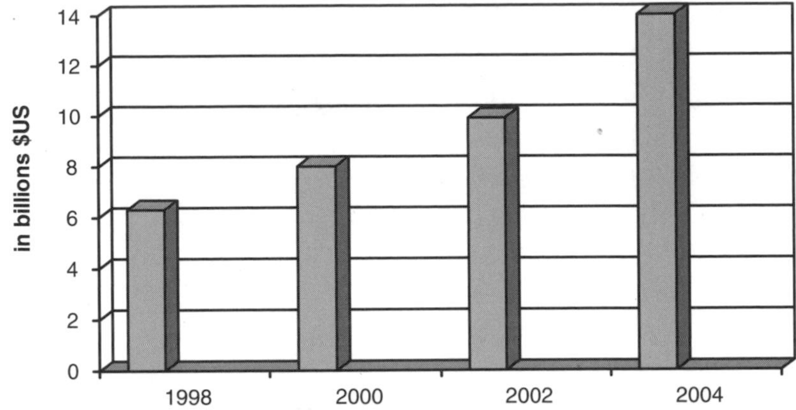

Figure 7-2 International growth of fiber

Let the Buying Begin

Faced with the many challenges of running a network, capacity planning, increased service needs, fiber depletion, and layered bandwidth management, the carriers need options to provide an economical capacity to withstand the onslaught of demand. One way to increase the fiber capacity is to lay more fiber. Where the cost of laying new fiber is minimal, this becomes the better solution. Unfortunately, laying new fiber will not necessarily enable service providers to provide new services or use the bandwidth management capability of a unifying optical layer.

A second choice is to increase the bit rate using TDM. Traditionally, this has been the carriers' choice (DS-1, DS-2, DS-3, and so on). However, when the carriers use this approach exclusively, they must make quantum leaps in one step, so they do not have to do this on a regular basis. This leads them to buy more than they initially need. Based on the SONET hierarchy, the next incremental step from OC-192 is OC-768 (10 to 40 Gbps). This method has been used with various networks based on SONET or SDH. Regardless of the location or technology, the carriers are making large investments in their infrastructure.

Is There an Alternative in the House?

The alternative for the carriers is DWDM. This increases the capacity of embedded fiber by first assigning incoming optical signals to specific frequencies within a designated frequency band and then multiplexing the resulting signals out onto one fiber. The technology that enables this high-speed, high-volume transmission is the optical amplifier. A network using such an amplifier could easily handle terabits of information.

Think of a highway, where one fiber can be thought of as a multilane highway. Now let's think of only one lane open and barriers on the rest (like the barrels we are accustomed to seeing on highway systems). Traditional TDM systems use a single lane of this highway and increase capacity by moving faster on this single lane. Using DWDM is similar to opening up the unused lanes on the highway (increasing the number of wavelengths on the existing fiber) to gain access to an incredible amount of untapped capacity in the fiber. An additional benefit of optical networking is that the highway is blind to the type of traffic that travels on it. Consequently, the vehicles on the highway can be trucks (IP datagrams), tractor-trailers (SONET), or sports cars (ATM cells). This analogy is shown in Figure 7-3.

As the demand increases, the market share and the spending will not slow down for some time to come. In fact, spending in United States for SONET transport equipment, cross-connects, and DWDM is expected to increase from $10 billion in 1998 to $24 billion by 2002, and predictions take us out to as much as $45 billion by the 2004. With this growth factor shown in Figure 7-4, one can see why the manufacturers are so excited.

Starting with DWDM, carriers can grow their networks on demand in the overall infrastructure. This enables them to add present-day and next-generation TDM systems. Moreover, DWDM gives the carriers sufficient flexibility to expand any portion of their networks—a definite advantage of the technology. Carriers seeking new and creative ways to generate revenue can benefit from a DWDM infrastructure while meeting demanding customers' needs.

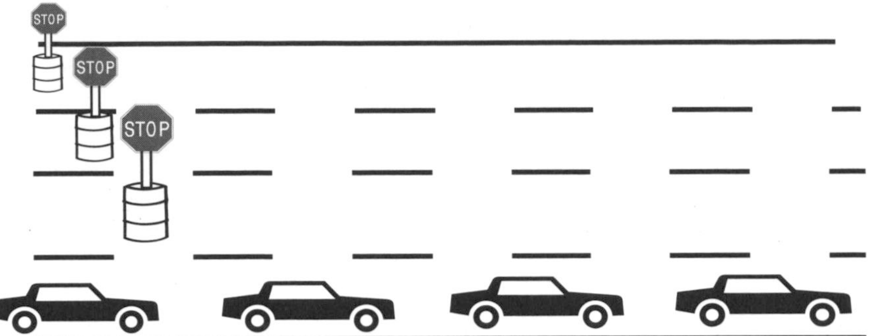

Figure 7-3 By opening up additional lanes, many more cars get on the highway.

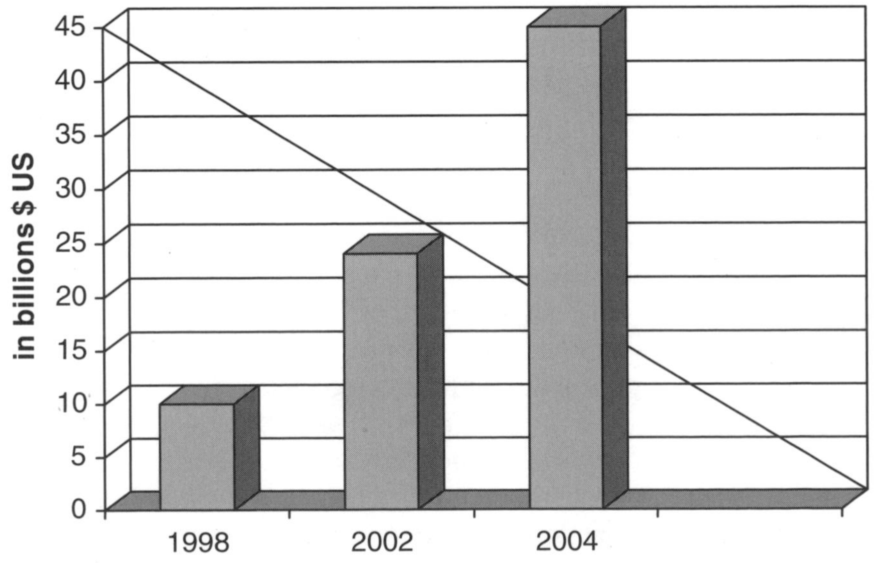

Figure 7-4 The growth curve for combined fiber-based systems

By partitioning and maintaining different dedicated wavelengths for different customers, they can lease individual wavelengths—as opposed to an entire fiber—to their high-use business customers.

Compared with older equipment applications, DWDM also increases the distances between network elements. This saves the carriers significant upfront costs as they build out their networks. The optical amplifier component of the DWDM system saves costs by amplifying optical signals without converting them to electrical signals.

Pay as You Grow

A DWDM infrastructure provides a graceful network evolution for carriers who need to meet their customers' increasing capacity demands. Because a DWDM infrastructure can deliver the necessary capacity expansion, driving a stake in the ground with DWDM is the best place to begin the migration to newer and more powerful technology. Taking smaller steps with DWDM enables the carriers to reduce initial costs while planning for future needs.

Some industry analysts rank DWDM as the perfect technology for networks requiring more bandwidth. However, these experts have noted the conditions for this fit: a DWDM system must be scalable. Even though a carrier may install an OC-48 today with 32+ channels per fiber and it may seem as overkill, it will prove to be visionary and efficient two years hence. Thus, carriers can add bandwidth and turn on what they need when they need it. This provides them the flexibility to grow without the big "hurdles" every time.

Bandwidth Demand Driven by Growing Competition

Since 1984, a trend developed throughout the world to encourage competition in the telecommunications sector through government deregulation and market-driven economic stimulation. Since competition was introduced, revenues and access lines have grown 40 percent. However, investment in outside plant has increased 60 percent. The 1996 Telecommunications Reform Act gave way to myriad new operators in the long-distance and local exchange markets. These new providers offered the promise of driving down costs. They also offered to create demand for additional services and capacity. Moreover, early competition among long-distance carriers was based mainly on price reduction. Today's competitive advantage is built on maximizing the capacity of the network and enhancing reliability through aggressive *service-level agreements* (SLAs).

Bandwidth demand increased as the carriers guaranteed fail-safe networks. Telecommunications is critical to businesses and individuals today. Carriers agreed to guarantee fault tolerance and immunity from outages. In many cases, telephone companies include service-level guarantees in their contracts, with severe financial penalties should outages occur.

To meet these requirements, carriers have broadened route diversity through either redundant rings or 1:1 point-to-point networks. Backup capacity is provided on alternate fibers. Achieving 100 percent reliability requires that spare capacity be set aside and dedicated only to a backup function. This can effectively double the bandwidth needed for an already strained and overloaded system because the "protective" path must equal the capacity of the "working path."

New Applications

Concurrently, the carriers are enhancing network survivability and accommodating escalating demand for services such as video, high-resolution graphics, and large-volume data processing. Each application requires insatiable amounts of bandwidth. Frame Relay and ATM also add to the demand. Internet usage, which is growing by 100 percent annually, is threatening to overwhelm access networks.

Over the past 20 years, the telecommunications infrastructure has been migrating to massive computerization and extensive use of fiberoptic cables. The widespread use of fiber has been made possible, in part, by the industry's acceptance of SONET and SDH as the standards for signal generation. Using SONET/SDH standards, telephone companies gradually expanded capacity by increasing data rates to 2.488 to 10 Gbps.

Applications for DWDM

As with any new technology, the potential applications for DWDM are in their infancy. Many new applications will emerge that can take advantage of the capacities and capabilities of DWDM. Already it has proven to be particularly well suited for several vital applications.

DWDM is ready-made for long-distance companies that use point-to-point or ring topologies. The immediate access to 16 new transmission channels—replacing one—dramatically increases the operator's chances of success and acceptance by the user community.

This increased capacity is critical to self-healing rings, which characterize today's most sophisticated telecom networks. Deploying DWDM enables a carrier to construct a 100 percent protected ring using two fibers. Operators building or expanding their networks also will find DWDM as an economical opportunity to incrementally increase capacity. Network wholesalers can take advantage of DWDM to lease capacity, rather than entire fibers, either to existing operators or to new market entrants. DWDM will be especially attractive to companies that have low-fiber-count cables that were installed primarily for internal operations but that could now be used to generate telecommunications revenue.

If You Cannot Build It, Buy It

With all the movement in the industry, we also have to look at the overall structure of the industry providers. In the early stages of the optical networks, carriers and manufacturers emerged. These providers were poised to build on the existing technologies and increase the capacity, drive new demand, and innovate wherever possible. However, the market heated up so quickly that many of the stodgy manufacturers were caught with their trunks down. They simply did not have the capacity in their trunking systems, nor were major capacity improvements on the horizon. Consequently, a new feeding frenzy began. In 1998, the industry was thrust into a major reeling under the inexplicable demands it had not anticipated. Thus the stage was set for the acquisitions and merger mania that followed. In the year 1999-2000, the amount of activity exceeded US$110 billion in acquisitions (representing $25 billion in 1999 and $85 billion through October 2000). This is shown in Figure 7-5. Table 7-4 is a more detailed listing of the action with the buyer, the company it bought, and the valuation of the company. This is not an all-inclusive list, but it represents many of the larger transactions that took place over these two years.

The graph Figure 7-6 is a breakdown of the major investments, but a word of caution is in order: Many of these manufacturers have undisclosed amounts that they have invested in some of their acquisitions that are not shown here. This graph shows where the major money came from in the form of stock or cash purchases.

Building Block of the Photonic Network

DWDM is established as the fiberoptic system preferred for providing bandwidth relief. Several carriers have settled on DWDM with 16 OC-48s as the technology of choice. With 16-channel DWDM

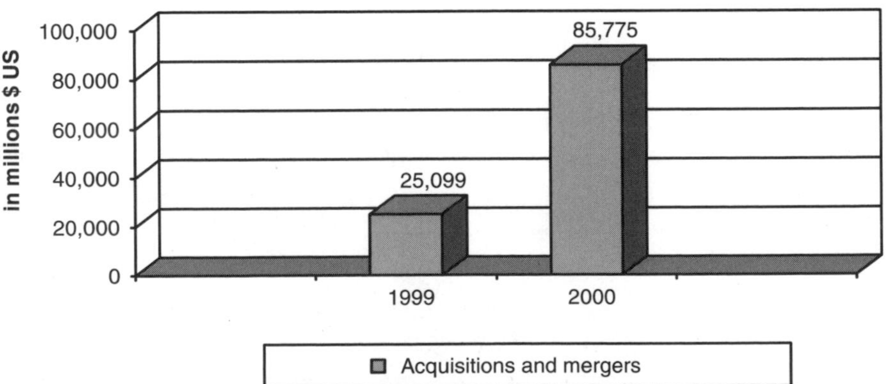

Figure 7-5 The value of acquisitions and mergers in 1999-2000

Table 7-4

Acquisitions by Vendor

Buying Company	Company Bought	Date	Value
Nortel Networks	Cambrian Systems	Dec 98-Jan 99	$300 million
Lucent Technologies	Sybarus Technologies	Feb 99	Undisclosed
GEC	Reltec Corporation	Mar 99	$2.1 billion
Applied Micro Circuits Corp.	Cimaron Communications	Mar 99	$115 million
SDL, Inc.	IOC International	Mar 99	$46 million
ADC Telecommunications	Spectracom	May 99	$105 million
Optical Networks	Object-Mart, Inc.	May 99	Undisclosed
E-TEK Dynamics	ElectroPhotonics Corp.	May 99	$40 million
Cypress Semiconductor	Arcus Technology	Jun 99	$20 million
Cisco Systems	Monterey Networks	Aug 99	$500 million
Cisco Systems	Cerent Corp.	Aug 99	$7.2 billion
JDS Uniphase	Ramar Corp.	Oct 99	Undisclosed
JDS Uniphase	SIFAM, Ltd.	Nov 99	$2.8 billion
Redback Networks	Siara Systems	Nov 99	$4.7 billion
Corning	Siemens AG Worldwide Optical	Dec 99	$1.4 billion
Nortel Networks	Qtera	Dec 99	$3.25 billion
Cisco Systems	Pirelli Optical Systems	Dec 99	$2.15 billion
Conextant Systems	Microcosm Communications	Jan 00	$180 million
JDS Uniphase	E-TEK Dynamics	Jan 00	$15 billion
Lucent Technologies	Ortel	Feb 00	$2.95 billion
Corning	NetOptix	Feb 00	$2 billion
Agilent	CSELT Optical R&D	Feb 00	Undisclosed
ADVA Optical	Storage Area Networks	Feb 00	$83 million

continued

Table 7-4 cont.

Acquisitions by Vendor

Buying Company	Company Bought	Date	Value
ADVA Optical	Broadband Gmbh	Feb 00	$22.9 million
SDL	Veritech Microwave	Feb 00	$590 million
Lucent Technologies	Ignitus Communications	Mar 00	Undisclosed
Nortel Networks	Xros	Mar 00	$3.25 billion
Intel	Giga A/S	Mar 00	$1.25 billion
Nortel Networks	CoreTek	Mar 00	$1.43 billion
JDS Uniphase	Cronos	Apr 00	$750 million
Cisco Systems	PentaCom	Apr 00	$118 million
Corning	NZ Applied Technologies	Apr 00	$150 million
Agilent	American Holographic	Apr 00	Undisclosed
MRV	Quantum Optech	Apr 00	Undisclosed
MRV	Optronics International	Apr 00	$234 million
MRV	JOLT	Apr 00	Undisclosed
ADC	IBSEN	May 00	$80 million
ADC	Altitun	May 00	$872 million
Corvis	Algety Telecom	May 00	Undisclosed
SDL	Photonic Integration Research	May 00	$1.8 billion
Kymata	BBV Design	May 00	Undisclosed
Cisco Systems	Qeyton Systems	May 00	$800 million
Avanex	Holographix	May 00	$75 million
Nortel Networks	Photonic Technologies	May 00	$35.5 million
Lucent Technologies	Chromatis Networks	May 00	$4.5 billion
ADVA Optical	First Fibre	Jun 00	$83 million
Sycamore Networks	Sirocco Systems	Jun 00	$2.9 billion

continued

Table 7-4 cont.

Acquisitions by Vendor

Buying Company	Company Bought	Date	Value
Lucent Technologies	Hermann Technology	Jun 00	$438 million
Alcatel	Innovative Fibers	Jul 00	$175 million
JDS Uniphase	SDL, Inc.	Jul 00	$41 billion
Cypress Semiconductor	Silicon Light Machines	Jul 00	$169 million
Corning	Willow Systems	Aug 00	Undisclosed
Broadcom	NewPort Communications	Aug 00	$1.25 billion
Corning	Pirelli Optical Components	Sep 00	$3.6 billion
Kymata	Total Micro Products	Oct 00	Undisclosed

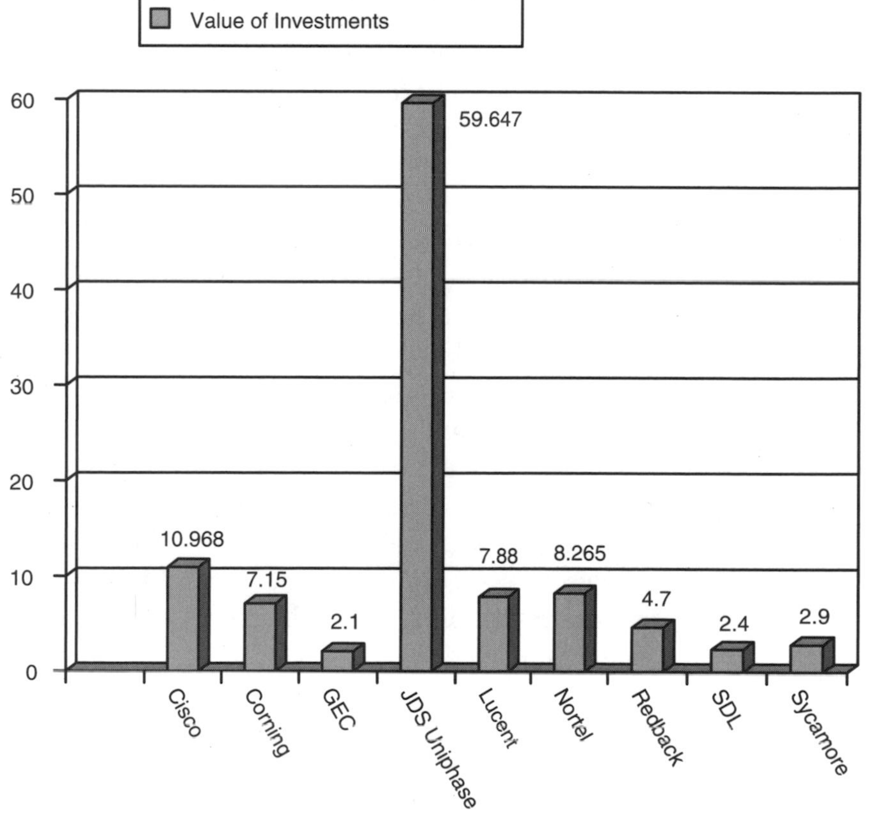

Figure 7-6
Categories of major investments by vendor

now deployed throughout the carrier infrastructure, and with a 128-channel system coming, DWDM certainly will be a key ingredient for interoffice interconnectivity. Indeed, deployment of DWDM is a critical first step toward the establishment of photonic networks in the access, interoffice, and interexchange segments of today's telecommunications infrastructure.

Given the rapidly changing and unpredictable nature of the telecommunications industry, it is imperative that today's DWDM systems adapt to future deployments and network configurations. Open DWDM systems provide such flexibility to aid the carriers in planning their future photonic network.

DWDM systems with open interfaces incorporate SONET/SDH, ATM, Frame Relay, asynchronous/PDH, and other protocols over the same fiber. Open systems also eliminate additional high-performance optical transmitters to interface with specific protocols. Rather, open systems enable service providers to quickly adapt new technologies to the optical network with "off the shelf," relatively inexpensive, and readily available transmitters.

Conversely, proprietary DWDM equipment locks the carrier into a single vendor, whereas open systems provide more freedom to provide services and reduce long-term costs. Proprietary systems, in which SONET/SDH equipment is integrated into the optical multiplexer-demultiplexer unit, are adequate for straight point-to-point configurations. Nevertheless, they require additional and costly transmission equipment when deployed in meshed networks.

DWDM systems complying with the ITU standards assure the carriers that they have systems with recognized industry standards and the flexibility to grow their optical networks into long-distance, local exchange, and access networks. Given the amount of growth and flexibility available, Table 7-6 shows where the vendors will sell their equipment and the marketplace for the near future. These figures represent specific categories of users, along with U.S.-based providers only. Considering other market segments will increase the numbers dramatically. This is still a place where we will expect to see much activity.

Table 7-6

U.S. DWDM Market Projections for Users of DWDM (US$ Millions)

DWDM System:	1999	2003	2005
IXC/ISP backbones	3,300	3,376	3,700
ILEC	21	1,302	2,965
CLEC	52	581	1,890
Cable television	81	909	2,167
Enterprise	56	168	337
Optical cross-connects	12	1,299	2,387
TOTAL	3,521	7,935	13,446

The Final List

One final list of vendors, which can never be all-inclusive, is definitely something that warrants some consideration. This list is impressive if only by sheer size. The intent is not to endorse one company over another but to list some of the players that fall into the categories of optical networking suppliers. Table 7-7 is the list of vendors, but as stated, not 100 percent. This list is current as of this writing, but if a user is interested in any one of the providers, then additional research is necessary.

Table 7-7

Vendor List (partial)

Accelight Networks
www.accelight.com

Acorn Networks
www.acorn-networks.com

ADC Telecommunications
www.adc.com

ADVA Optical Networking
www.advaoptical.com

Aetian Networks
www.aetian.com

continued

Table 7-7 cont.

Company	Web site
AFC	www.afctek.com
Agility Communications	www.agilitycom.com
Air Fiber	www.airfiber.com
Alcatel Optronics	www.alcatel.com/telecom/optronics
Algety Telecom	www.algety.fr
Alidian Networks	www.alidian.com
Allied Signal	www.honeywell.com
AllOptic, Inc.	www.alloptic.com
Altitun AB	www.altitun.com
Amber Networks	www.ambernetworks.com
AMP	www.amp.com
Anda Networks	www.andanetworks.com
Anritsu	www.global.anritsu.com
Appian Communications	www.appiancom.com
Apollo Photonics	www.apollophoton.com
Astral Point	www.astralpoint.com
Astroterra	www.astroterra.com

continued

Table 7-7 cont.

Atoga Systems
www.atoga.com

Atrica, Inc.
www.atrica.com

Atoga Systems
www.atoga.com

Aurora Networks
www.aurora.com

Axsun Technologies
www.axsun.com

Avanex
www.avanex.com

Avici Systems
www.avici.com

Bandwidth9
www.bw9.com

Bay Microsystems
www.baymicrosystems.com

Blaze Network Products
www.blazenp.com

Bookham Technologies
www.bookham.com

Bragg Photonics
www.braggphotonics.com

BrightLink Networks
www.corvia.com

Calient Networks
www.calient.net

Calix Networks
www.calix-networks.com

Caspian Networks
www.caspiannetworks.com

Catamaran Communications
www.catamarancom.com

continued

Table 7-7 cont.

Centerpoint Broadband
www.centerpoint.com

Cerent Corporation
www.cerent.com

Chiaro Networks
www.chiaro.com

Chorum Technologies
www.chorumtech.com

Chromatis Networks
www.chromatis.com

Cicada Semiconductor
www.cicada-semi.com

Cidra
www.cidra.com

Cielo Communications
www.cieloinc.com

Ciena
www.ciena.com

Cierra Photonics
www.cierraphotonics.com

Cinta
www.cinta-corp.com

Cirrex
www.cirrex.com

Cisco Systems
www.cisco.com

Codeon Corporation
www.codeoncorp.com

Cognigine
www.cognigine.com

Coherent Systems
www.coherentinc.com

CoreTek
www.coretekinc.com

Table 7-7 cont.

Coriolis Networks
www.coriolisnet.com

Corvis
www.corvis.com

Corning
www.corning.com

Crescent Networks
www.crescentnets.com

Cronos Integrated Microsystems
www.memsrus.com

Cspeed
www.cspeed.com

CyOptics
www.cyoptics.com

Cyras
www.cyras.com

DiCon Fiberoptics
www.diconfiberoptics.com

Digital Lightwave
www.lightwave.com

Digital Optics, Inc.
www.doc.com

Discovery Semiconductors
www.chipsat.com

Ditech
www.ditechcorp.com

Dynarc
www.dynarc.com

ECI Telecom
www.ecitele.com

Emcore
www.emcore.com

Ericsson
www.ericsson.com/transmission

Table 7-7 cont.

E-TEK Dynamics
www.e-tek.com

Equipe Communications
www.equipecom.com

ExceLight Communications
www.excelight.com

EZchip Technologies
www.ezchip.com

Finisar
www.finisar.com

Free Electron Technology
www.freeelectrontechnology.com

Fujitsu Network Communications
www.fnc.fujitsu.com

General Instrument
www.gi.com

Geyser Networks
www.geysernetworks.com

Gigabit Optics
www.gigabitoptics.com

Gotham Networks
www.gothamnetworks.com

Growth Networks (now Cisco)
www.growthnetworks.com

Harmonic, Inc.
www.harmonicinc.com

Hitachi Telecom
www.hitel.com

IONAS A/S
www.ionas.com

Ilotron
www.ilotron.com

Iolon
www.iolon.com

continued

Table 7-7 cont.

IP Photonics
www.iphotonics.com

Iridian Spectral Technologies
www.iridian.ca

Iris Group
www.irislabs.com

IronBridge Networks
www.ironbridgenetworks.com

ITF Optical Technologies
www.itfoptical.com

Jasmine Networks
www.jasminenetworks.com

K2 Optronics
www.k2optronics.com

Kestrel Solutions
www.kestrelsolutions.com

Kymata
www.kymata.com

Lambda Crossing
www.lambdax.com

Lantern Communications
www.lanterncom.com

LaserComm
www.lasercomm-inc.com

Latus Lightworks
www.latuslightworks.com

Laurel Networks
www.laurelnetworks.com

LGC Wireless
www.lgcwireless.com

LightChip
www.lightchip.com

LightConnect
www.lightconnect.com

continued

Table 7-7 cont.

LightLogic
www.lightlogic.com

LightSpeed Semiconductor
www.lightspeed.com

LiquidLight
www.liquidlightinc.com

Lightwave Microsystems
www.lightwavemicro.com

Lucent Technologies
www.lucent.com

Lumenon
www.lumenon.com

Lumentis
www.lumentis.se

Luminent
http://www.luminentinc.com

Luminous Networks
www.lumnet.com

Lumos Technologies
www.lumos.com

LuxCore
www.luxcore.com

LuxN
www.luxn.com

LuxPath Networks
www.luxpath.com

Lynx Photonic Networks
www.lynx-networks.com

Mainsail Networks
www.mainsailnet.com

Mahi Networks
www.mahinetworks.com

Maple Networks
www.maplenetworks.com

continued

Table 7-7 cont.

Mayan Networks
www.mayannetworks.com

Memlink
www.mem-link.com

Metera Networks
www.metera.com

Metro-Optix
www.metro-optix.com

MetroPhotonics
www.metrophotonics.com

Microcosm Technologies
www.memcad.com

Micro Photonics Integration
www.mpi-ioc.com

Molecular OptoElectronics Corporation
www.moec.com

Monterey Networks (now Cisco)
www.montereynets.com

MRV Communications
www.mrv.com

Nanovation Technologies
www.nanovation.com

NEC
www1e.mesh.ne.jp

Net Insight AB
www.netinsight.se

NetOptix
www.ofccorp.com

Network Photonics
www.networkphotonics.com

NewCore Networks
www.newcorenetworks.com

New Focus
www.newfocus.com

continued

Table 7-7 cont.

Newport
www.newportcom.com

Network Elements
www.networkelements.com

Network Photonics
www.networkphotonics.com

Nexsi
www.nexsi.com

Nishan Systems
www.nishansystems.com

Nortel Networks
www.nortelnetworks.com

Nova Crystals
www.novacrystals.com

Novalux
www.novalux.com

NZ Applied Tech (now Corning)
www.nzat.com

Ocean Optics
www.OceanOptics.com

Ocular Networks
www.ocularnetworks.com

ONI Systems
www.oni.com

Onix Microsystems
www.onixmicrosystems.com

Optical Micro Machines
www.omminc.com

Oplink Communications
www.oplink.com

OpNext
www.opnext.com

OptCom
www.scivac.com

continued

Table 7-7 cont.

Opthos
www.opthos.com

Optical Capital Group
www.opticalcapitalgroup.com

Optical Micro Machines
www.omminc.com

Optical Solutions
www.opticalsolutions.com

Optical Switch Corporation
www.opticalswitch.com

OptiMight Communications
www.optimight.com

OptiSphere
www.optisphere.com

Optiwave Corporation
www.optiwave.com

Optix Networks
www.optixnetworks.com

OptoSpeed
www.optospeed.com

Opto Tronic AB
www.optotronic.com

Optranet
www.optranet.com

Optun
www.optun.com

OptXCon
www.optxcon.com

Orika Networks
www.orikanetworks.com

Osicom
www.osicom.com

PacketLight Networks
www.packetlight.com

continued

Table 7-7 cont.

Pandatel
www.pandatel.com

Phaethon Communications
www.phaethoncommunications.com

Photonetics
www.photonetics.com

PhotonEx
www.photonex.com

Photonic Materials
www.photonicmaterials.com

Photuris
www.photuris.com

PicoLight
www.picolight.com

Pluris
www.pluris.com

Precision Optics Corporation
www.poci.com

Princeton Lightwave
www.princetonlightwave.com

Qeyton Systems
www.qeyton.com

Qtera Corporation (now Nortel)
www.qtera.com

Quake Technologies
www.quaketech.com

Quantum Bridge
www.quantumbridge.com

Quison Technologies
www.qusiontech.com

Rapid 5
www.rapid5.com

Roshnee
www.roshnee.com

continued

Table 7-7 cont.

Santec
www.santec.com

SAN Valley
www.sanvalley.com

Scientific Atlanta
www.sciatl.com

SiberCore Technologies, Inc.
www.sibercore.com

Sirocco Systems
www.siroccosystems.com

Southampton Photonics
www.southamptonphotonics.com

Spectra Switch
www.spectraswitch.com

Sumimoto Electric Lightwave Company
www.sel-rtp.com

Surface Technology Systems
www.stsystems.com

SwitchCore
www.switchcore.com

Sycamore Networks
www.sycamorenet.com

Tejas Networks
www.tejasnetworks.com

Tektronix
www.tek.com

Telica
www.telica.com

Teloptica
www.teloptica.com

Templex Technology
www.templex.com

Tellium
www.tellium.com

continued

Table 7-7 cont.

Tenor Networks
www.tenornetworks.com

TeraBeam
www.terabeam.com

Terawave Communications
www.terawave.com

Transcomm Technology Systems, Inc.
www.transcomm.com

Transmode
www.transmode.se

Trellis Photonics
www.trellis-photonics.com

Trillium Photonics
www.trilliumphotonics.com

Virtual Photonics
www.virtualphotonics.com

Velio
www.velio.com

Wavesplitter Technologies, Inc.
www.wavesplitter.com

World Wide Packets
www.worldwidepackets.com

Xros is now Nortel
www.xros.com

Xtera Communications
www.xtera.com

Yavo Networks
www.yafonet.com

Zaffire
www.zaffire.com

Zenstra
www.zenastra.com

CHAPTER 8

High-Speed Applications

Up to now, our discussions have dealt with the technologies, development, and competing products designed by the various manufacturers. Some limited discussion also has taken us through the steps of using the fiber and optical networking and switching at the carrier level. However, little discussion has taken place of the use of fiber and optical switching systems in the ever-increasing pool of applications for the end users, carriers, and manufacturers combined.

The time to discuss the application and use of the fiber-based systems is now. In this chapter, two major concepts must be addressed: making money and saving money. Making money represents the perspective of the manufacturers. They will invest in research and development efforts to create products and goods that others want. These manufacturers will concentrate their efforts on the biggest *return on investment* (ROI) that they can possibly achieve. That is a business statement, not a criticism of the efforts of manufacturers. Once manufacturers arrive at a product, they will market this product for everything they can get from it. At the same time, they will also look for spin-off applications to create a second wave of products and applications that will fit the need. This is where the vendors start. The goal is to offer the product or service that will return profits greater than their expenses, meaning they want to make money.

While manufacturers are making money on their new products, they will be replacing other (older) technologies and products that have lived through their life cycle and are returning less on their investment. Therefore, the new and improved product will create greater wealth with less cost. In this regard, the providers are saving money.

Simultaneously, the carriers will look at the new products and services offered by the manufacturers with one major goal in mind: Install this new product and create revenue streams that exceed their cost. Hence the carriers also want to use these new technologies to make money. With the implementation of these new products, some measure of benefit is achievable. This may include

- Reducing the numbers of devices
- Increasing the number of calls/connections per fiber
- Adding new service levels beyond what was available initially

In any of these choices, the outcome is that the carriers will reduce their overall cost of operation, gaining more bang for their buck. This creates the opportunity for the carriers to save money.

End users are continually working with manufacturers and carriers to realign their networks for their own benefit. While engaging both the manufacturers and carriers, the end-user community can create new networking strategies, such as

- Improved speeds
- Increased throughput
- New services
- Greater connectivity to their remote sites
- Redundancy at the access level
- Internet access for e-commerce
- New marketing campaigns

Regardless of the specific application, the end users are trying to do one of two things:

1. Make money by increasing access to them from their customers or by expanding their e-commerce solutions
2. Save money by reducing the number of individual links necessary to provide higher capacity or increasing the redundancy without installing additional circuitry

As one can see, the overall goals of the three main characters in this networking strategy happen to be the same. It is through the new and improved use of optical networks and switching componentry that this will occur for all three players.

Therefore, the next set of applications will deal with the use of SONET/SDH in a networking environment, along with the benefits that can be derived. Starting with the beginning stages, the course of action will include looking at the following:

- SONET/SDH
- WDM/DWDM
- Optical switching

Add-Drop Multiplexing: A SONET/SDH Application

A major application for using SONET/SDH is the ability to perform add-drop multiplexing. Although network elements are compatible at the OC-n/STM-n level, they may still differ from vendor to vendor. SONET/SDH does not attempt to restrict all vendors to providing a single product, nor does it require that they produce one of every type out there. One vendor may offer an add-drop multiplexer with access to the DS-1/E-1 level only, whereas another may offer access to DS-1/E-1 and DS-3/E-3 rates. The benefit of an add-drop multiplexer on a *wide-area network* (WAN) is to drop (demultiplex) only the portions of the optical stream required for a location and let the rest pass through without the demultiplexing process. It would be extremely inefficient to have to demultiplex an entire OC-12/STM-4, for example, only to drop out one DS-1/E-1. The ability to extract only what is necessary helps to prevent errors, loss of data, and other delays inherent in older technologies. The add-drop multiplexer makes this attractive for carriers to use in rural areas, where they may bundle many lower-speed communications channels onto a single OC-1 or OC-3/STM-1 to carry the information back to a central metropolitan area. Moreover, beyond just dropping a digital signal out of a higher-speed OC-n/STM-n, the carrier can fill in what has been vacated (for example, if a DS-1 is dropped off along the optical path, a new DS-1 can be multiplexed back into the OC-3 in its place). This provides the carriers with considerable flexibility. Figure 8-1 shows an add-drop multiplexer. Here, portions of the bandwidth can be dropped off and additional new signals can be added in place of the data stream dropped out of the higher-speed signal. A single-stage add-drop multiplexing function can multiplex various inputs into an OC-n signal. At an add-drop site, only those signals which need to be accessed are dropped and inserted. The remaining traffic continues through the network switching system without requiring special processing. The figure shows a local traffic convention whereby the necessary traffic is added or dropped as appropriate.

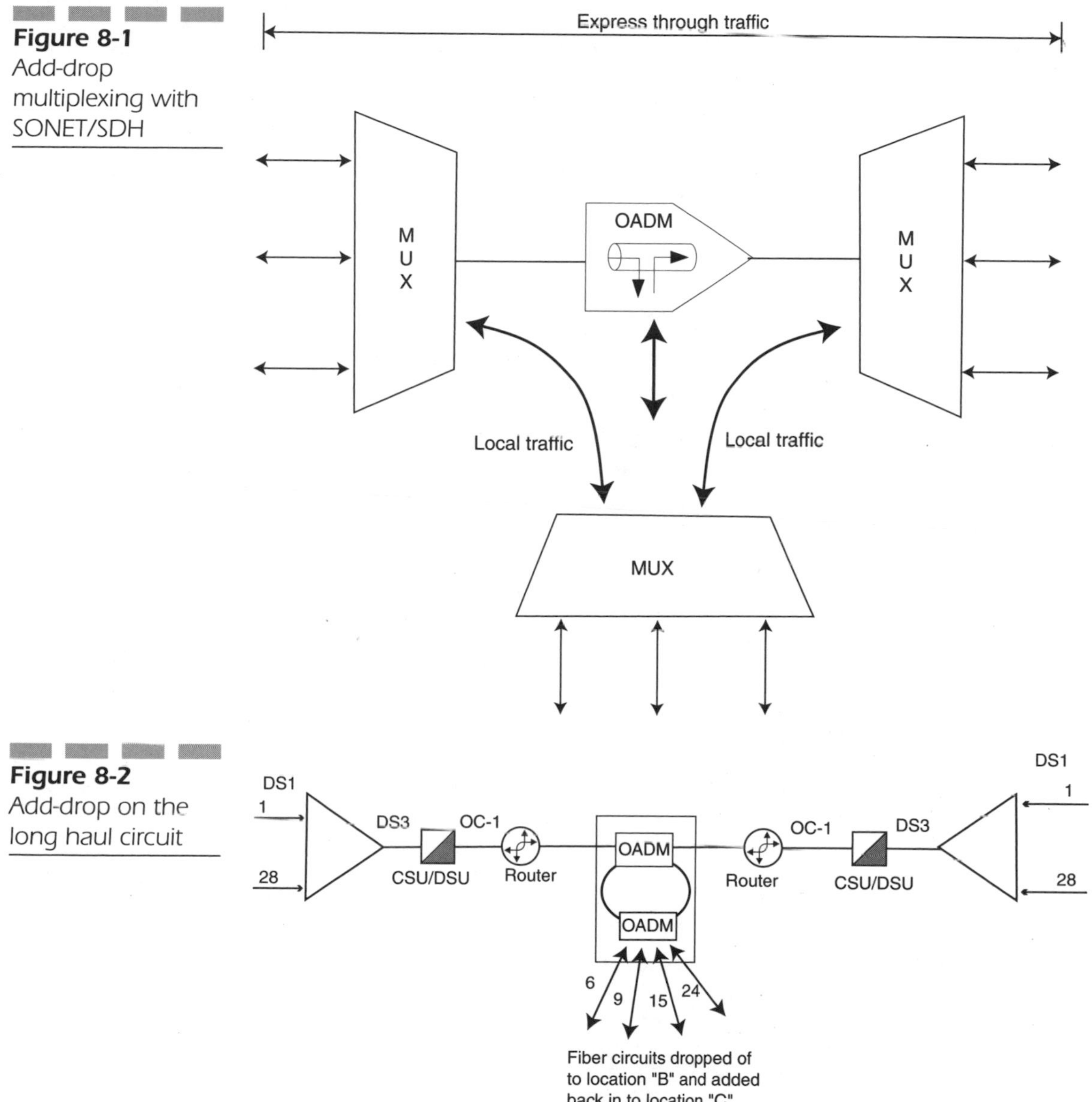

Figure 8-1 Add-drop multiplexing with SONET/SDH

Figure 8-2 Add-drop on the long haul circuit

Figure 8-2 provides a slightly more detailed look at the application of add-drop multiplexing within a longer-haul circuit. Here, the inputs at location A are multiplexed into a DS-3 and then onto a fiber-based OC-1. As the circuit is taken across the long-haul network, it may pass through amplifiers or regenerators in a SONET/SDH environment. At location B, a few DS-1s are dropped off, and new ones are inserted back into the empty time slots to be carried back to location A or on to location C depending on the need. This is a better way of viewing the true use of add-drop multiplexing.

SONET/SDH Topologies

Several different topologies can be employed in a SONET/SDH network, using the various multiplexers to satisfy the high-speed needs of the carrier or the end user. These include the normal topologies most networks have been accustomed to over the years, including

- Point-to-point
- Point-to-multipoint
- Hub-and-spoke
- Ring
- Dual counter-rotating rings

These variations provide the flexibility of SONET/SDH in local- and wide-area networks built by the carriers. These are now becoming the method of choice at many large organizations too. In each of the topologies, larger organizations are finding the benefits of installing highly reliable interoperable equipment at the private network interfaces and access to the public networks.

Point-to-Point

The SONET/SDH multiplexer, the entry level for an organization, acts as a concentrator for multiple lower-speed communications channels such as DS-1/E-1 and DS-3/E-3. This equipment may be acquired by the end user, or it may be provided as the *customer premises equipment* (CPE) by the carrier (ILEC, CLEC, and IEC). In its simplest form, two devices are connected with an optical fiber (with any repeaters as necessary) as a point-to-point circuit. As the entry-level point into SONET/SDH architecture, the inputs and outputs are identical. In this environment, the network can act as a stand-alone environment and not have to interface with the public switched networks. Figure 8-3 shows a point-to-point multiplexing arrangement.

While considering this, the application may be to bundle multiple communications channels together, replacing the leased lines installed for each application. If one considers the use of SONET/SDH, many lower-speed applications can be bundled together into a single high-speed communications channel using a point-to-point circuit. In this case, no add-drop multiplexing is required because all the bandwidth is used between the same two ends. Figure 8-4 shows some of the lower-speed communications channels.

Figure 8-5 shows the same services bundled together onto a single OC-1 to carry all the services between the two ends. Note that this figure goes beyond the replacement of individual slower circuits with a high-speed and accelerated communications channel to satisfy the demands that were not being met initially.

Figure 8-3 Point-to-point services with SONET/SDH

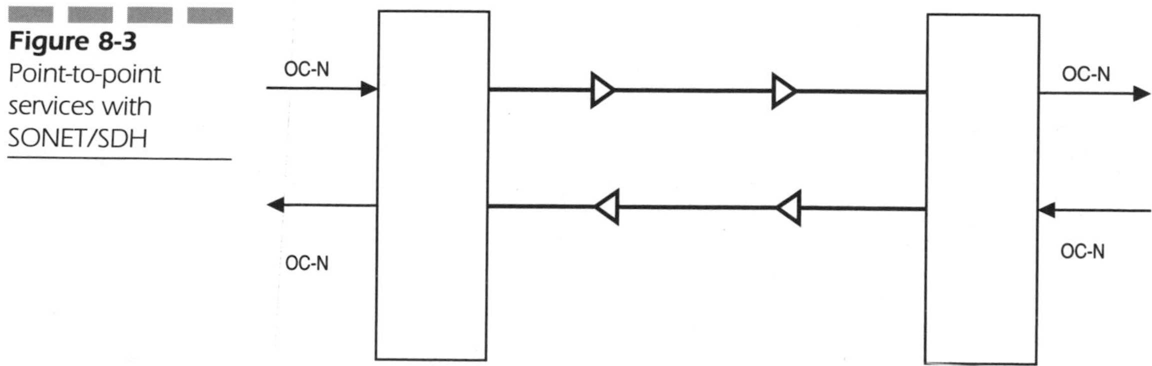

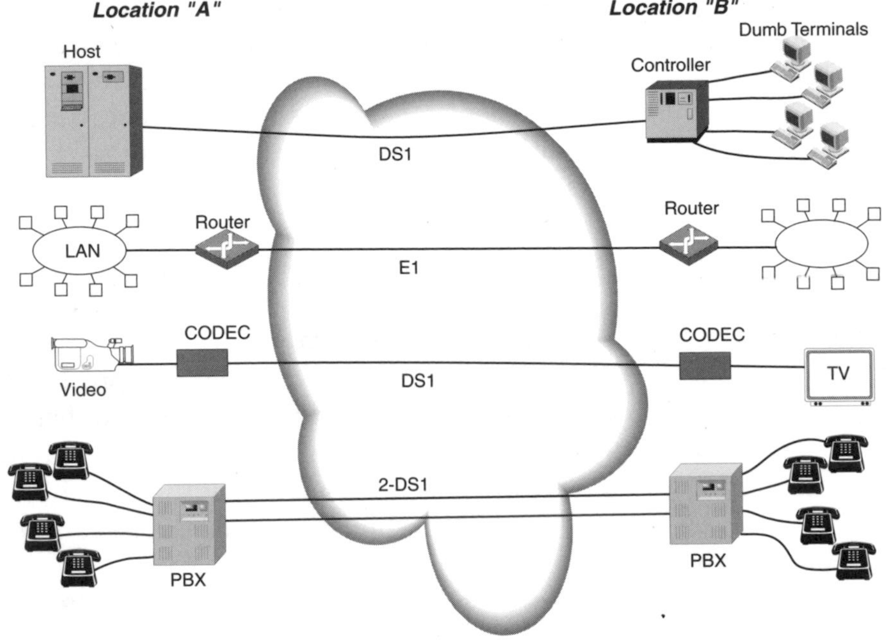

Figure 8-4 Point-to-point applications using low-speed communications

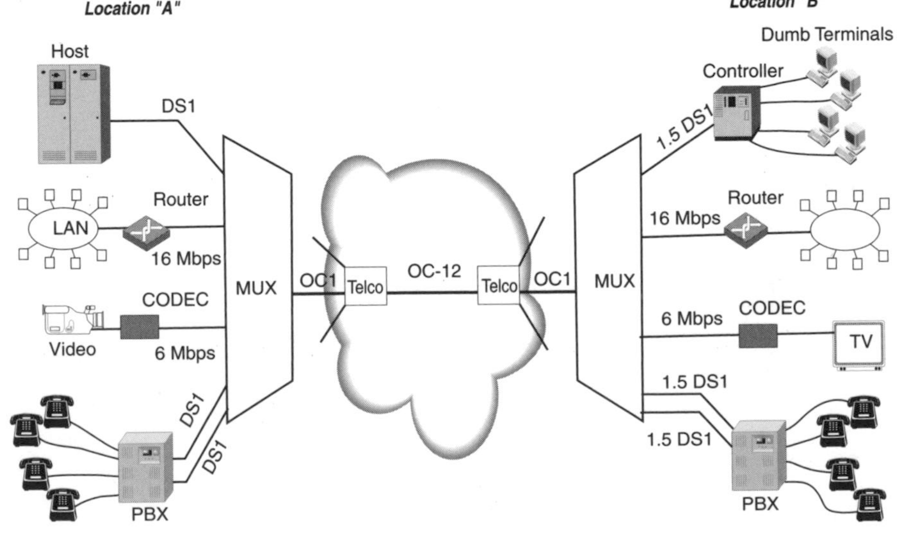

Figure 8-5 Bundled services on a point-to-point SONET OC-1 circuit

Point-to-Multipoint

The next step is to consider the point-to-multipoint arrangement. This will use a form of add-drop multiplexing to drop circuits off along the way. In a large corporate network spanning the country (or any subset), a single high-speed link may be employed. The SONET *add-drop multiplexer* (ADM) is used for the task at hand, dropping circuits out without demultiplexing the entire high-speed signal. Figure 8-6 shows an ADM installed between two far-end locations so that signals can be added or dropped off as necessary. This is a better solution than renting three different circuits between points AB, AC, and BC, which adds to the complexity and cost. By using a circuit from A to B to C with ADMs, the service usually can be accommodated more efficiently.

Hub-and-Spoke

The hub-and-spoke method (sometimes referred to as a star network) enables some added flexibility in case of unpredicted growth or constant changes in the architecture of the network. A SONET/SDH

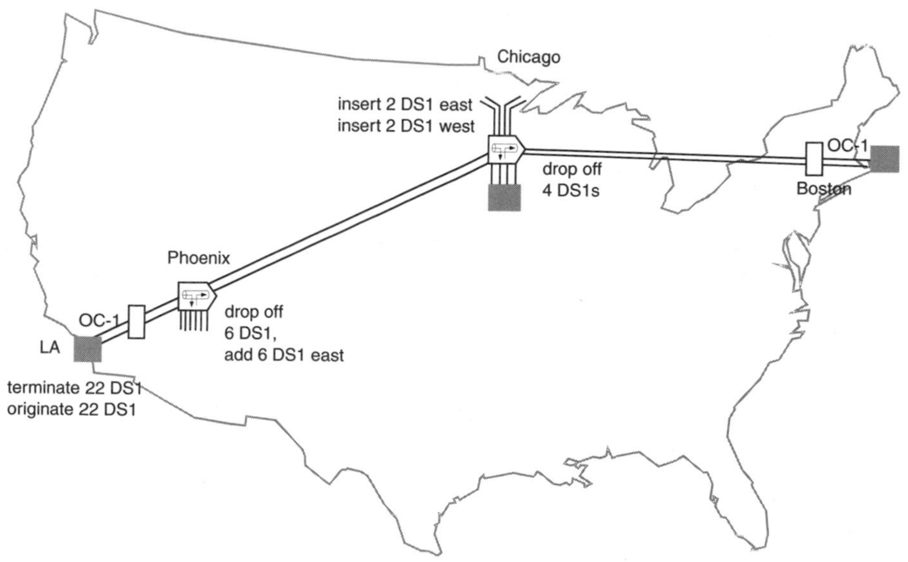

Figure 8-6 ADMs installed along the way of a multipoint circuit

multiplexer can be hubbed into a digital cross-connect, where it is concentrated and then forwarded onto the next node. This is used in many larger organizations where regional offices are located and district or branch offices are tied into the network through the hub. Again, the flexibility is available if a major change occurs in the network architecture or in case of major campaigns in the organization. Hubs will act as the cross-connect points to link the various echelons in the network together. These may be developed in a blocking or nonblocking manner. Typically, some blocking may be allowed. The hub-and-spoke arrangement is shown in Figure 8-7.

Ring

In a ring architecture, where SONET/SDH automatic protection switching is employed, the best of all worlds comes to fruition. The ring topology uses ADMs throughout the network, and a series of point-to-point links is installed between adjoining neighbors. The bidirectional capability places the most robustness into the network; however, unidirectional services also can be installed. The primary advantage of the ring architecture is survivability in case of a cable cut or a failure in a network node. The multiplexers have sufficient intelligence to reroute or reverse direction in case of a failure. If more than one fiber link is installed, the systems could use alternate paths, but they must recover in *milliseconds* (ms) which APS on

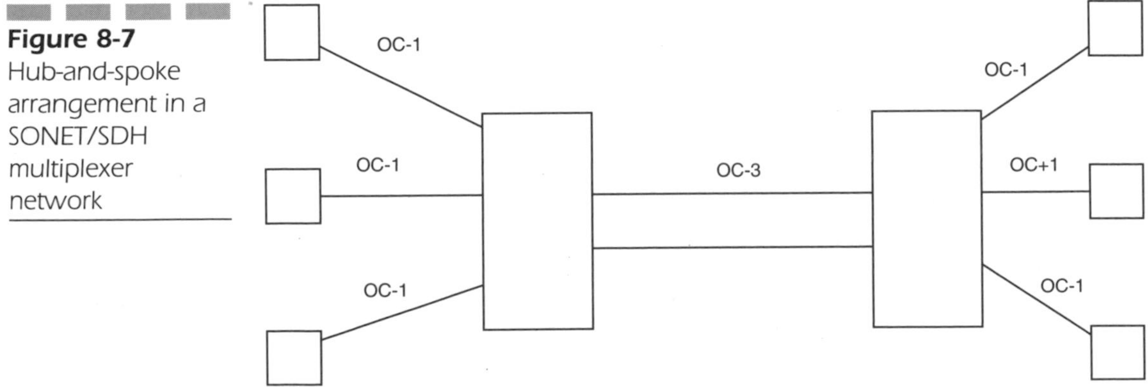

Figure 8-7 Hub-and-spoke arrangement in a SONET/SDH multiplexer network

SONET/SDH is designed to do. Figure 8-8 shows the ring topology with dual fibers run (bidirectional service) between the ADMs.

Ring topologies also may be used as access methods to provide robust services to the Internet. Figure 8-9 shows a ring of OC-3s installed for a large organization looking for redundancy and resiliency in the network. In this case, the access methods are installed by the carriers to different carriers (AT&T World Net and UUNet). If a single failure occurs, the network will begin to immediately close the circle and offer the customer high-speed and reliable communications all at the same time. Regardless of the application, this redundant-ring topology assures the customer of availability without the wait. The network will likely heal and begin the alternate routing in less than 10 ms. At one point, this form of internetworking would have been too expensive for customers to afford and for carriers to install. With all the changes in bandwidth allocation and the technology improvements, networks like this are becoming common.

Access Methods

One of the major issues always facing end users and local carriers is that of access. Users are now more sophisticated in their desires. They no longer want to settle for just any service. Instead, they

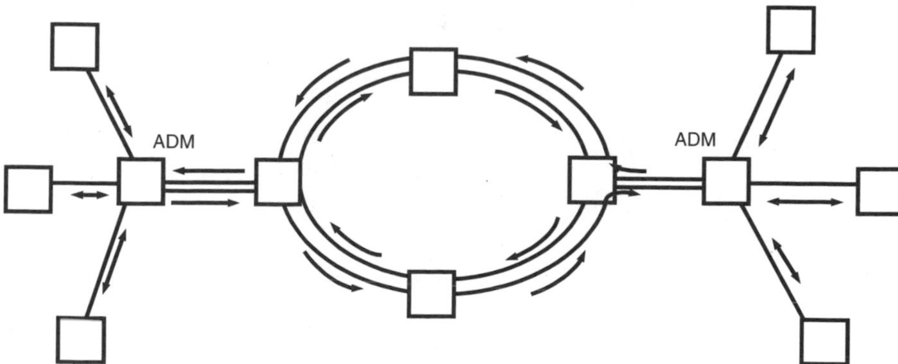

Figure 8-8 Ring architecture of SONET/SDH multiplexers

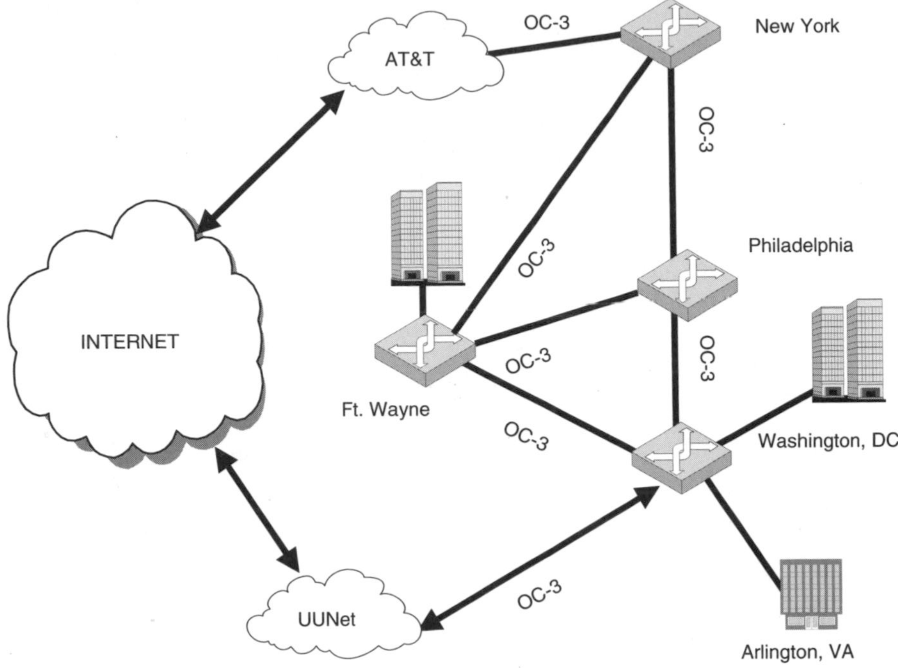

Figure 8-9 Redundant access to the Internet

expect and demand higher-speed services to satisfy their access needs. Figure 8-9 illustrated a means of accessing the Internet with a dual feed to different suppliers. In this scenario, the user will demand service levels that are far greater than what was available from local providers in the past. This feat is possible because of the various methods of using the fiber to the door and the high-speed multiplexing of many plesiochronous and synchronous inputs at the SONET/SDH level. Using our example here, dual access to the Internet is possible and very realistic. In particular, high-speed access is also needed because at most organizations the actual desktop (LAN) is working with 100-Mbps Ethernet. We now need to move data across wider networks unimpeded.

Beyond basic access to the Internet, we face the ever-present issue of fiber to the door. Yes, this will likely be inevitable. However, for the time being, access may start at the consumer's door on copper. Here, the user may use a special copper feed at whatever rate of speed that can be sustained on such a local feed. At the *incumbent local exchange carrier* (ILEC) (or *competitive local exchange carrier* [CLEC]) office, a digital cross-connect system will bundle the access lines together onto a SONET/SDH channel at OC-1, OC-3/STM-1, OC-12/STM-4, or higher. This is shown in Figure 8-10, where the local loop is still copper, but fiber services are applied at the ILEC office. An alternative to the copper feed is the possibility that the *local exchange carrier* (LEC) may have a digital subscriber loop, using fiber on what it calls the *digital loop carrier* (DLC). In this case, the fiber enables higher-speed access.

Another possibility, shown in Figure 8-11, is the use of integrated access services. The customer may choose to install a DS-3 (T-3) to the door to support the following services:

- Voice at the PBX, which may be using one or more T-1s
- LAN using a 10-Mbps feed from an Ethernet router
- Other data services

Figure 8-10 Looking outward from the consumer's door

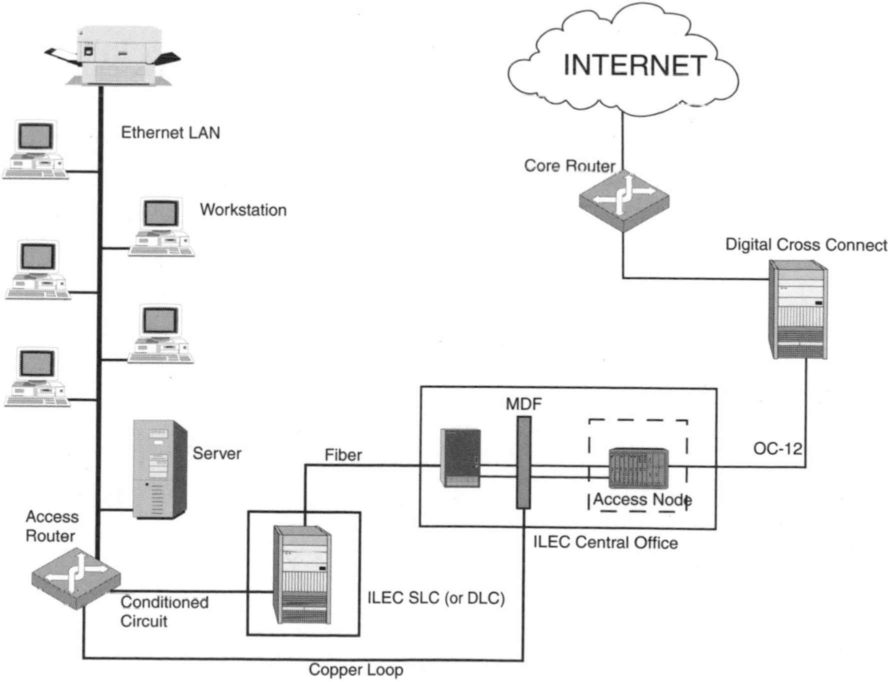

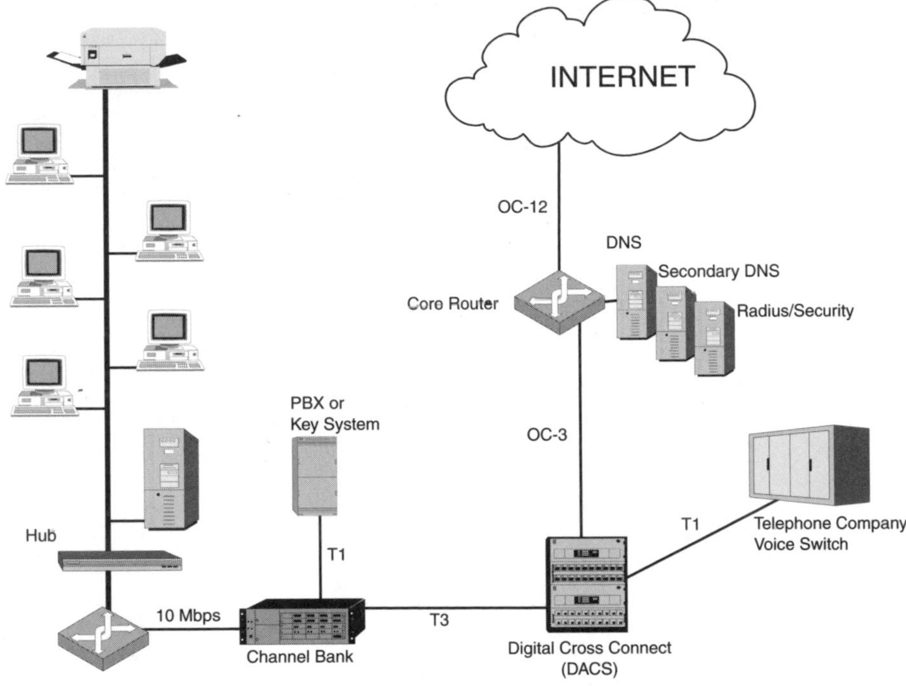

Figure 8-11 Combining services onto a DS-3 and then multiplexing onto SONET

These can all be combined at the local loop and then carried through a channel bank or multiplexer to the LEC office. At the LEC office, the T-1s can be dropped off into the voice switch for circuit-switching needs (dial-up voice). Meanwhile, the data continues through a digital cross-connect system to a core router. This will enable Internet access at 10 Mbps. Combinations of such services are almost endless. The common denominator is the use of high-end multiplexers in the LEC office to bundle the services onto a fiber-based architecture such as SONET/SDH.

Alternative Approaches to Multiple Services Delivery

As we continue to escalate the speed of data networks, we hear many arguments about the best way to carry the traffic. The *Internet Protocol* (IP) is now the most common form of data that we need to send across our networks. A lot of discussion entered the market regarding the use of IP over various data networking protocols and different layers of the OSI model.

IP will run anywhere that we want it. The issue is not whether it can be done, but whether we want to do it? Sales and marketing people with a personal stake in selling specific products entered the foray with a statement that *Asynchronous Transfer Mode* (ATM) was too expensive to use for IP datagrams (packets). Therefore, data communications manufacturers developed a marketing strategy to handle IP over SONET (POS) instead of ATM. At the time, the entire industry was leaning toward IP over ATM. Soon everyone was expounding the benefits of running IP over SONET. Therefore, enter a new group of people who began to espouse the benefits of running IP over *dense-wave-division multiplexing* (DWDM) without the use of ATM or SONET.

A number of alternative approaches were developed to address the limitations of traditional SONET in multiservice access networks. These alternatives include IP over ATM over SONET, IP over SONET (packet on SONET), and IP over DWDM. The protocol stacks for these three approaches are shown in Figure 8-12.

Figure 8-12 Various approaches to carrying IP

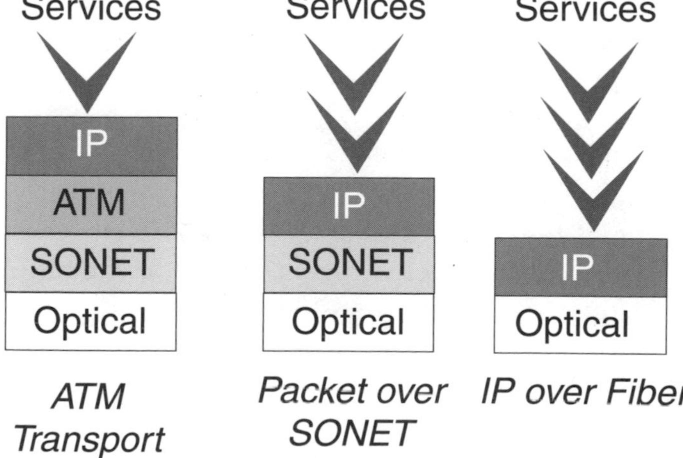

The first approach adapts all services to ATM cells, which are then transported over an optical network using a concatenated SONET frame. Several standards address this approach, including Telcordia GR-2837, which defines ATM virtual path support on SONET rings, and Telcordia GR-2842, which presents requirements for ATM-based access multiplexers. The second approach adapts services to IP frames for transport over an optical network using either a channelized or a concatenated SONET frame. The IETF *multiprotocol label switching* (MPLS), *differentiated services* (Diffserv), and *resource reservation services protocol* (RSVP) standards address a number of issues associated with this approach. The third approach again adapts all services to IP frames for transport directly over an optical network. However, this approach eliminates the intermediate SONET layer. Each of these approaches has the potential to increase bandwidth utilization on fiber access networks.

Many network operators plan to use ATM over SONET for integrated delivery of services because of its support for a wide range of service types and its robust and mature *quality-of-service* (QoS) features. Telcordia's GR-2837 standard defines several approaches to support of ATM traffic on fiberoptic rings. The most efficient of the approaches uses a concatenated SONET frame, eliminating the SONET *virtual tributary* (VT) structure while retaining the section and line overhead bytes. Using ATM technology increases the granularity of transport bandwidth to minimize the wasted bandwidth resulting from using the traditional SONET hierarchy. ATM over SONET technology also supports fast automatic protection switching at the ATM virtual path level or the SONET layer. This addresses one drawback of earlier approaches to protection switching using ATM virtual channels or IP routing table recalculations, which were much slower. Finally, current ATM over SONET technology accommodates ring network topologies rather than assuming point-to-point or mesh topologies. This enables the technology to be used on fiber access rings that are prevalent in many parts of the United States. Figure 8-13 is a representation of what can be gained or lost by eliminating any of the protocols or layers in the OSI.

Services may be established on an on-demand basis using ATM *switched virtual circuit* (SVC) signaling. QoS features also include more efficient allocation of bandwidth on access networks by provid-

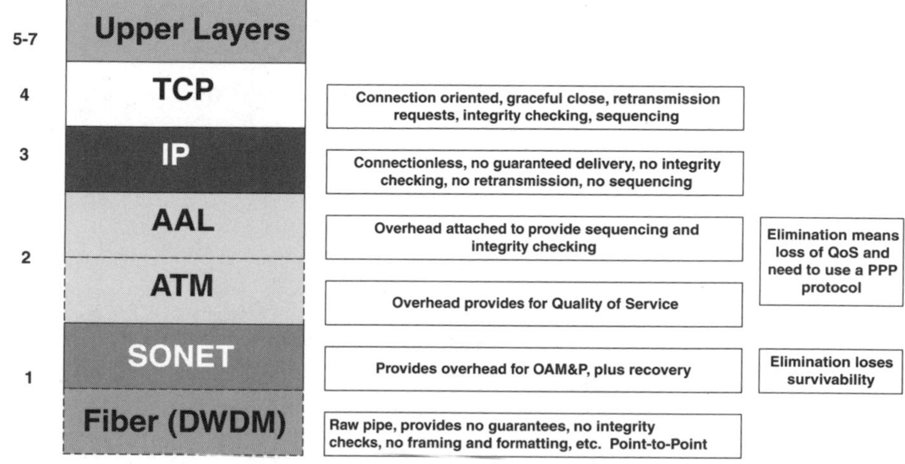
5-7
Upper Layers
4
TCP
Connection oriented, graceful close, retransmission requests, integrity checking, sequencing
3
IP
Connectionless, no guaranteed delivery, no integrity checking, no retransmission, no sequencing
AAL
Overhead attached to provide sequencing and integrity checking
2
ATM
Overhead provides for Quality of Service
Elimination means loss of QoS and need to use a PPP protocol
SONET
Provides overhead for OAM&P, plus recovery
Elimination loses survivability
1
Fiber (DWDM)
Raw pipe, provides no guarantees, no integrity checks, no framing and formatting, etc. Point-to-Point

Figure 8-13 Summary of protocol layers and benefits

ing statistical gain for bursty services while ensuring that the bandwidth and latency requirements of leased-line and *time-division multiplexing* (TDM) voice services are also met.

These features enable an OC-12 fiberoptic access ring using ATM over SONET technology to support over 100 10baseT transparent LAN services, assuming a 2-Mbps sustainable rate on each service. Increasing the utilization of access networks enables network operators to postpone upgrades of these networks to higher rates and minimizes the need to acquire additional leased access facilities.

Packets can be sent over ATM and then over SONET by going through several steps of preparation. In Figure 8-14, data must be sent. The data file can be multimegabytes large. The sequence will follow as:

1. The multimegabyte file is passed to TCP.
2. TCP segments the data into 64-kB segments.
3. TCP passes the segment to IP.
4. IP creates the default datagrams of 576 bytes (or some other size).
5. The datagrams are passed to the *Asynchronous Transfer Mode* (ATM), *ATM Adaption Layer* (AAL) (typically AAL5) and broken down into the *segmentation and reassembly* (SAR) of 48 bytes.

6. The SAR is passed to the ATM layer, where the 5-byte header is attached, creating the cell.
7. The 53-byte cells are mapped onto a SONET frame in a horizontal format.
8. The SONET frame is transmitted across the fiber link.

What about the Metropolitan-Area Networks?

Manufacturers are now addressing the metropolitan-area optical-transport architecture based on dedicated optical networks connecting wavelength-routed and traditional IP systems. New products are appearing with DWDM, adding dynamic add-drop functions and using broadband active optical amplifiers, when necessary, to extend system reach or cut the number of optoelectronic conversions within the metropolitan region.

Passive DWDM was limited in metropolitan areas compared with the success of long-haul systems. This is due mainly to the LECs (ILECs and CLECs) being separated from the protection switching and provisioning capabilities in a DWDM environment. The newer systems were designed to overcome these limitations by providing either protected or unprotected channels. The optical subsystem uses 1,310-*nanometer* (nm) short-reach lasers. Transceivers can be configured via software for OC-3, OC-12, or OC-48 rates.

Essentially, two choices are available for community networks in the metropolitan areas: lease or build. Most large corporations with metropolitan-area networking needs lease services from carriers. Many carriers have built their own highly resilient SONET rings in urban areas to serve various customers with leased lines connecting to that ring. Common services include T-1, T-3, Frame Relay, and OC-3 dedicated lines. This is shown in Figure 8-15, where the configuration uses a SONET architecture.

A real need exists among local communities, governments, and school districts today to obtain cost-effective high-speed communications access to enable new multimedia applications such as distance

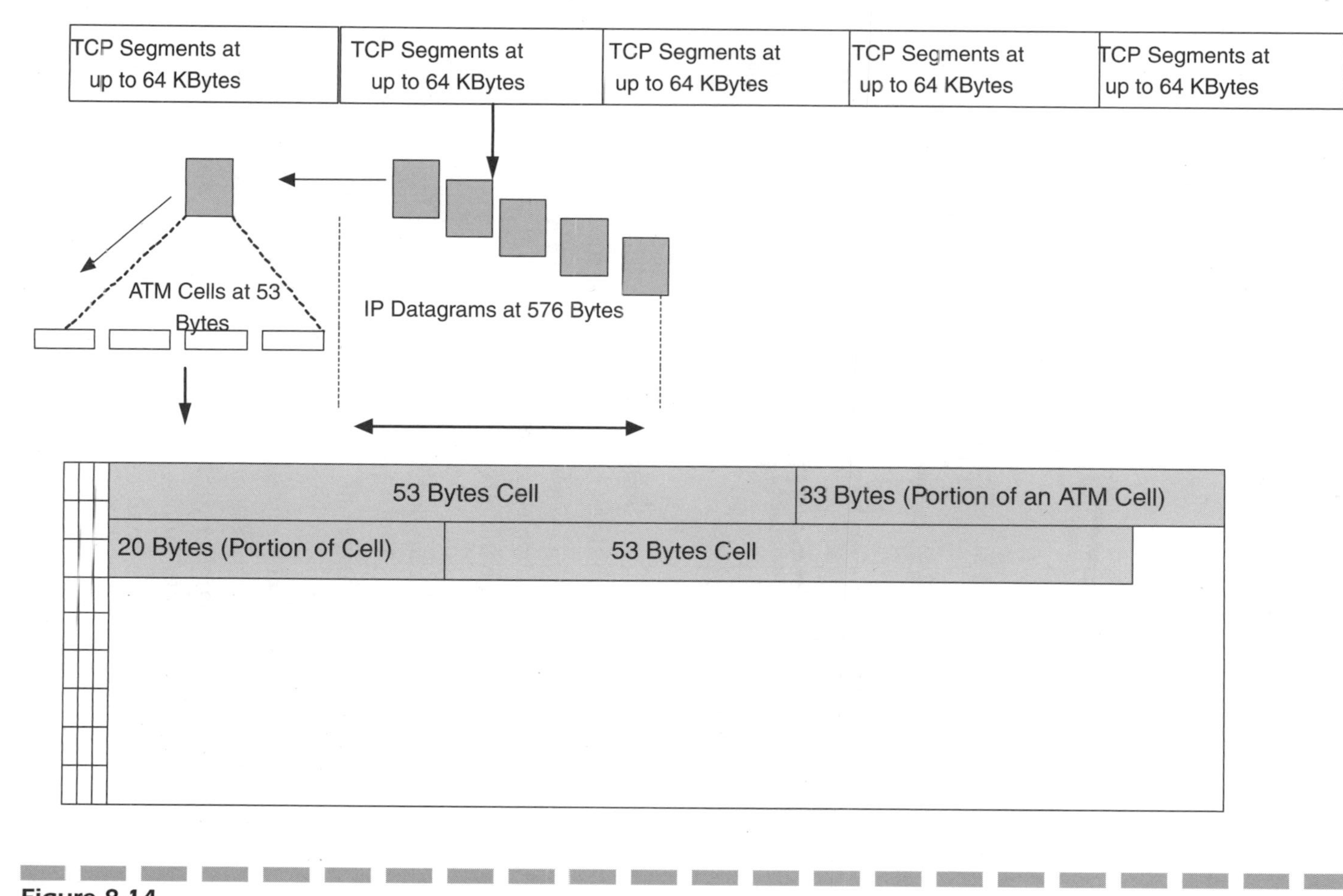

Figure 8-14
Multistep process of handling IP over SONET

Figure 8-15
The metropolitan SONET network

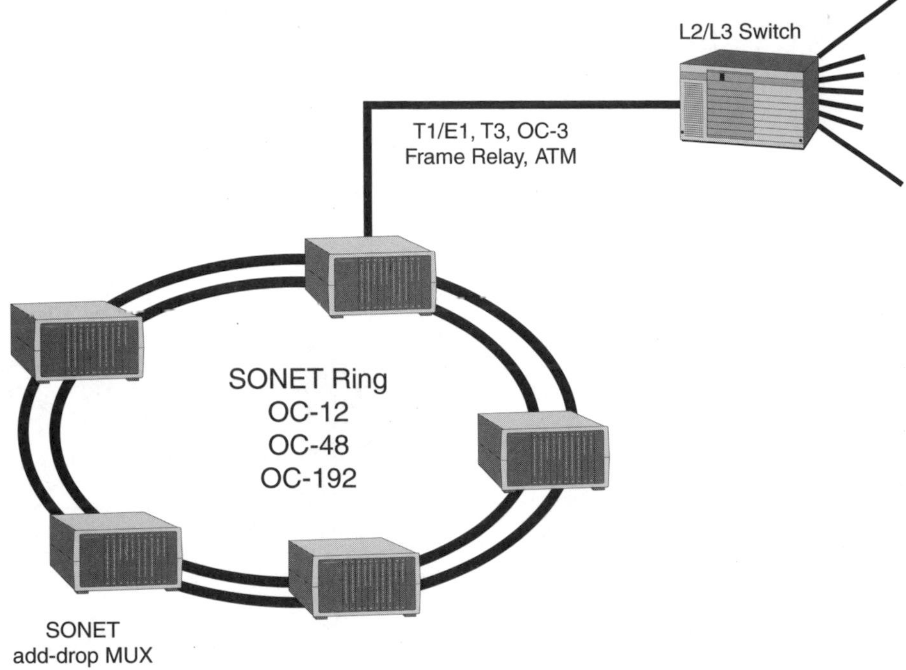

learning/training, telemedicine, global information systems, intranets for e-mail and shared databases/applications for e-government, and *business-to-government* (B2G) and extranet access. Individual agencies and school districts usually build independent islands of information technology around themselves, isolated from each other. Different software and hardware platforms are deployed, and information cannot be shared. These entities failed to leverage their economies of scale for greater buying power. This has resulted in higher communications and information technology costs and duplication of effort.

Things are changing, however. Innovative communities are collaborating to pool resources to create new network infrastructures that enable higher-performance networked applications at lower overall costs. By building a high-speed communications grid among public entities, a community may be able to break down traditional barriers and streamline operations by reducing duplicated efforts. Figure 8-16 shows how this might work.

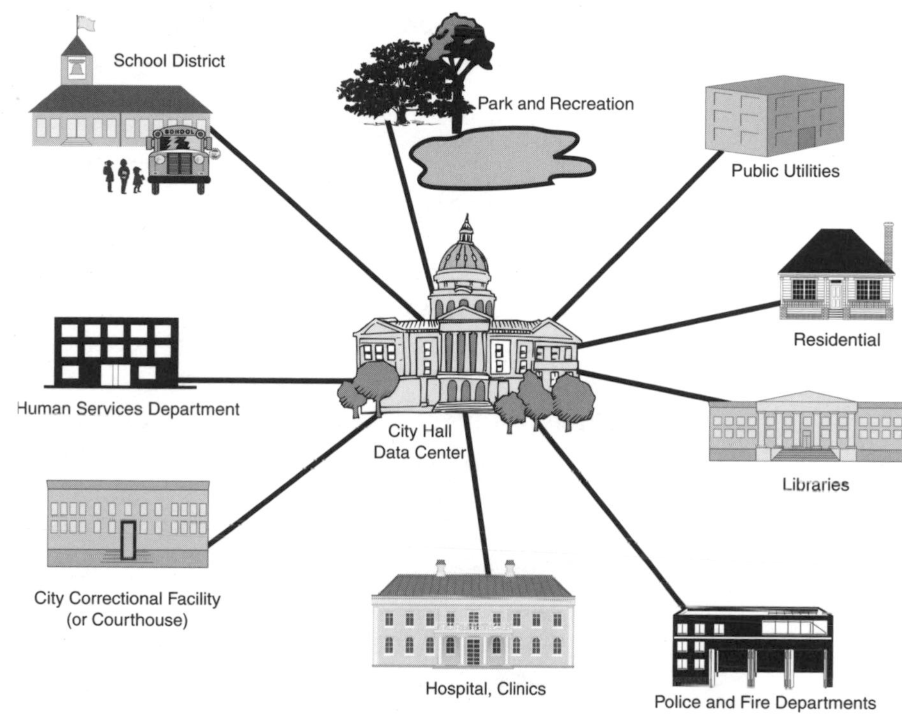

Figure 8-16 Communities of interest are emerging (3Com)

Applications for DWDM

As with many new technologies, the potential for DWDM is still in its infancy. However, the technology already has proven to be particularly well suited for several vital applications. DWDM is ready-made for long-distance telecommunications operators that use either point-to-point or ring topology. The sudden availability of many new transmission channels as opposed to only one increases a carrier's ability to expand capacity and simultaneously set aside backup bandwidth without installing new fiber.

The huge capacity afforded by DWDM is critical to the development of self-healing rings, which is characteristic of most sophisticated telecom networks. By deploying DWDM terminals, an operator can construct a 100 percent protected 40-Gbps ring with multiple communications signals using only two fibers.

Carriers planning their capacity for current or future needs also find DWDM as an economical way to do the following:

- Incrementally increase capacity
- Rapidly provision new equipment for needed expansion
- Future-proof their infrastructure against unforeseen bandwidth demands

Wholesalers can take advantage of DWDM to lease capacity (rather than entire fibers) either to existing operators or to new market entrants. DWDM will be especially attractive to companies that have low-fiber-count cables that were installed primarily for internal operations but that could now be used to generate telecommunications revenue. In the past, many carriers were smug with the idea that they installed plenty of spare fibers in their rights of way. Therefore, these carriers stated that they could just light up another fiber rather than install the DWDM multiplexers and switches. This may have been true in the past, but as things progressed, the fibers were consumed, and the demand for new bandwidth continued to escalate. Using DWDM in the metropolitan area breathes new life into these carriers' networks.

DWDM system transparency to various bit rates and protocols will enable carriers to tailor and segregate services to various customers along the same transmission routes. DWDM enables a carrier to provide STM-4/OC-12 service to one customer and STM-16/OC-48 service to another all on a shared ring. In regions with a fast-growing industrial base, DWDM is one way to utilize the existing thin fiber plant to quickly meet burgeoning demand.

Building Block of the Optical Network

DWDM is now entrenched as the preferred method to relieve the bandwidth constraint many carriers face. Several U.S. carriers have settled on DWDM at 16 times the OC-48 rate to gain more capacity. DWDM deployments throughout the carrier infrastructure will continue to be an essential element of future interoffice fiber systems. DWDM is a critical first step toward the establishment of photonic networks in the access, interoffice, and interexchange segments of the telecommunication infrastructure. Figure 8-17 is an example of optical access links using the DWDM architecture in the metropolitan area.

DWDM systems with open interfaces give operators the flexibility to provide SONET/SDH, asynchronous/PDH, ATM, Frame Relay, and other protocols over the same fiber. Open systems enable the carriers to quickly adapt new technologies to the optical network using "off-the-shelf," relatively inexpensive, and readily available transmitters.

Open interfaces provide operators with greater freedom to provision services and reduce long-term costs. Proprietary-based systems, in which SONET/SDH equipment is integrated into the optical multiplexer-demultiplexer unit, are adequate for straight point-to-point

Figure 8-17 Optical access in metropolitan networks (Alcatel)

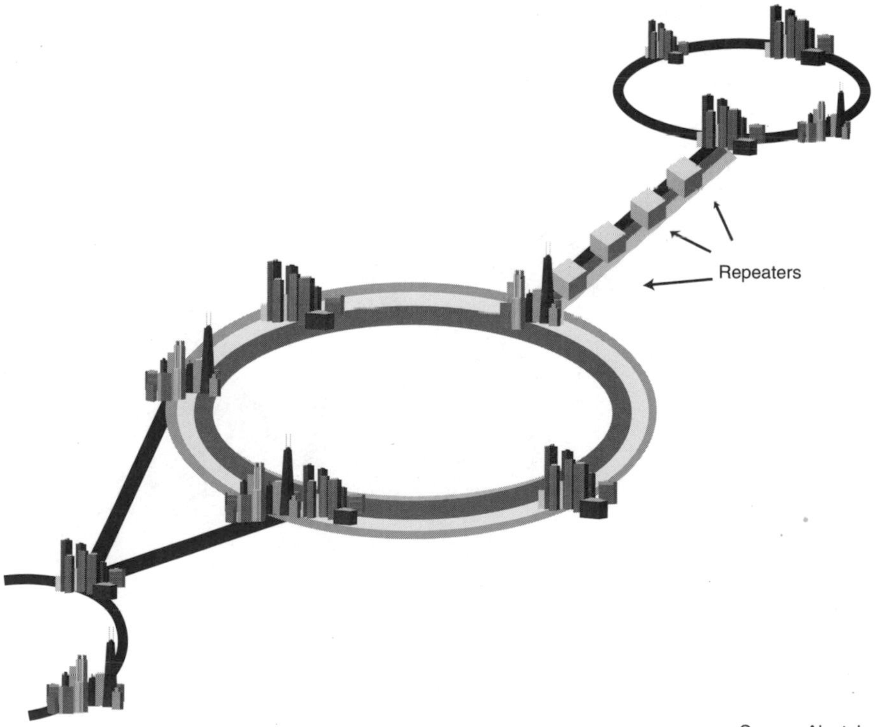

configurations. However, they require additional and costly transmission equipment when used in meshed networks.

In just under two years, DWDM has become an industry standard that will find acceptance in any carrier environment. Therefore, DWDM

- Allows new services to come online more quickly.
- Contains costs so that customers can afford new services.
- Overcomes technological barriers associated with more traditional solutions.

Newer applications emerge using the hybrid combinations of *passive optical networks* (PONs) in a community alongside of the coaxial systems serving broadband communications in the business and residential market. The use of different wavelengths in this market makes the combinations that much more attractive and economical. This combined networking strategy with DWDM in the metropolitan area is shown in Figure 8-18.

Figure 8-18
Combining services in the metropolitan area (Alcatel)

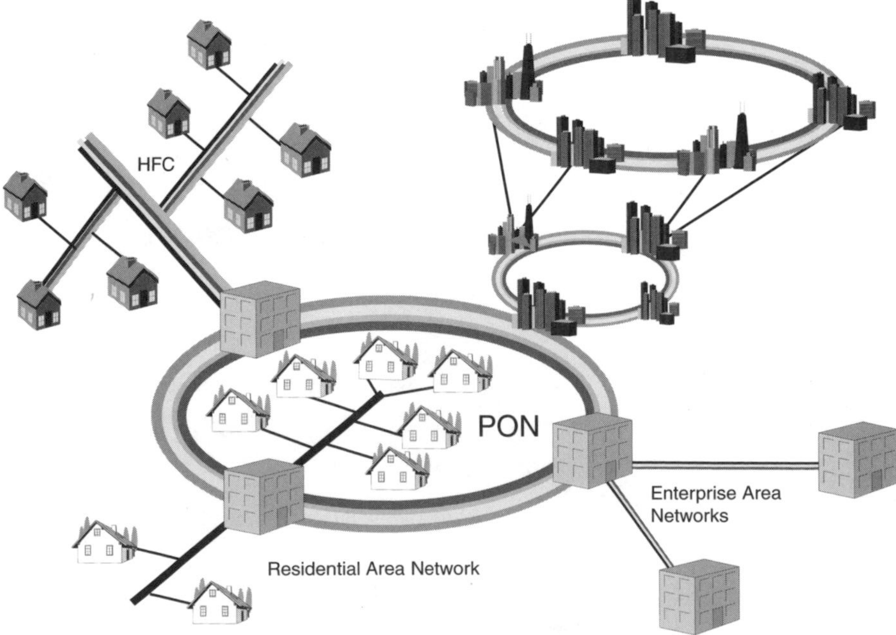

Metropolitan-area networks (MANs) are "hot buttons" for various providers. The current state of innovation and integration is shifting away from the WANs to the last mile and across citywide-area networking strategies. These core networks are changing the way carriers perceive their ability to use and deploy their bandwidth. WANs were the building blocks in the middle to late 1990s. However, the new century marks the investment strategies for the ILECs and CLECs (data CLECs also). Tremendous growth in access capacity is the new marketplace for the infrastructure. These MANs will span the range of applications from the areas covered in Table 8-1.

The services we saw earlier in the discussion of technologies are not different. Each has a need for dedicated high-speed or shared high-speed communications across the MAN. Figure 8-19 shows the areas of concentration as the primary means of using the MAN and separate wavelengths in support of each of the market drivers.

One additional area is the use of a combination of localized communications access methods through a multiplexer (that is, OC 48/192) connected into a digital cross-connect system at the local carrier network. At the carrier location, the introduction of wave-division multiplexers (WDM/DWDM) into the same cross-connect system will be handled. From there, the fibers will carry the various wavelengths to a switch, where the information will be optically

Table 8-1 Services Driving the Use of DWDM across MANs

Services
Data center operations across town
Financial institutions with personnel spread across the broad area of a city
Planning for disaster recovery services to a "hot site" location
Mainframe access and Escon services to legacy applications
Backup and storage of network appliances and services
High-speed Internet access
Mission-critical services such as storage-area networks
FDDI distribution and MAN access
Multimedia applications

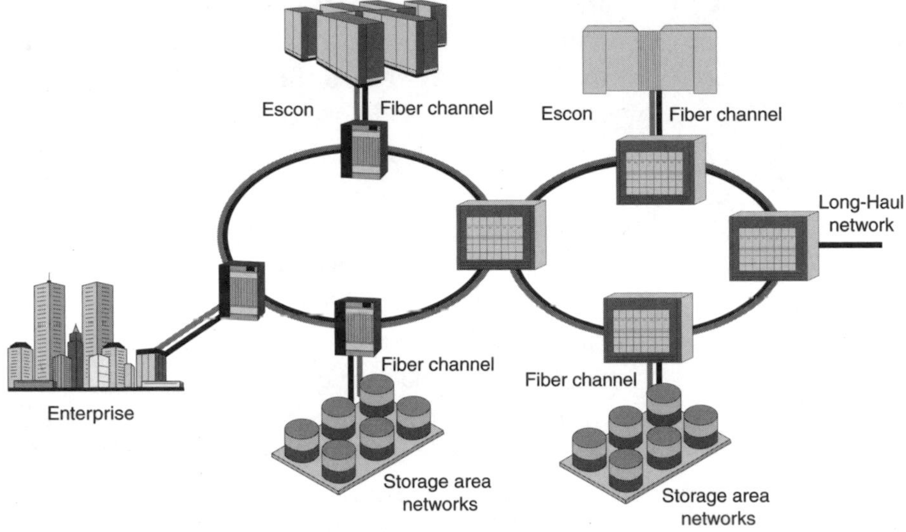

Figure 8-19 The services using the bandwidth

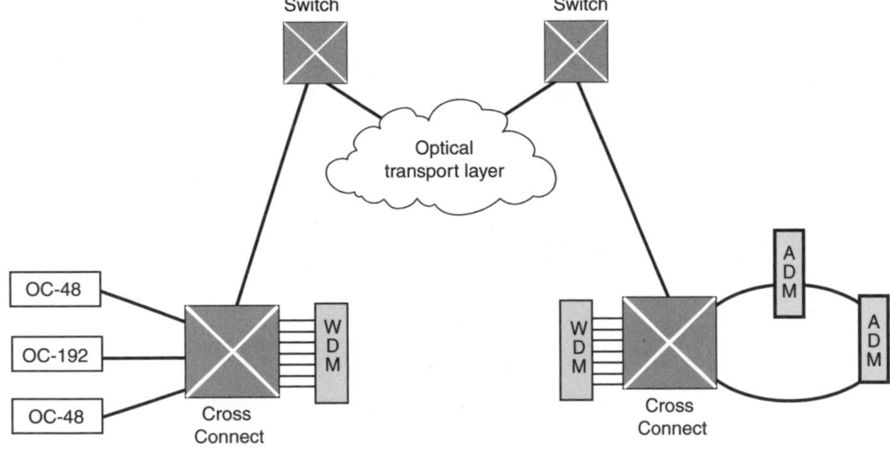

Figure 8-20 Local switching in an optical architecture (NEC)

switched across town at the optical layer. Finally, the information will be extracted in the reverse order back down to the cross-connect and to any multiplexers on a local ring or multiplexer as necessary. This configuration is shown in Figure 8-20.

The Wide-Area Network

When provisioning for the long-haul networks, the carriers have to take into account that they will interface with local providers, that is, unless they become the local provider too. However the interconnection is made, the wide area is where most of the infrastructure was built in the past because of the economics of providing the fiber-based (SONET/SDH) networks to carry long-distance traffic and consolidated data communications. This worked, but as seen, the new battlefront is at the metropolitan area. Thus, when the communications providers use their interconnectivity, they must take into account how they will link the metropolitan and wide areas together. An example of this form of interconnection is the use of data and voice communications linked together on a WAN. In this application, a combination of access methods can be suitable, such as Frame Relay, ATM, and Internet leased-line access through the metropolitan network and interconnected across the wider area, as shown in Figure 8-21.

In some cases, the long-distance network will be used to provision a high-speed data network for a large organization at OC-3/OC-12 speed (or STM-1/STM-4) to link corporate sites with a dedicated private-line network service. In this case, the application is raw speed at the 622-Mbps rate, but this can be subdivided into multiple lower-speed communications channels, or it can be packetized and carry

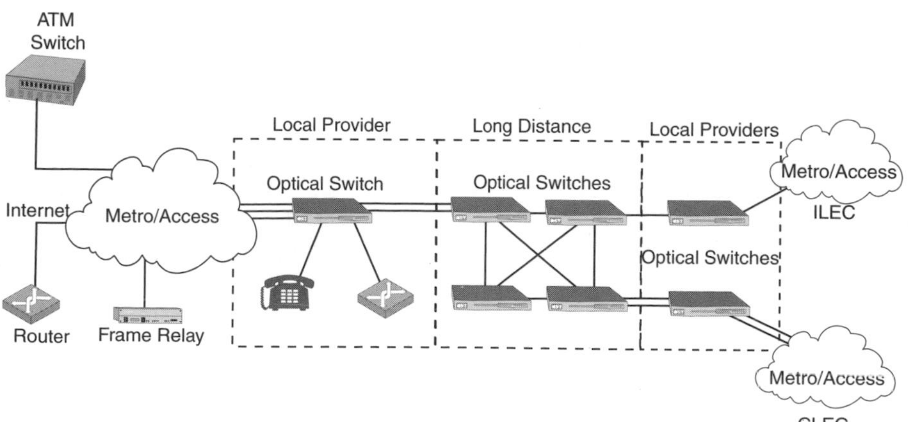

Figure 8-21 Interconnecting MANs and WANs

voice over data, data, video, and multimedia on the same communications channels. This provision enables the long-distance carriers to allocate and multiplex as much bandwidth as the customer needs in a private-line service between the two ends, as shown in Figure 8-22.

In the long-distance network, the SONET and SDH services can be used to provide a series of interconnected ring topologies that enables the carrier to provide the redundancy and resiliency of the network as needed. Figure 8-23 shows a series of interlocking rings used to provide full service and availability in case of a disaster (for example, backhoe fade when a backhoe digs up the cables). These interconnected rings may provide a full 1:1 protection circuit for the entire OC 12/48 network, or they may be 1:n (where n is 3, 4, or 5), enabling mission-critical services to be covered even though some lower-priority circuits may not be 100 percent backed up. This enables the carrier to provision as much as necessary in order to meet the critical need without overpopulating a network for nonessential services. This is more of an economic decision than any other consideration. Regardless of the level of backup coverage, the carriers use the interconnected rings for their benefit as well as for that of the customer.

Figure 8-22 The data private line

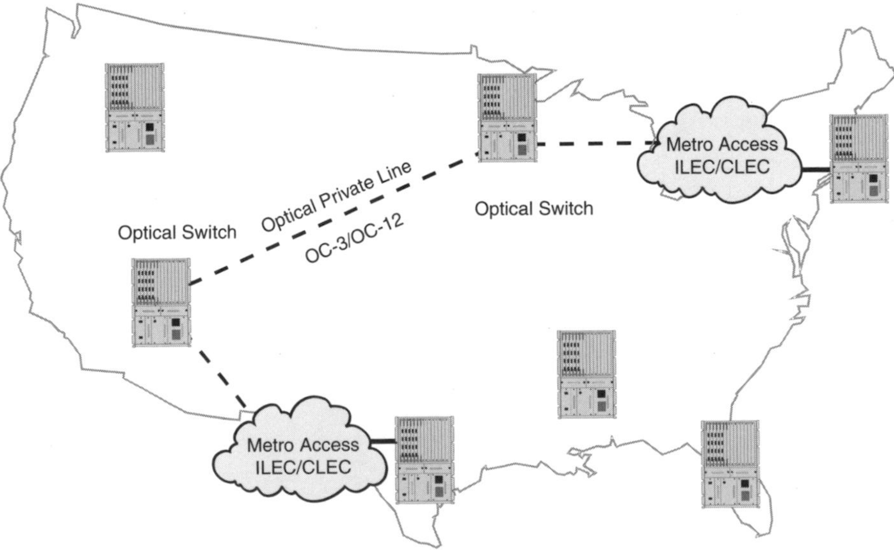

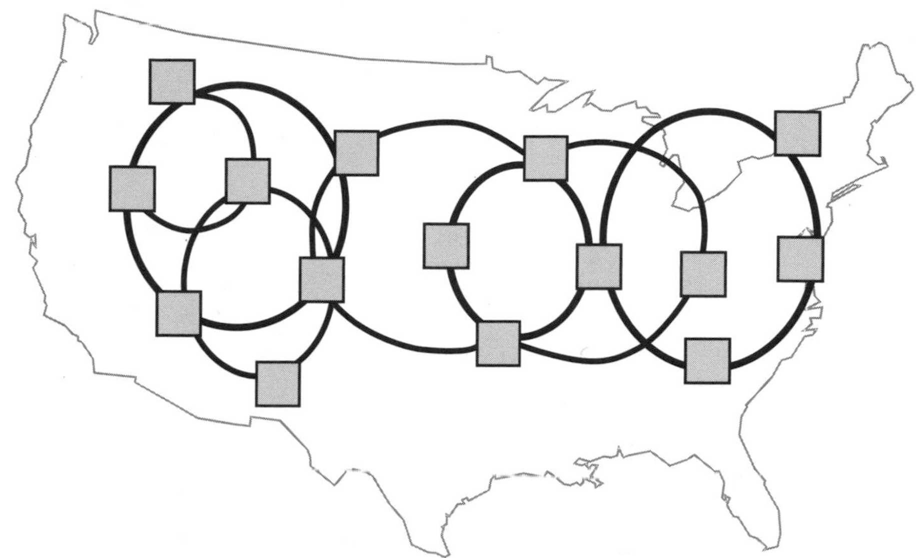

Figure 8-23 Interconnected rings across a WAN

CHAPTER 9

Cost Implications and Financial Trending

Whenever a new service is introduced, one can expect that the costs and pricing models are going to be at their highest levels. Over time, as mass production takes place and more systems and services are implemented, the pricing begins to fall. There is nothing new here, except that the timing of this model has been somewhat slow in occurring and shifting. Consider that the use of fiberoptics initially made its way into the telecommunications industry in the 1960s. Furthermore, the development of worldwide standards in the form of SONET and SDH took almost 30 years to be implemented. At the point when SONET became a standard (followed soon thereafter by SDH), the pricing models began to shift. The industry saw the influx of new fiber-based architectures in the long-distance marketplace with companies like Sprint, Williams Telecommunications, MCI/WorldCom, and AT&T. These carriers were fast to install their infrastructure because the model brought a new form of cost-efficiencies into the long-distance arena. The long-distance market is very lucrative. In the late 1980s (shortly after SONET became a standard), the long-distance portion of the industry amounted to approximately $80 billion in North America alone. The profitability was extraordinary, with carriers making between 30 and 40 percent profits.

At the local loop, however, things were different. Telephone companies were slow to implement because of the cost implications and the fact that they depreciate their infrastructure over a 25- to 30-year term. The local dial tone market during the same period amounted to $115 billion in North America, yet the incentive to invest was limited. Many of the companies held back because no one saw a need for high-speed fiber to the consumer's door. Besides, only one provider existed for the local loop. When changes began to occur in 1996 with telecommunications deregulation at the local loop, the picture also changed dramatically for providers:

1. Newer markets were opened.
2. Many new competitors appeared.
3. Telephone companies had to offer the local copper to the competitor at a reduced price.

With this competition, the carriers were faced with the risk of losing their installed base of customers unless they changed the way they provided services. SONET became a mainstay for large corporations. Telephone companies sustained their operation by offering higher-speed access and lower costs at the same time. Carriers will be able to upgrade network connections more easily and may end up with excess capacity on their networks in the future. To entice corporate enterprises to use this capacity, carriers are expected to reduce prices or develop novel value-added services. A very close friend of mine has become a "designer carrier," offering specialty product and bandwidth on a user-by-user basis. Although the benefits of fiberoptic technology have been very clear for 20 years or more, the medium has been 20 to 40 percent more expensive than coaxial cable connections. Fiber's complexity is one reason, but a lack of reliable standards also contributes to the sharp price differential.

Sometimes It Is the Fiber

As light beams travel along a fiberoptic cable, they can splinter, bump into each other, and disrupt the connection. The greater the wavelength density, the higher the risk of this occurring. This makes sense, because the more light beams (wavelengths) we use, the more chance there is of something getting in the way. To solve the problem, suppliers have delivered amplifiers that regenerate wavelengths as they travel along a line. Amplifiers can be expensive, costing $50,000 to $100,000 per unit. Therefore, equipment vendors have been developing new technologies, such as *Spatial Mode Transformation* (SMT),[1] that boosts the maximum distance between amplifiers.

The type of fiber that carriers have in place also determines how much amplification is needed. Carriers have largely deployed single-mode fiber, whereas multimode fiber has become the staple in enterprise networks. Most single-mode fiber was not designed to carry such dense transmissions. Corning's LEAF single-mode fiber, introduced in February 1998, does not need as much regeneration nor does it need to consume as much power as traditional single-mode fiber lines. Consequently, it can support transmissions traveling more than 31 miles. Most fiber was optimized to approximately a 6.2-mile connection. Corning sold 1 million kilometers of LEAF fiber

[1]Spatial Mode Transformation is a product of LaserComm.

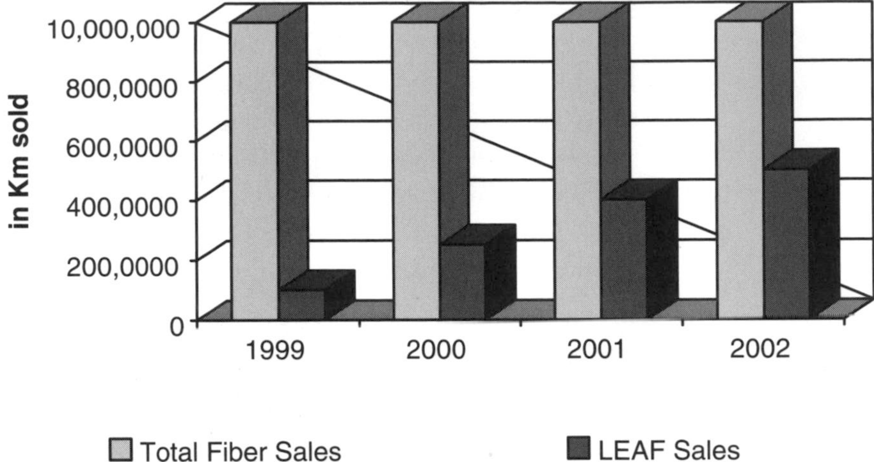

Figure 9-1 Sales of LEAF fiber by Corning

in 1999, which accounted for about 10 to 15 percent of all its fiber sales. Expectations are that the number will increase to the 20 to 25 percent range by the end of 2000. Expectations of growth of this type of fiber are shown in Figure 9-1. However, the total sales have been kept stable to show the percentage increases in perspective.

Equipment vendors face another challenge in taking advantage of these new high-bandwidth options. According to Ciena Corp., the carriers want systems that meet the following criteria:

- Compact
- Low power consumption
- No heat generation

Suppliers think that microprocessor improvements can solve these problems and lead to delivery of higher-speed *dense-wave-division multiplexing* (DWDM) systems. By the end of 2000, products supporting 160 separate 10-Gbps wavelengths (1.6 Tbps of bandwidth) began to emerge from vendor's test labs and into carrier networks for trials. Most of this bandwidth will be used in long-haul connections.

Carrier interest in the new wares is high. *Internet service providers* (ISPs) see the products as a way to differentiate their services by offering customers higher-speed Internet connections. *Competitive local exchange carriers* (CLECs) need the bandwidth to compete with the incumbent *local exchange carriers* (ILECs).

Cable & Wireless USA, Inc., plans to install DWDM multiplexers in 60 metropolitan areas across the country. The plan calls for the first 60 cities to be completed between 2000 and 2001. Because of such rapid deployments, research houses expect North American carrier purchases of local DWDM equipment to increase from $115 million to $923 million in 2003, as shown in Figure 9-2.

As this ramp-up on the local loop occurs, the source of network bottlenecks could very well shift again. Corporations and employees can fill this bandwidth with various multimedia applications, such as videoconferencing. Services may quickly use the extra capacity in the long-haul network, and suppliers will be looking for ways to push DWDM capacity even higher.

It Is in the Glass

Optical fever has swept Wall Street and Silicon Valley. Internet traffic doubles every three months, placing an insatiable demand for bandwidth with which it is tough for the providers to keep pace. The demand has brought the once high-minded and academic discipline of light physics from the back room of laboratory research into the

Figure 9-2 Increased installation of DWDM equipment.

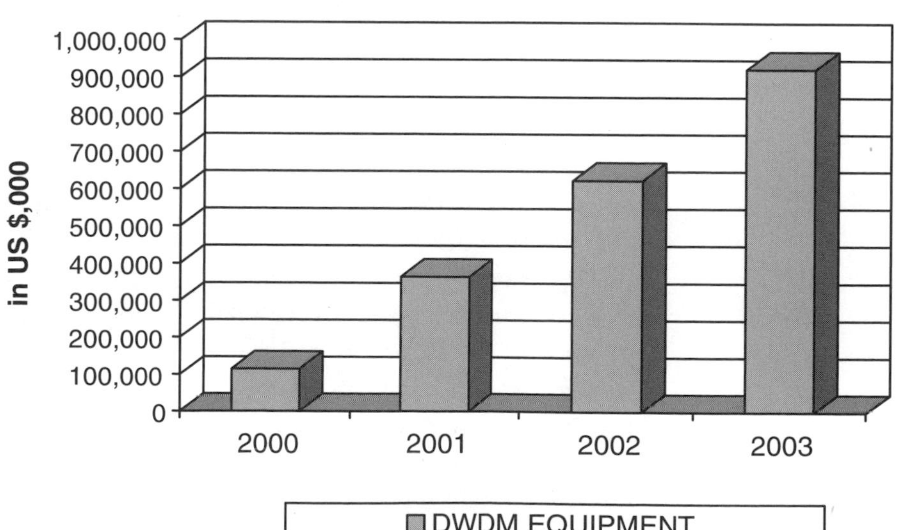

Internet spotlight. The valuations of optical companies have been multiplied by this single act. The craziness slowed a bit at the end of 2000, but it is expected to regain momentum again. An industry that is only five years old has created a gold rush that pits the three networking giants (that is, Cisco, Lucent Technologies, and Nortel Networks) against one another.

The long-term goal is to make a pure optical network in which a light packet shuttles digital data at tremendous speed without ever having to be converted into electrical signals. A group of optical start-ups is aiming to deliver the components and new technologies in order to make end-to-end optical a reality. No one is sure when all-optical networks will become the norm, but within 10 years, these networks should be deployed at major companies. Plenty of research and development dollars and effort will be directed toward pure optical switches and optical technologies for metropolitan markets.

The pace of this fiber network buildout has been nothing short of astonishing. Carriers such as Qwest Communications International, Level 3 Communications, and Global Crossing have snapped up optical gear (lasers, amplifiers, and other components) so fast that shortages have occurred. Manufacturers and start-ups cannot ramp up production quickly enough to meet the demand. The companies supplying the underlying components, such as Nortel, Lucent, and Cisco, are also struggling to keep up with the demand. Nortel estimates that it will spend $260 million to boost its production by 30 percent in 2001. One telecom research company expects annual spending on optical networking equipment to quadruple over three years, to $23 billion, which can be seen in Figure 9-3.

The economics of optical networking are now starting to appear and are becoming very favorable. For example, the cost of installing optical networks over the traditional *time-division multiplexed* (TDM) networks of the past are favorable, representing as much as a 50 percent savings over traditional TDM installation costs. Figure 9-4 attempts to show this relationship of installed costs for optical versus TDM equipment. The savings for long-haul networks can mount up quickly in this way.

This figure shows that there is a 50 percent or better savings at the representative number of OC-48s installed. Carriers like the average savings per *point of presence* (POP) of $520,000. This allows

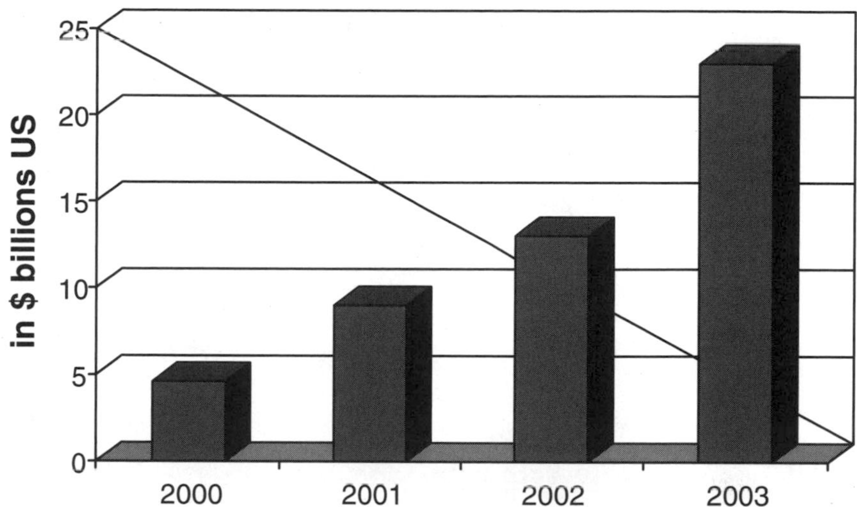

Figure 9-3 Growth in optical networking equipment

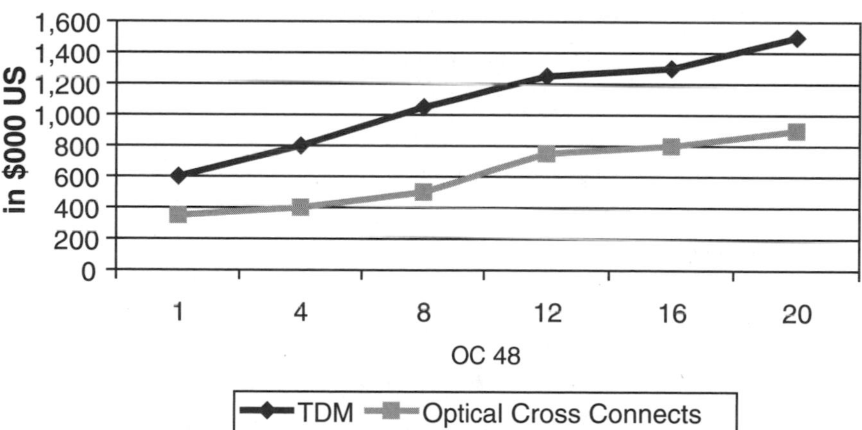

Figure 9-4 Comparison of OC-48s on TDM versus optical cross-connect systems

them more flexibility to install more equipment at lower rates. Moreover, when the carriers want to install their optical networking components, differences play into another part of the equation. The two different ways to install fiber networks are

1. Transparent
2. Opaque

Transparent Optical Networks

For more than 10 years, optical systems have been tested and built based on certain theories and test beds. Transparency is a desired feature in developing optical networks because the signal is carried through the entire network transparently (optically) without having to perform conversions.

Opaque Optical Networks

In the past, conversion was needed at the amplifiers. The change was from optical to electrical and then back to optical again (OEO). Because this conversion was necessary, the following was present:

- A risk of degradation of the signal
- Added equipment required to perform the conversions
- Latency built into the overall performance of the network

This conversion adds to the overall cost of the network, increases the maintenance of equipment, and increases the risk and complexity. The alternative to this was to use opaque networks.

Several advantages and disadvantages exist for both transparent and opaque networking strategies. One also can imagine that in between the two end points, several hybrid or in-between models exist. The carriers and manufacturers are involved in providing the best cost advantages as soon as possible so that network build-out can be accommodated. Yet the risk of having to bring in a forklift and remove older equipment is one that is minimized wherever possible. It is through this combined approach of the ends that the networks have been deployed. The advantage of using transparent networks is shown in Figure 9-5 in that it is less expensive to operate. Transparent networks also operate independently of the data rate passing through them. Introducing a new data rate requires little changes. This provides for the overall "future proofing" of the network so that mass equipment changes are not required.

Of course, the disadvantages also must be viewed as the other side of the coin, as shown in Figure 9-6. The following are several of the disadvantages of transparent networks:

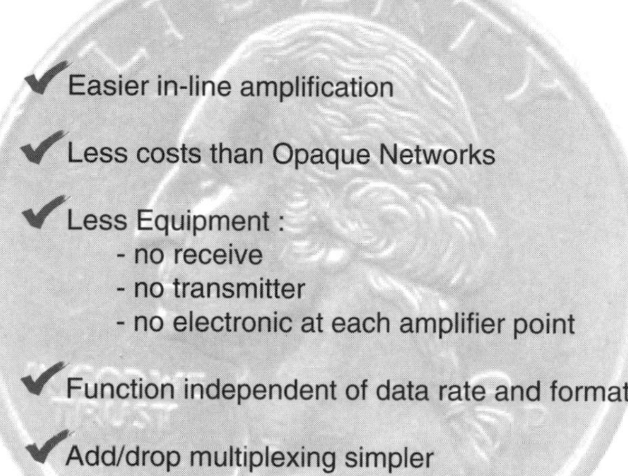

Easier in-line amplification
Less costs than Opaque Networks
Less Equipment :
- no receive
- no transmitter
- no electronic at each amplifier point
Function independent of data rate and format
Add/drop multiplexing simpler

Figure 9-5 The advantages of transparent networks

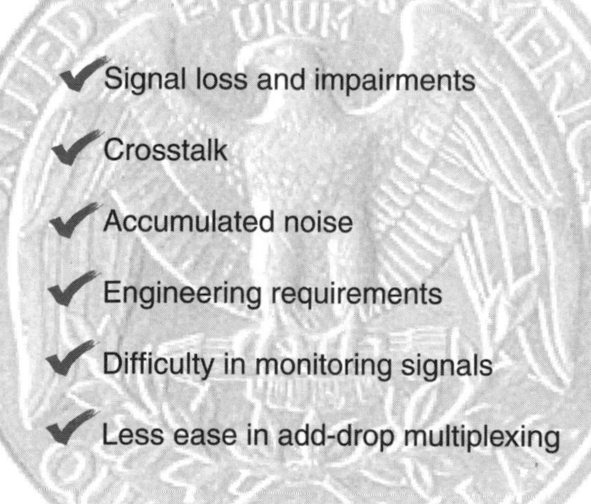

Signal loss and impairments
Crosstalk
Accumulated noise
Engineering requirements
Difficulty in monitoring signals
Less ease in add-drop multiplexing

Figure 9-6 The disadvantages of transparent networks

- Reduced optical signal strength due to cross-talk, attenuation, and other accumulated impairments
- "Creeping" impairments that can slip into the overall construction and degrade the network
- Some added complexity in design
- More problematic in monitoring the overall quality of individual signals running on the wires

Advantages of opaque networks include the following:

- They require less overall engineering concerns when they are being laid out.
- They can be engineered with a span-by-span (building block) approach.
- For now, considerable ease of implementation exists for add-drop multiplexing and multicasting.

Several different approaches will be taken by carriers and manufacturers to develop the use of transparency in the network of the future. This is so because the model is still in its infancy. Given the cost advantages of transparent networking, we can expect to see much more emphasis on add-drop multiplexing and increases in demand for these systems. Some issues have yet to be resolved in the engineering side of transparent networks, but for moderate and small networks, the use of transparency in multiplexing, multicasting, and add-drop multiplexing will grow in the near term. Figure 9-7 is a representation of a cost model for add-drop nodes with different configurations. The darker bar on the chart represents a system cost based on four add-drop channels of a 16-channel system in the node. The lighter bar is the cost value of the node based on eight add-drop channels of a 32-channel system.

DWDM Capabilities

DWDM enables the network to be more powerful and flexible. For example, *optical add-drop multiplexers* (OADM) can be installed between two end terminals on any route. These enable the operator

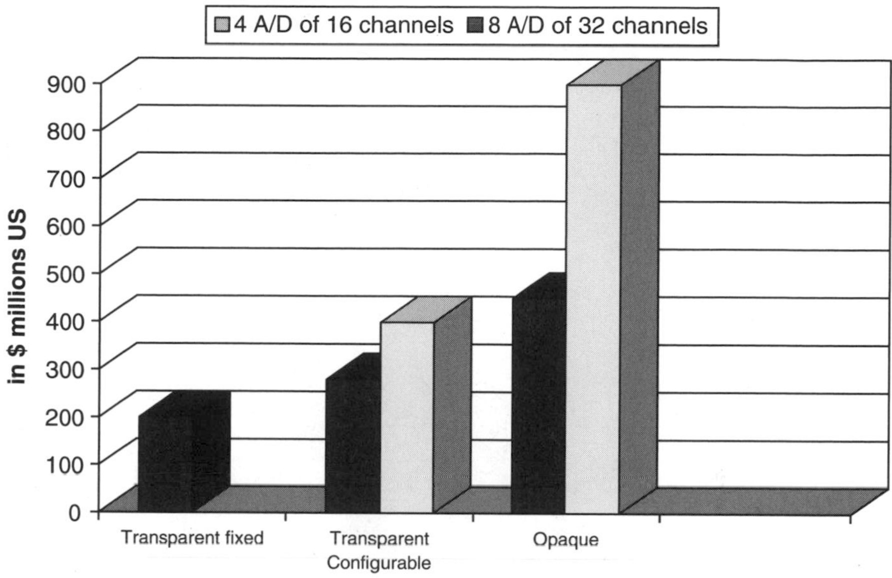

Figure 9-7 Cost ratios for transparent and opaque systems

to add and/or drop four OC-48 channels between DWDM terminals, as seen in Figure 9-7.

This feature provides the flexibility of allowing some channels to pass through the hub and create express channels. Carriers can tailor services to specific customers, and revenue-generating traffic can be distributed. All this is possible while costs are reduced for installing end terminals at low-traffic areas.

In addition, DWDM systems with an open architecture can greatly assist operators in keeping pace with the constantly changing industry. These systems enable operators to provide SONET/SDH, asynchronous/PDH, Fast Ethernet, and ATM traffic on the same fiber. Operators will easily adapt to new technologies without adding optical transmitters for a specific protocol. Using a meshed network of sorts, the optical mesh will enable an open architecture to simplify the protocols and bandwidth-carrying capacities for the future. Figure 9- 8 shows an optical mesh network capable of providing the necessary protection and added bandwidth for several protection routes. Instead of having the carriers provide 100 percent redundancy, a much lesser percentage of redundancy is possible with

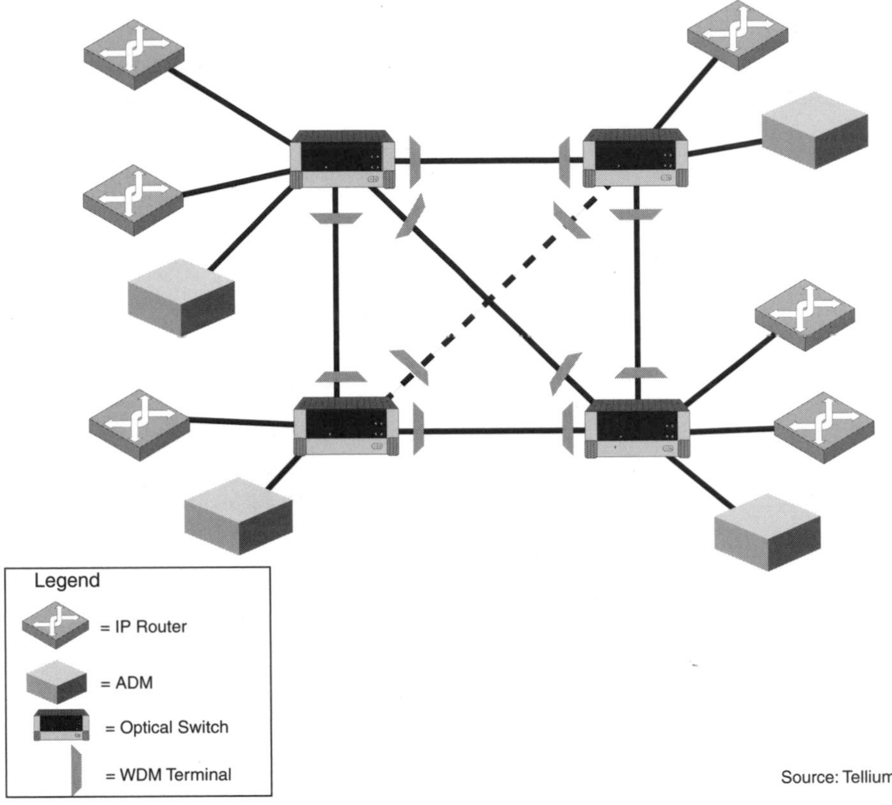

Figure 9-8 The optical meshed network (Tellium)

meshed networks. Less than 50 percent redundancy links are more representative, saving carriers a fortune on the lost bandwidth of the past.

Handling the Bandwidth Crunch

DWDM is the logical choice for the majority of bandwidth traffic jams, such as

- Data-intensive applications
- Internet access
- Voice over data protocols (VoIP, VoFR, VToA)
- Multimedia

- Streaming audio and video files
- LAN to WAN communications

These new DWDM systems will be able to transport a massive amount of video, telephony, and voice traffic over a single fiber. This type of system will multiply the capacity up to 128 or more times, with anticipated cost savings compared with traditional fiberoptic network architectures.

A 128λ DWDM system meshes well with cable operators' current requirements. In one scenario, five optical wavelengths are dedicated to 80 video channels, one for pay per view premium channels and two for cable modem, telephony, and other two-way traffic. DWDM technology not only lowers initial costs but also represents efficient revenue-generation capability by enabling traditional core services to operate on the same network with two-way DS-3 and Ethernet-based services. When these advantages are combined with the latest optical amplifier technology, DWDM becomes a powerful solution for meeting the bandwidth needs of today's cable networks, as well as providing tremendous capacity for the future.

Optical Cross-Connects

Digital cross-connect systems have been around for two decades. These were based on the use of electrical communications using standard TDM strategies. The cross-connect systems were designed to handle the provisioning, protection (automatic protection switching), and restoration of the larger networks. The volumes of traffic passing through a *digital cross-connect system* (DCS) required active monitoring and maintenance capabilities on the signals passing through. Newer cross-connect systems are now using an optical WDM architecture to satisfy the larger capacities and traffic volumes on the network. The size of these networks mandates that attention be paid to signal attrition (attenuation) and careful design efforts in using them. Carriers are actually demanding initial cross-connects that will support several hundred OC-48s today. However, in the future these carriers will be looking for systems with thousands of ports as the network grows and the wavelength management becomes more available. A typical cross-connect is shown in Figure 9-9, where a TDM architecture is used inside the network node but a WDM architecture is used across the long-haul network using 16λ on the fiber backbone. This figure looks at the equivalent of 48 OC-48s cross-connected across DS-3 TDM multiplexers. This allows a 2400 × 2400 digital cross-connect system.

An alternative to this figure is to use an optical cross-connect in a WDM mesh architecture that enables a 64 × 64 cross-connect with 16 OC-48 to DS-3 multiplexers. This is shown in Figure 9-10 using a meshed WDM as contrasted with TDM networks. These systems yield benefits as already described and summarized in the followiing list:

- Patch panel replacements
- OC-n switching
- Remote access
- Video and multicast
- Protection rings

Figure 9-9 Traditional DCS in WDM network (Tellium)

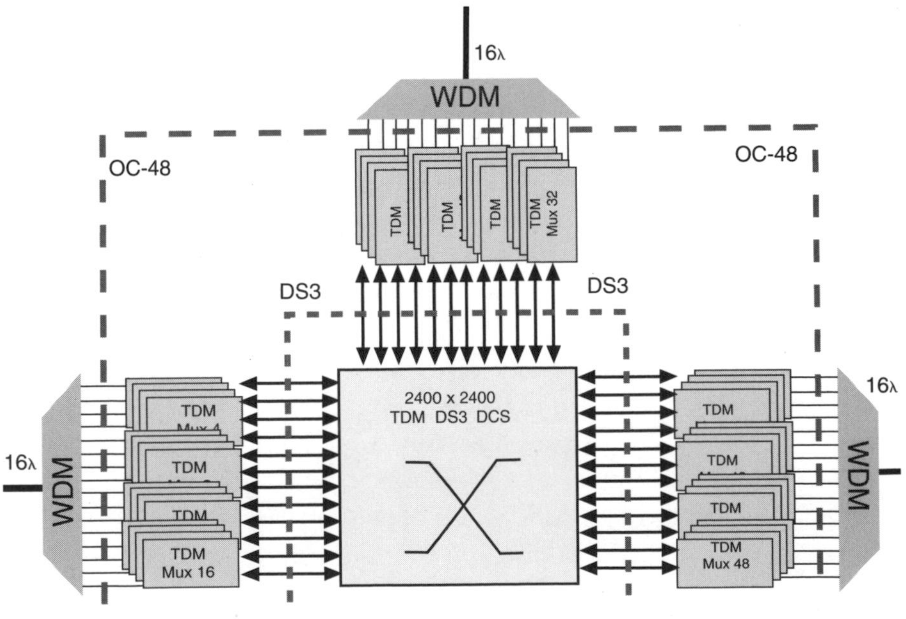

Source: Tellium

- Ring internetworking
- Mesh and restoration products

All these features save the carriers significant amounts of money in their local and long-haul networks. This, of course, is the goal and is being met daily with the products that are in development or in actual networks today.

Implementing DWDM

Deploying more fibers has been the primary choice for many years for expanding network capabilities. Each new fiber could add up to 2.4 Gbps. This has always been an expensive procedure, but

Figure 9-10 Optical cross-connect in WDM mesh (Tellium)

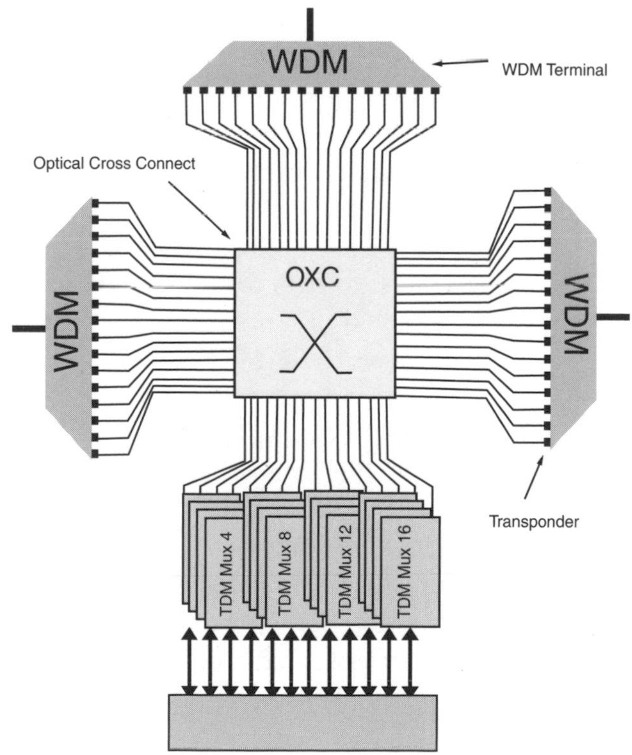

increases in associated costs have made it an even greater investment. First, the average price for deploying new cable is estimated to be $70,000 to $100,000 per mile, and this can be even higher in densely populated areas. This does not include expenses for support systems and electronics. Think of the cost of trying to excavate downtown Manhattan to lay new fibers in the streets. One must look at the reasonableness of such a maneuver before just considering the overall costs. The rights of way are getting congested, so every time a new dig begins, every other cable in the ground is placed at risk of backhoe fade (cable cuts). Many times the same vendor who laid the cables cuts the cables when digging anew for another carrier. The impact of downtime and disruptions is significantly higher than the cost of splicing (fixing) the cables.

DWDM therefore has been accepted as a cost-effective alternative when insufficient fiber is in place to meet requirements. Many carriers pulled sufficient fiber for their primary head-end interconnect routes. As additional hubs were added to the primary ring, certain segments may contain insufficient fiber, thus placing the carrier at odds of what to do.

As a simple cost comparison, Scientific-Atlanta created a model to estimate the cost of DWDM versus the cost of fiber. The model uses a regional fiber network with a single head end and up to five offshoots. Each of the hubs was spaced 30 miles apart. In this model, six fibers were used in the head-end-to-hub interconnect. Using DWDM, 16 video channels would be delivered over each OC-48, making the ring capable of transporting either 96 uncompressed analog video channels or 16 QAM IF digital channels and 80 uncompressed analog video channels—all over a single fiber.

Figure 9-11 compares the cost of using DWDM in this application with the direct cost of fiber cable. The DWDM estimated cost includes 1,550-nm OC-48 lasers, a DWDM multiplexer, and a DWDM demultiplexer. For fiber cable, only the estimated cost of the cable and splicing is considered. Construction costs are not included.

As expected, the model shows that the estimated cost of DWDM is favorable to the cost of the alternative option of constructing new fiber routes. What was not anticipated is the favorable degree of the DWDM interconnection. The DWDM approach for the model is expected to reach cost parity with the cost of dedicated fiber for a sin-

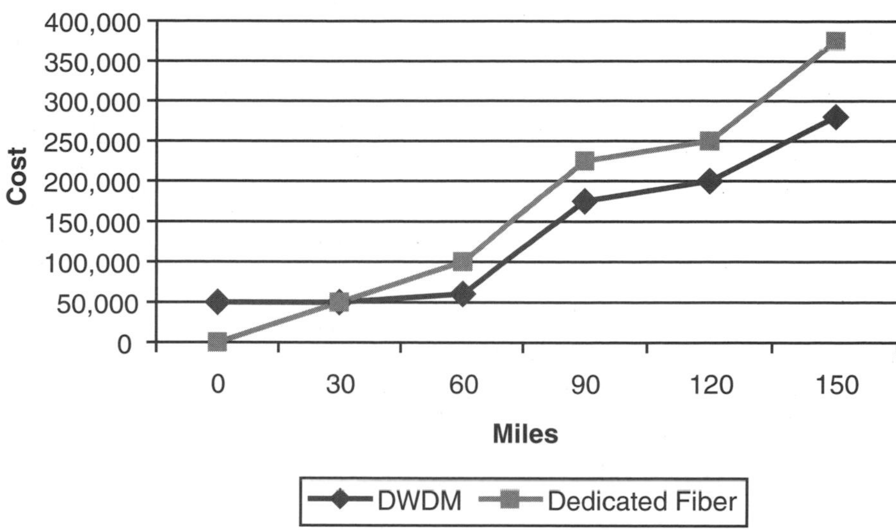

Figure 9-11 Cost model of dedicated fiber versus DWDM (Scientific Atlanta)

Source: Scientific Atlanta

gle head-end-to-hub link at just over 30 route miles, or at the initial hub location. After the initial interconnect, the expected cost differential is obvious. Savings for DWDM, compared with the cost of fiber, range from 12 to 30 percent. The implications of this simple analysis are significant. DWDM technology is expected to prove cost-effective for the case of insufficient fiber, but also another strong business case for DWDM may be realizable even when sufficient fiber does exist.

Costs for the Metropolitan Networks

Not all networks need to be long distance to save considerable amounts of money. In metropolitan networks, the savings can mount quickly using DWDM and optical cross-connection systems. Comparing the optical networking and SONET architectures in a metropolitan area shows between 20 and 40 percent overall savings, with all things being equal. Let's look at a scenario of using optical switching and cross-connection with a WDM attitude. Compare this with a

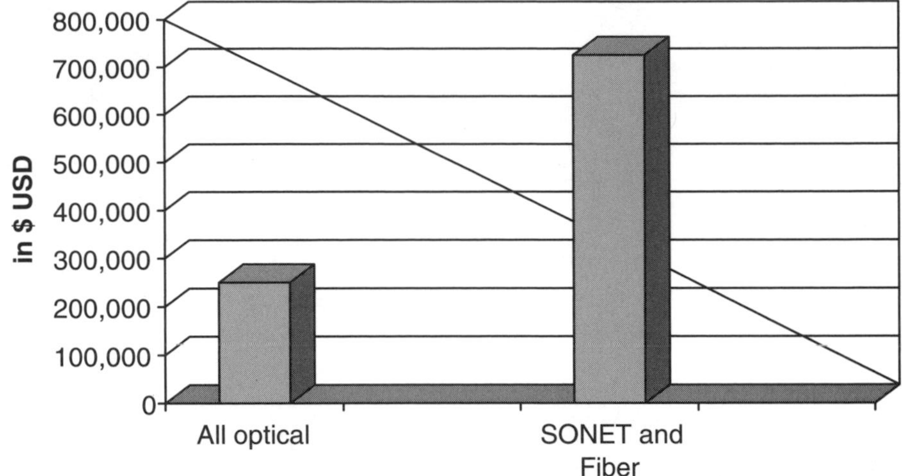

Figure 9-12 Capital costs for a metropolitan-area network

TDM digital cross-connect and fiber-based architecture such as SONET or SDH. Figure 9-12 shows the differences in pricing the systems out in a metropolitan network where a carrier may be planning a new architecture. This figure shows that the older architectures are rapidly becoming obsolete as all-optical networking strategies and components become the method of choice.

DWDM Application Drivers

Beyond cost savings associated with using DWDM technology compared with the cost of dedicated fiber, two other forms of savings should be considered. These are related to the cost of future upgrades and the opportunity costs of fiber.

Future Upgrades

In the mid-1990s in the telephone industry, many carriers believed their fiber capacity was sufficient for many years of expansion. Internet and data communications placed unanticipated demands on networks, causing the bandwidth consumption to outpace capacity. This also could happen to *cable TV* (CATV) operators. Using DWDM technology, cable operators can multiplex numerous services while saving fiber capacity for future expansion.

It should be less expensive to include DWDM during the initial system installation rather than wait until all the bandwidth is consumed. An upgrade from dedicated fiber requires a laser transmitter as well as the DWDM multiplexing and demultiplexing equipment. Postponing the DWDM installation only prolongs a problem that will occur eventually. Fiber capacity will become saturated, requiring the upgrade and the replacement of costly lasers. Furthermore, delays experienced while the new electronics are ordered and installed and service disruptions during the upgrade will all serve to frustrate both carriers and consumers. Installing DWDM upfront is also less expensive because a small initial premium prevents having to change the entire system in the future.

Opportunity Costs

Because carriers typically focus on core services (such as voice, analog broadcast video, and interactive data), they may overlook other opportunities that fiber offers. Because the infrastructure passes many business and residential *small office and home office* (SOHO) users, fiber lines can be leased to businesses for LAN-to-LAN internetworking. Moreover, newer broadband services, including cable modems, telephony, and multimedia applications, can be added with few cost implications. With local DS-3 tariffs ranging from $3,000 to $8,000 per month, carriers can create additional revenue by leasing excess fiber to businesses at competitive prices. Their mainstay core services can still be provided using DWDM technology. These revenue opportunities can be significant in the future, thereby offsetting the incremental costs of using DWDM.

Faster, Better, Cheaper

What is apparent thus far is that the movement from carriers and manufacturers is to develop the systems that operate faster, better, and cheaper. The older (if this is a realistic word) networks were based on voice-centric services. Voice was and still is the primary revenue producer for the carriers; therefore, they cannot ignore its importance. If all we needed to provide were voice and low-speed data, then we could continue to use the optical systems of the past, providing one wavelength on each fiber and using TDM in the form of SONET/SDH. The existing networks as we know them are shown in Figure 9-13 with the combination of older technologies in place. These systems still work; there should be no mistake about this. However, as we have seen, these systems are becoming passé. The need to manipulate the bandwidth and provide more raw power is becoming evident, but making it happen as a quality transition is also important. The networks of the past will not scale to the degree we need for the future bandwidth needs of other services.

The voice communications architecture was disrupted by the explosion of the Internet when IP protocols brought about cheaper, faster, and better ways to handle data traffic. Shortly after the changes brought about by the Internet, we saw the migration of voice architecture onto packet data networks. Optical networks and switching systems represent the same positive disruption to the backbone networks. Carriers now will be able to handle massive amounts of information for a lower cost per bit than ever before. What is more interesting is that the cost of ownership and construction of these higher-speed networks is 60 percent lower than the cost of the initial rings (SONET/SDH) installed in the 1980s and 1990s. Moreover, the need for redundancy is lessened with wavelength manipulation, creating a faster recovery methodology. The providers can move away from slower protocols and unreliable transport systems. They also can move away from SONET multiplexers and create optical switching at lower cost. The network can be minimized, and the amount of infrastructure can be lowered. An example of this is reflected in the number of new fiber miles that are being installed. Figure 9-14 shows that the need for new fiber is diminishing,

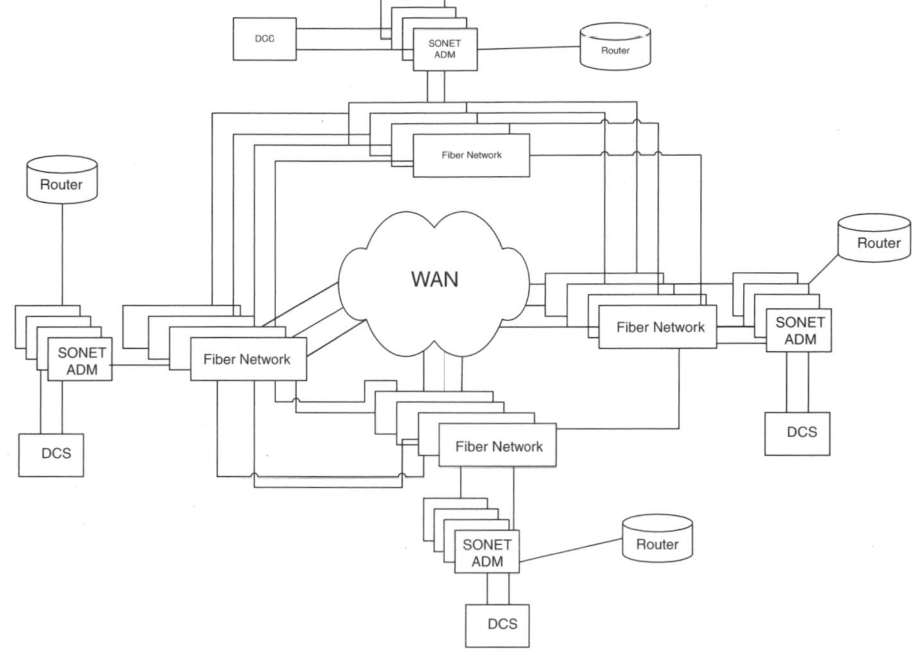

Figure 9-13 Current fiber networks

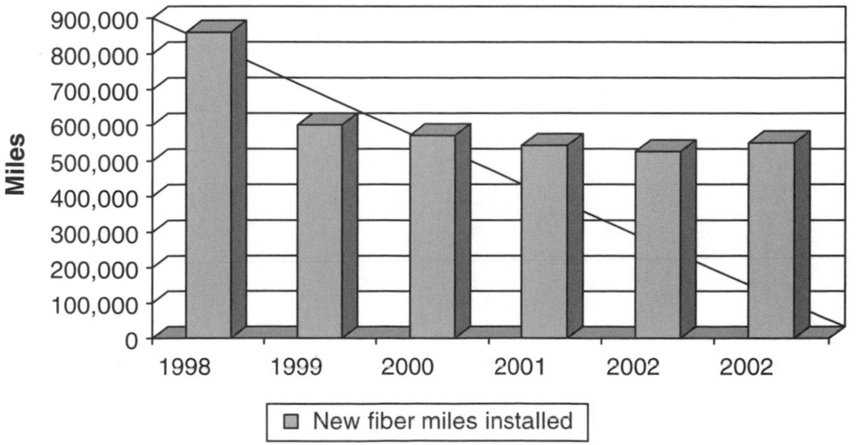

Figure 9-14 Projection of new fiber miles installed

whereas the capacities of each fiber are increasing. This may be a short-term anomaly in the industry, but one can expect that new fibers will carry considerably more traffic than older systems. Notice that in 2002 the number may begin to rise again because by then the capacities may be exhausted. However, the amount of traffic carried on each new fiber will be exponentially higher. This anomaly may be one that uses up the existing capacity, or it may be representative of the need for new miles in rural and remote locations.

CHAPTER 10

The Future of Optical Networking (Where Is It All Heading?)

We have journeyed through many of the technical (although hopefully not too technical) details including the following:

- How and why fiber was invented
- The different forms of fiber optics
- The basis of *Synchronous Optical Network* (SONET) standards
- The International *Synchronous Digital Hierarchy* (SDH) standards
- The use of various colors of light in *Dense Wave Division Multiplexins* (DWDM)
- Optical switching and cross connects
- The applications that require the bandwidth
- The market

Each of the building blocks that we stacked upon each other is designed to get us to an end. The point is that once we know how all the pieces fit together (as shown in Figure 10-1) we can then project where it will take us in the future.

After reviewing what we learned, what can we do with all this bandwidth? Let's think about what we may need for the future. Over the next five to 10 years, the thought process is that we will want high-speed bandwidth to the door. That door may be business locations, or it may be residential. Broadband communications for the future is what everyone keeps touting, but few have actually caused this to materialize.

So that I do not sound cynical, few "killer" applications will demand the bandwidth about which everyone is talking. We all hear about the Internet enabling technologies that will bring interactive two-way multimedia applications to the door. That will happen, but it has to be reasonably priced before the masses jump up and sign on. So what else can there be?

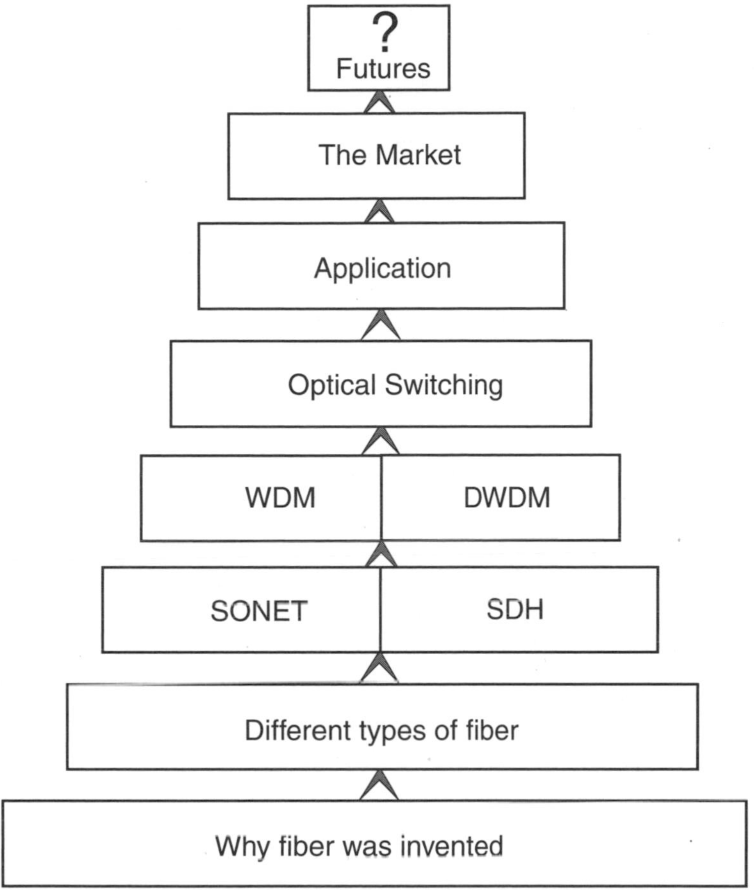

Figure 10-1 Building block approach used

Changes in Infrastructure

In 1993, the Internet was a telecommunications network that ran on a T-3 backbone and supported on-ramps (access) at T-1 speeds. For the smaller organization, the access was on a 56-Kbps *digital data-phone service* (DDS). From a networking perspective, the net looked like a centrally controlled core of communications infrastructure with smaller feeds leading into larger ones. As the number of end-users grew exponentially, so did the traffic demands. The more end points we added to the net, the greater the demand on the backbone to support more data and more dense graphics. Figure 10-2 is a representation of the users' speeds.

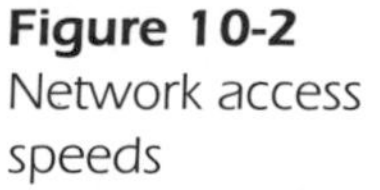

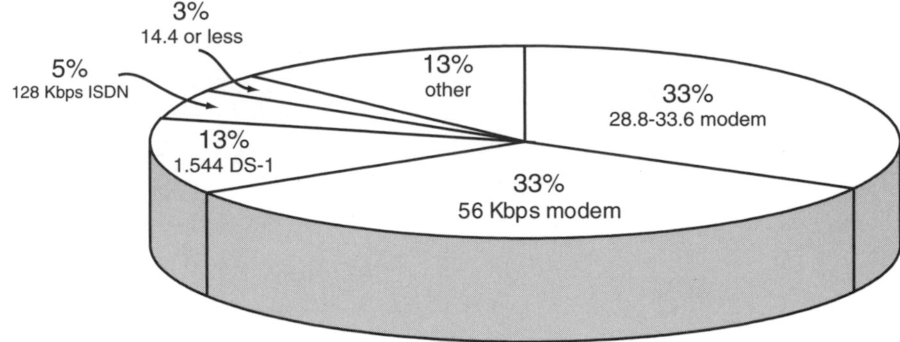

Figure 10-2 Network access speeds

In 1996, a major change began to take shape in the telecommunications industry. The *Incumbent Local Exchange Carriers* (ILECs) and the *Competitive Local Exchange Carrier* (CLECs) were faced with the dilemma of satisfying the explosive demand for connections to the Internet. This, of course, was done initially using dial-up communications. At the time, modem speeds of 14.4 to 56 Kbps were common and users were happy just to be logged on. However, the term World Wide Wait began to express the frustration people were experiencing when they logged on to an *Internet Service Provider* (ISP) who had insufficient capacities to satisfy the demand. Moreover, these ISPs were consuming all the bandwidth in the telephone company's *central office* (CO) because the typical user in a telephony environment talked for three to five minutes. However, the typical Web surfer stayed on the line for hours. This meant that the telephone companies were caught with their trunks down. They simply did not have enough ports to support the demand, causing congestion at the CO and in the network.

Armed with this new set of needs and the rising demand curve, the telephone companies sought help from the manufacturers. Initially, the carriers began espousing the death of the *Public Switched Telephone Network* (PSTN) as we know it. Circuit switching is supposed to be dead, and packet switching is alive and well. The argument was that if we could selectively route the voice calls into the voice side of the network and the data calls directly into the Internet, then the bandwidth would be better utilized. As shown in Figure 10-3, a front-end system was used to receive the dial-up telephone calls and analyze them. The calls were routed into the network based on the dialed digits or the modem tones preceding the call setup. This worked for a while, but it was a stopgap measure that had a short life span.

Next came the dedicated links for separate voice traffic and data access. In Figure 10-4, a company may have a T1 circuit installed to the building for voice communications multiplexed at 64-Kbps voice *Time-Division Multiplexing* (TDM) calls. The second T1 was used as a dedicated access link into the Internet (or a corporate private network). This works, but it is expensive and inefficient.

The topology changed as the progression wore on. The Internet no longer is a single network; it is made up of thousands of interlocking networks each owned and operated by independent organizations (ILEC, ISP, CLEC, and end-user). These multiple backbones carry different types of traffic. The number of applications supported has also grown exponentially.

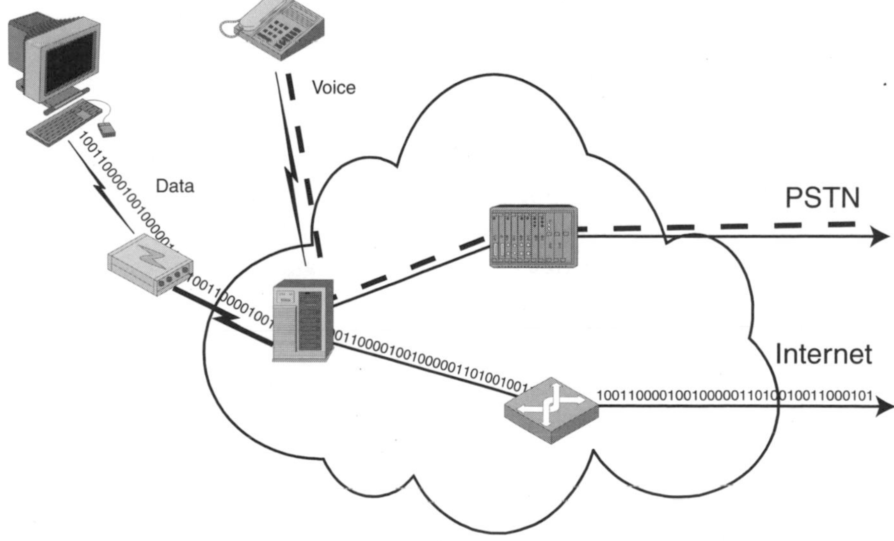

Figure 10-3 The front-end on the network decided where traffic went.

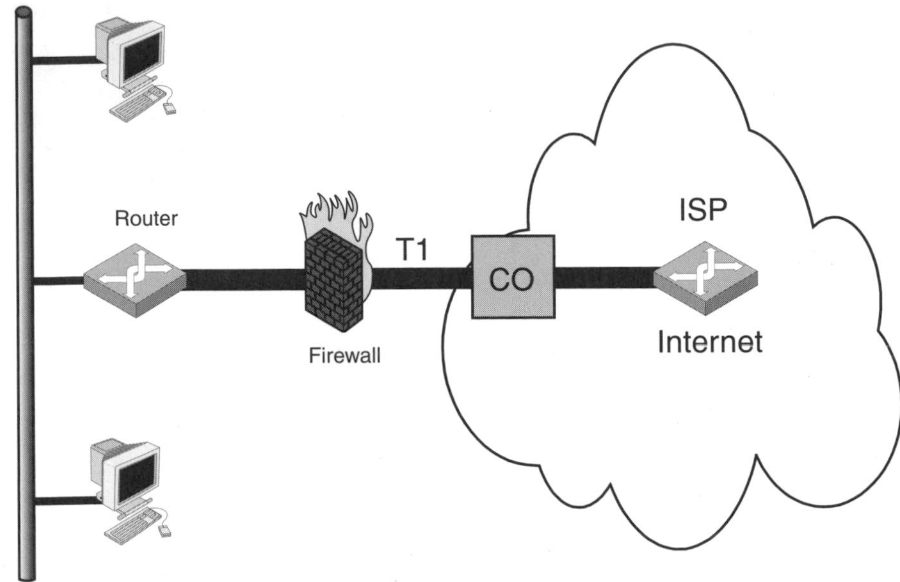

Figure 10-4 Dedicated access to the Internet for large organizations

Enter the Packet-Switching World

To facilitate the integration and convergence of the voice and data worlds, the industry quickly evolved to the idea of conducting all of our business using the *Internet protocol* (IP). The terms that quickly appeared were as follows:

- *Voice over IP* (VoIP)
- Video over IP
- Fax over IP

Each of the industry segments was engulfed in a means of making these real-time, time-sensitive applications work on the IP protocols and creating an efficiency improvement in the circuit-switched network by changing to a packet-switched architecture. We heard that using a compressed voice conversation and a packet-switching mechanism, we could gain an 11- to 13-fold increase in the number of calls that could be handled on the existing circuits in the long-distance and local networks. The model was modified to reflect these changes by creating a VoIP service and the protocols to support this new use of existing applications. In Figure 10-5, telephone-to-telephone over the Internet was being offered as the mainstay for the carriers.

What carrier would ignore the benefit of gaining 11- to 13-fold more calls across the existing set of circuits that are already installed? As a matter of fact, the TCP/IP protocol stack was vigorously attacked and modified to support this new application of the *real-time protocols* (RTPs), as shown in Figure 10-6 with the introduction of the upper layer protocols to support real-time applications like VoIP and video over IP.

However, more problems emerged with the demand for real-time video, streaming video, and interactive multimedia. The network just could not sustain the demand and the rapid onslaught. For example, the growth in volume for Internet users has been phenomenal, as shown in Figure 10-7. This growth showed us that the circuit-switching world was becoming passe and that packet switching would be more efficient for our voice, data, and video applications.

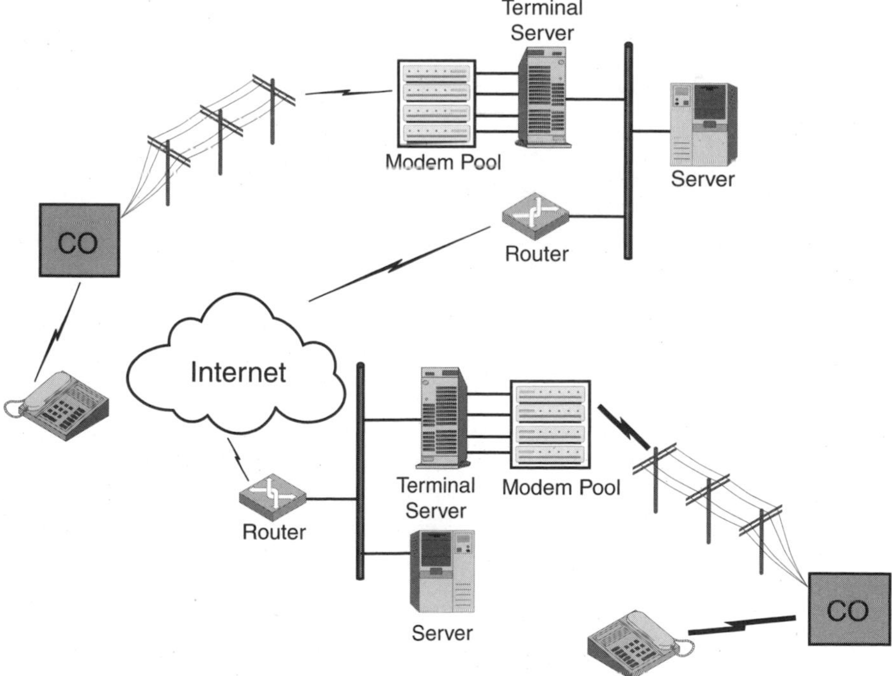

Figure 10-5 Telephone-to-telephone across the Internet using VoIP

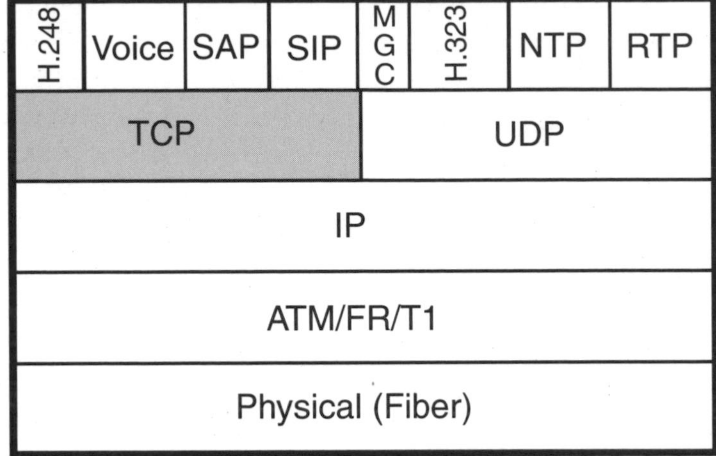

Figure 10-6 Changes in the model add the RTP to the application layer

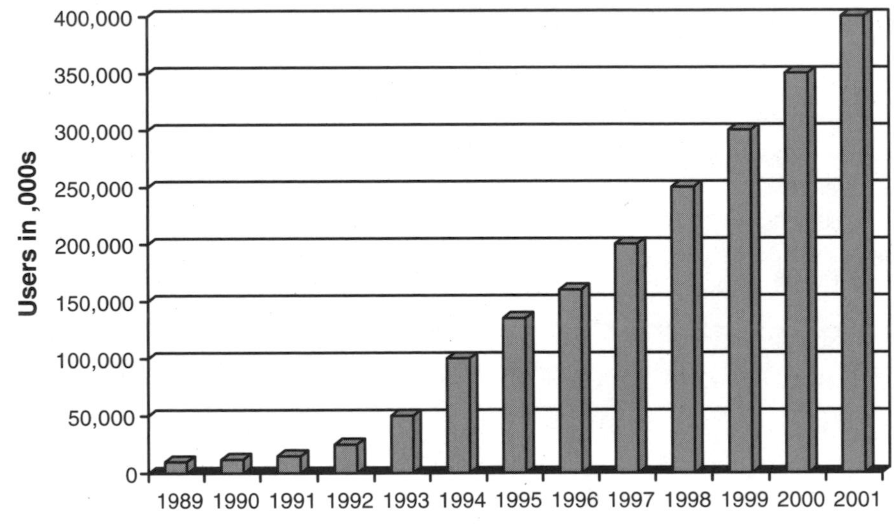

Figure 10-7 The growth In the volume of users

Much of the decisions were based on the fact that the telecommunications networks were built on TDM architectures and SONET/SDH. SONET ran out of steam as the network grew beyond the capacities that were well known and comfortable. In the normal way of delivering the data speed communications, SONET devices (specifically the add/drop multiplexers) were exclusively used to drop off smaller subscriber circuits from a larger communications channel. The *add-drop multiplexer* (ADM) was generally complemented by a *digital cross-connect system* (DACS) that acts as the in-between box for the channels as they travel across the backbone networks. Figure 10-8 shows where the DACS sits in front of the ADM.

Legacy Systems

The older SONET multiplexers are transparent to the type of traffic being carried. Therefore, they only act as they are programmed and they operate on all traffic the same way. This means that these legacy systems are somewhat inflexible and cannot differentiate the type of services being carried. Consequently, the legacy multiplexers are incapable of dynamically allocating bandwidth "on the fly," creating some inconsistencies in the way the IP traffic is being generated. This lack of flexibility and integration in the network elements limits the amount and type of traffic we can carry on the architecture. Problems like this are common; however, they do get in the way of progress.

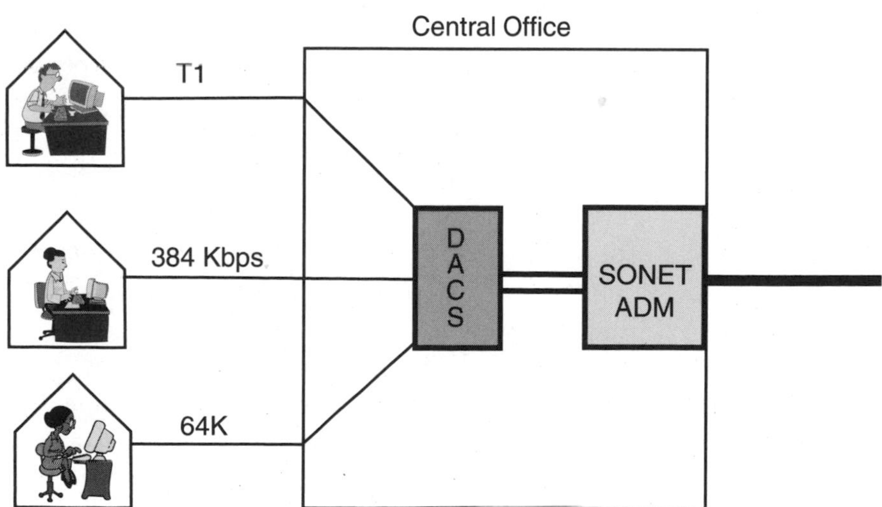

Figure 10-8 DACS in front of the ADM

Migration Is the Solution

To solve this problem, significant investments have been made to satisfy the demands of the network and make improvements on the SONET equipment. Intelligence was designed for the network. These improvements had to be backward-compatible and standards compliant. Thus, ATM and Frame Relay switching systems were used to provide much of the intelligence, while SONET ADMs were merely the transport systems acting as the carriers. Optical switches and intelligent cross connects were also created to alleviate the problems at layers 1 and 2.

What began was the movement for the industry pundits to declare that SONET was dead and that optical switching was the heir apparent. To give equal coverage, these same folks also told us that ATM was dead. They are getting better at guessing. They have not been right yet. However, they have seen a migration from older SONET-based systems into a newer generation of services. SONET has changed and morphed like a chameleon creating some exciting changes.

As we moved forward, with a new generation of SONET equipment being complemented by the optical cross connects and switches, the application came back into focus. The metropolitan networks became the new playing field, as we saw for the optical switching systems. The due diligence effort played out a new application of moving the high-speed data and video across the metropolitan area. However, the use of the bandwidth in the localized communities demanded significant investments from the ILECs, CLECs, and the *data LECs* (DLECs) in order to meet the growing demand.

Yet the killer application has still not emerged to justify many of these investments in rural (and some metropolitan) communities. What we do know is that in the past, bandwidth requirements doubled every 24 to 30 months, as shown in Figure 10-9. The installed fiber met these demands without much problem. In the 1990s, unparalleled growth in telecommunications became the norm. Bottlenecks began to occur on the existing fibers. Carriers struggled to add more fibers to keep pace with the unending demand. Economics also played an important role in the buildout of more fibers in the routes because of capital intensity.

Figure 10-9
North American data rate growth

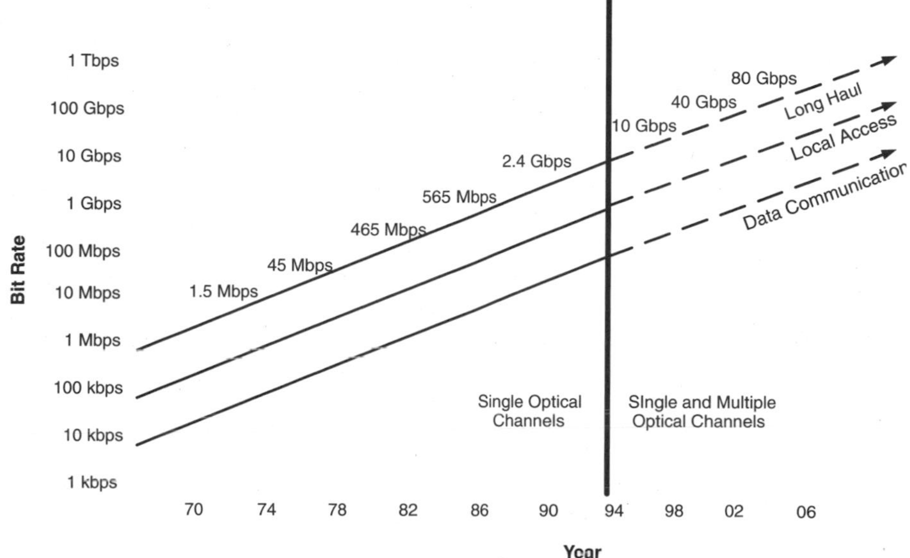

DWDM Created the Sizzle

DWDM became the preferred architecture to derive the bandwidth that the carriers so desperately needed. Several U.S.-based carriers have already settled on DWDM, using OC-48 rates as their technology of choice. With a minimum of 16 channels in DWDM and with 40 to 128 channels coming quickly, this architecture will be a critical component of future networking standards. The actual rollout of DWDM becomes the initial step in building a new photonic network in three main areas:

- Access
- Interoffice (Metropolitan)
- Interexchange (Long haul)

Understanding that the changes occurring in the industry are escalating at a terrific pace, it becomes imperative to ensue that the future growth can be established on the components being installed today. The openness of the network architecture for the future will depend on the ability to change quickly, adapt with limited modification, and prepare new offerings in the photonic world instead of the electrical world. These new systems must address open systems interfaces with the following:

- ATM
- *Plesiochronous Digital Hierarchy* (PDH)
- SONET/SDH
- *Digital Signal-level n* (DS-n), for example, DS-1, DS-3, and so on.

Each of the services above must be dealt with transparently in order to achieve acceptance and openness in the carrier communities. That transparency will be passed along to the end-user (consumer) in a mix of new service offerings where bandwidth will not be an issue. Instead, the bandwidth will become the underlying transport that no one really worries about, but it is assumed that it will be there, it will be reliable, and it will be affordable. Without achieving these parameters, the systems will fail to deliver upon the promises of the past.

Using the DWDM architectures, the migration and provisioning of the networks will help keep in mind the need to expand and grow gracefully. Systems will be required to support the services as shown in Figure 10-10.

The point of this is not so much that the pipes are bigger. The flow of the data into these pipes has become dramatically large, thus the challenges are different. As the data continues to escalate in size and complexity, the carriers are faced with installing and maintaining the optical mechanisms to preserve the integrity of the network and

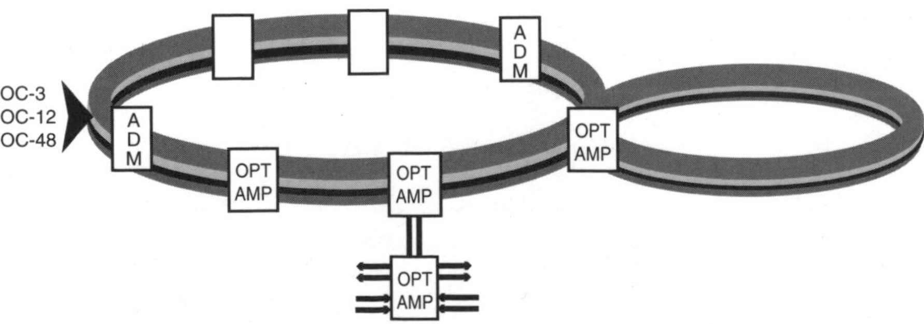

Figure 10-10 Photonic networks with DWDM

the data simultaneously. Traditionally, the light was great for the transport of huge quantities of information. However, light did not control the gating mechanisms that constitute the inner workings of the switches and networks. To instill the controls necessary, the light must be converted into electrical (optical/electronic/optical) so that the chipsets can determine what is expected of them to switch and route the traffic. These have been the challenges of the past.

So What About Now?

The changes taking place in the industry are many. However, looking forward, over the next five to 10 years we can expect to see a myriad of changes. What goes around comes around! In the development of the Internet architecture, we have seen that the movement to packet-switched architecture was accepted as the replacement for our networks. The basis of this decision, as already discussed, was to satisfy the growth and the demand for more data. As development continues in the WDM marketplace, we can expect that the use of eight or 16 lambdas (wavelengths) will become passé. Instead, we can expect the providers to continue pushing the envelope and producing 128 to 256 and even 1,000 different wavelengths on a single fiber. The fiber cables being installed consist of 96 to 192 fibers in a bundle (or many more in the long haul network). If we have 192 fibers and can place 1,000 different wavelengths on each fiber, we will have

$$192 \times 1000 = 192{,}000 \text{ different wavelengths } (\lambda)$$

Extending that number to a lambda carrying OC-192 today at approximately 10 Gbps, the result is

$$192{,}000 \times 10 \text{ Gbps per l} = 1{,}920{,}000{,}000{,}000{,}000 \text{ bps or}$$
$$1.920 \text{ Petra bits per second}$$

That is a consolidated figure, but it is a significant number. However, the snapshot is using the OC-192 at 10 Gbps for the overall data rate. The newer OC-768 operates at 40 Gbps. If we extend that same logic, the results are as follows:

$$192 \text{ fibers} \times 40 \text{ Gbps per (l)} \times 1{,}000 \text{ l per fiber} = 7.680 \text{ Petra bits per second}$$

We are now approaching some very respectable increases on a fiber bundle. The carriers can effectively change out the infrastructure components and achieve this growth on their existing fiber routes.

The newer zero dispersion fiber will support this and more for the future, opening the possibilities of even greater returns on the investment. Newer developments with the equipment manufacturers also add additional sub-multiplexing on the sidebands of the wavelength creating the possibility of 100 different subchannels (in *Radio Frequency* [RF]), creating as much as 100,000 carriers on a single fiber. This means that low-speed channels can be created to meet the demands of the end user at perhaps 100 Mbps each. Note the operative word here is low-speed. By setting up connections at 100 Mbps, we can literally create a 100-Mbps Ethernet connection across the *Metropolitan Area Network* (MAN) or the *Wide Area Network* (WAN), as shown in Figure 10-11. This, of course, meets some of the future demands for the *Small Office and Home Office* (SOHO) and *Residential Office and Branch Office* (ROBO).

Moreover, the future of the larger organization will require 1-Gbps Ethernet or 10-Gbps Ethernet in the *Campus Area Network* (CAN) that will be required to connect across the WAN for location independence, as shown in Figure 10-12. This is where the motion is taking the industry and the fibers must be able to support the concatenation of the bandwidth demands to meet the need of the customer. This creates some of the "killer" applications for the future.

Through optical switching techniques, the packet-switched networks that have been emerging in the past few years to support the convergence of voice, data, video, and multimedia applications will also change. The packet-switching efficiencies have been displacing the circuit-switching architecture of the telephony networks. However, when optical switching becomes a reality and is deployed en

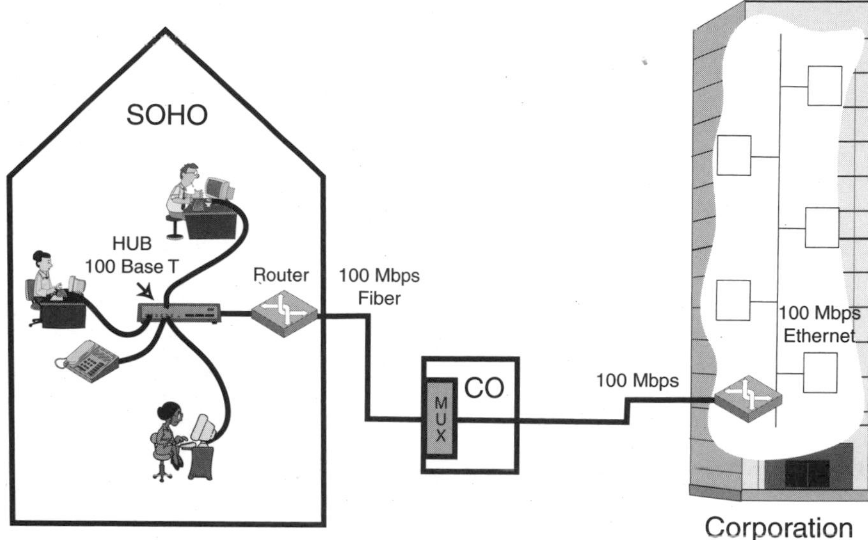

Figure 10-11 SOHO connections at 100-Mbps Ethernet

masse the world may change again. What was considered a dead technology—circuit switching—can now emerge to be the way we use our networks in the future. Optical provisioning that took weeks, if not months, will become a circuit-switched operation that can happen in seconds. If this is possible, the end user will be able to provision a wavelength between two ends in the future. A nailed-up connection can be created using a different lambda (l) to carry an immense amount of data and video at the 10 to 40 Gbps rate, as shown in Figure 10-13. Because the optical systems will have extra bandwidth available, a user can literally establish a point-to-point connection and nail it up for the duration of the need (minutes, hours, days). The cost of the bandwidth will plummet as we continue to proceed through this decade, thus making on-demand dial-up provisioning a reality and an economical choice.

This means that we are in the never-ending shift of technological innovation. The industry has evolved from circuit switching to packet switching. Next, we will evolve from packet switching to wavelength (circuit) switching. What goes around comes around. There must be some way to predict what the impact of this shift is going to have on the carriers. Functionally, we can expect that the cost per bit, cost per minute, or the cost per transaction will contin-

Figure 10-12 One- or 10-Gbps Ethernet connections across the WAN

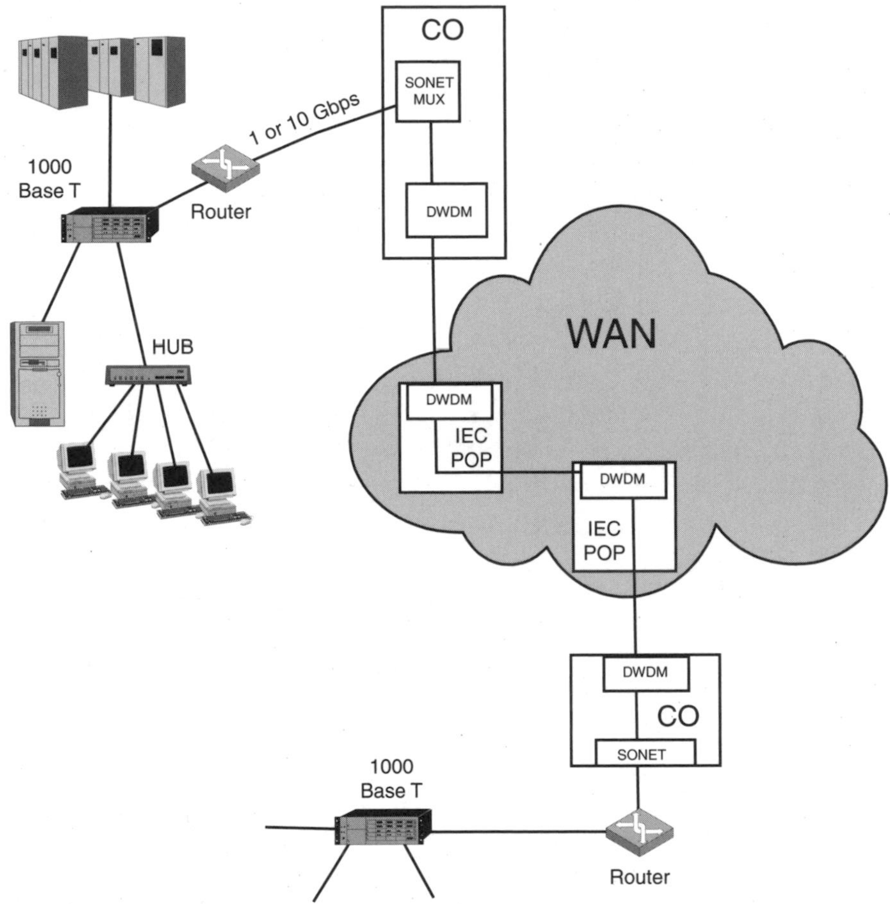

ually decline to a point very close to being free. There is no such thing as free! Thus, we will pay a flat rate for unlimited use of the bandwidth. Flat rate pricing will encourage us to generate more data, or at least stop constraining our data transmissions because of the cost. Instead of deliberately waiting for some magic formula to fall in place, the carriers will likely orchestrate an on-demand dial-up arrangement by the wavelength of 2.4, 10, or 40 Gbps, depending on the need. This, of course, will make it far more attractive for the community to develop more applications that are less sensitive to bandwidth and more sensitive to timing or throughput.

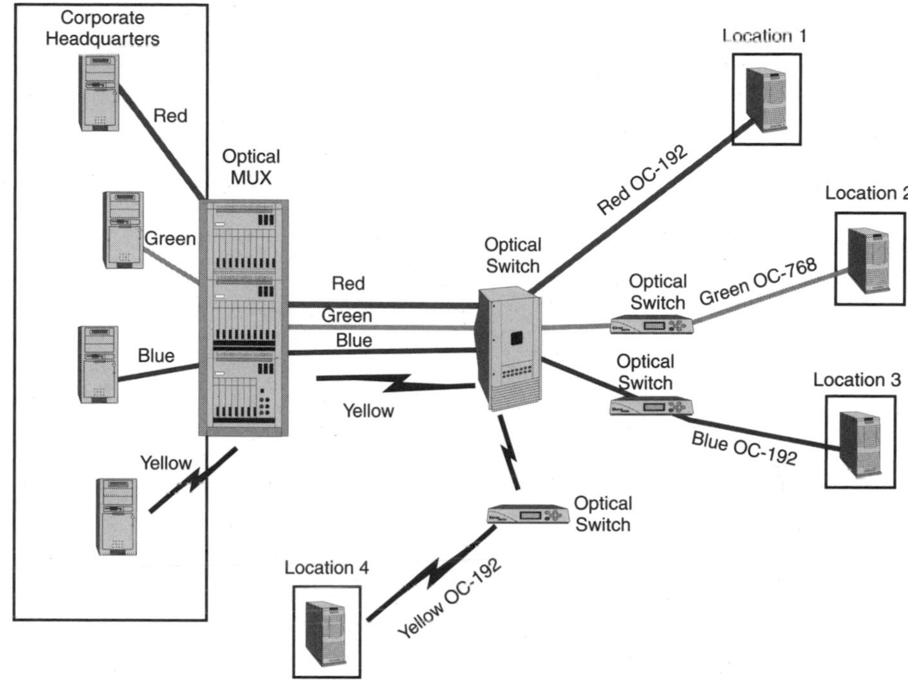

Figure 10-13 Circuit-switched nailed connections at the OC-192 or OC-768 rate

QoS a Reality!

Somewhere along the way to this magical world of unlimited bandwidth on demand, we will also meet the monster that has been looming in the background of our network. The issue of *quality of service* (QoS) has not been assured yet. Too often we have been relegated to choosing the type of data we must send at a specific time or date. This is because of the delay and latency in the networks. In the future with the unlimited bandwidth, we shall see less dependency on trying to handle the data and more independence in the type of data. Real-time voice and video applications can once again be a reality without concern. If we need more bandwidth, we can dial it up. If we need to transfer a huge file between two points, we can dial up a guaranteed throughput by dedicating a wavelength between the two points for the duration of the connection. This is the best part of the two converging network themes of packet and circuit switching coming together. If we converge and take the best of both worlds, we can migrate to what appears in Figure 10-14 and have a combined networking strategy, which is what the other services have been trying to achieve.

Another Thought

In 1992, I wrote a book on disaster recovery planning for telecommunications networks. In that book, several concepts were discussed regarding the guaranteed connections, the redundant networking strategies, and the recovery efforts for an end-user and carrier alike. The main thought was to use the dual-fed fiber in a building and place half of the mission-critical services on each of the feeds. That way, in the event of backhoe fade (a cable cut), only half of the mission-critical services would be potentially impacted. Moreover, by having SONET architecture, we could automatically recover by using the benefits of the ring topology.

The assumption that I made when writing about this was that the carriers would have fiber to the door for all of their business customers. That fiber would also be fed via a SONET ring. The reality is that this has not happened as quickly as we expected and it has only recently begun to appear. Large customers can take advantage of the fiber feeds to a building and they are using the range of OC-1 to OC-3. That means that the end users are still stuck on 50- to 155-

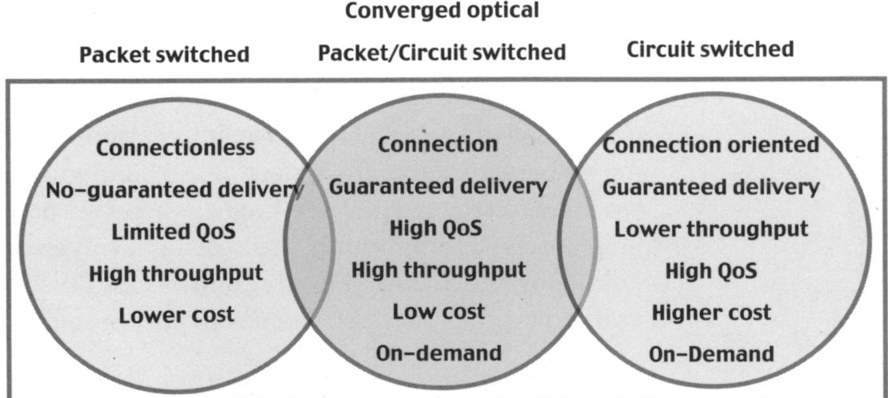

Figure 10-14 Convergence in the future

Mbps outward communications. Very few corporate clients have moved to OC-12 at 622 Mbps or above. A dozen or so clients have actually installed high-speed communications networks connecting their campus environment to another site across town. In this case, they may have an OC-48 at 2.488 Gbps installed on campus. However, to link the two sites together, they still have to step down to OC-3 or OC-12, as shown in Figure 10-15. The reason should be obvious: cost!

When the bandwidth becomes readily available, as we saw in earlier chapters in the metropolitan networks, then we can expect the raw bandwidth and power. This unfortunately is going to take a few years. Sure, some of the larger customers will become pilot programs, as the local carriers want to deploy this bandwidth. For the masses, however, the wait will be much longer. The thought here is that we have been talking about this capability for nearly a decade, and it is only now becoming a reality. Therefore, one can expect that although time is becoming shorter for these implementations, we are still five to seven years away from having the services we really want.

Figure 10-15 Linking two sites together

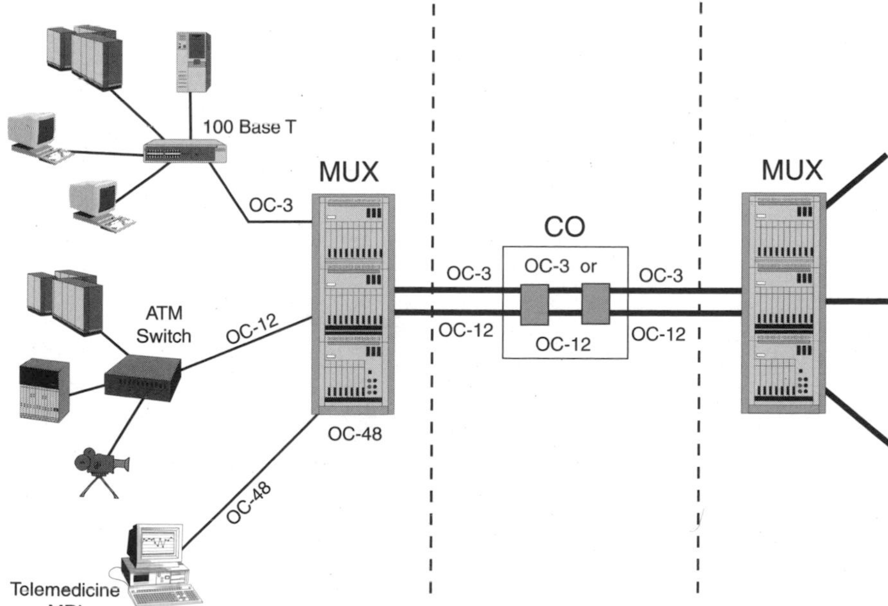

What Then Can We Do?

Another topic that I addressed in the disaster recovery planning book was to use what I termed "free space optics." At the time, I outlined that in order to overcome the hesitation of installing fiber to everyone's door, the carriers may implement the speed and bandwidth necessary over the airwaves. In the free space optics definition, I discussed that we could get hundreds of Mbps in the air to manage our bandwidth needs. At the time, the choices were for RF capability. The choices are outlined in Table 10-1.

Note that the speeds available were limited to 50 Mbps and less for many of these choices. Some were also very slow compared to our demands increasing exponentially. The motion for *Local Multipoint Distribution Services* (LMDSs) and *Multichannel Multipoint Distribution Services* (MMDSs) at the wireless local loop emerged as a possible substitute to a fiber or copper to the door. Unfortunately, the RF choices available topped out at the 64-Mbps and below availability. Moreover, the availability of the frequencies and the infrastructure took too long to deploy for a customer to be satisfied. The ability to dynamically add on capacity is not as easy as one would like. A representation of the RF choice with LMDS and MMDS is shown in Figures 10-16 and 10-17 respectively.

Table 10-1

Choices for Local Access

Technique	Speed	Distance	Problem
Microwave radio dedicated to the customer door	8 T-1s is at 1544 Mbps T-3 at 44736 Mbps	7-10 miles for local access	Licensing is a problem
Infrared light-based systems	6.312 Mbps	Up to 1 1/2 mile local access	Limited distance and environmental conditions
Cellular radio	64 Kbps up to 1.544 Mbps	3 to 5 miles	Eavesdropping, availability, and cost
Fiber optics	622 Mbps	20 miles without repeaters	Availability and cost

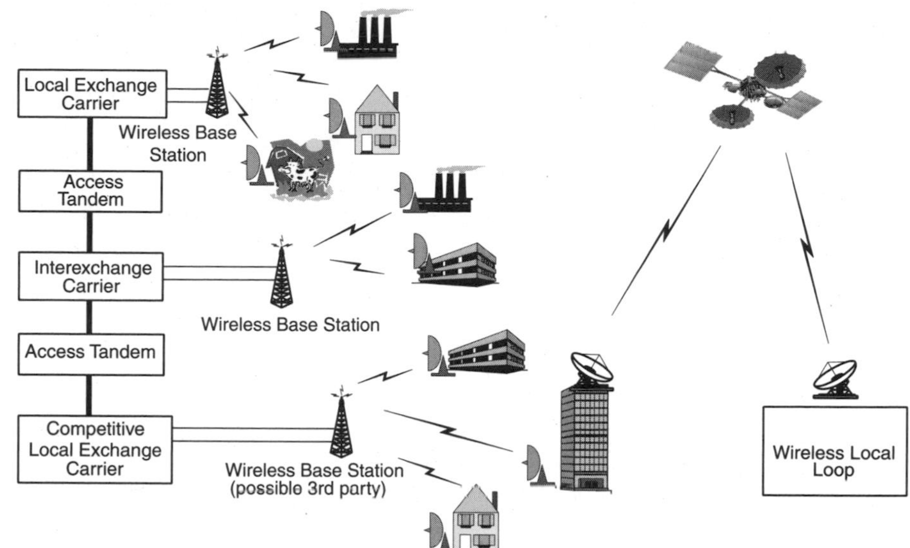

Figure 10-16
LMDS

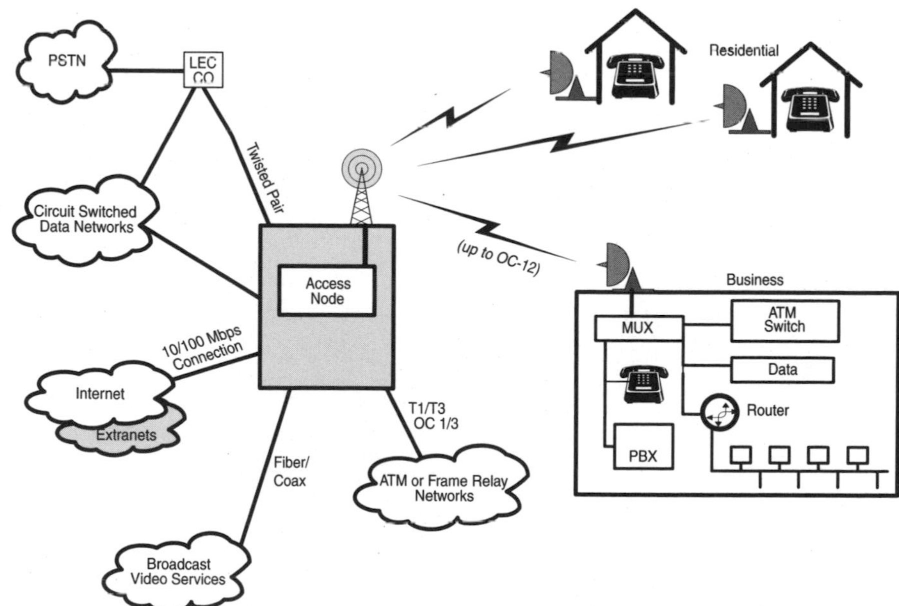

Figure 10-17
MMDS

Satisfying the Last Mile

National and international networks send data from city to city over thousands of miles of fiber at the speed of light. At the urban termination point of these long-haul networks, the data must traverse the last mile to reach each customer site. The infrastructure that delivers data over this last mile is usually unshielded twisted pairs of copper and offers

- Low bandwidth
- Long lead times to provision
- Noisy channels
- Error-prone conditions

This does not sound like the goal of high-speed communicators. Efforts to solve the access problem by extending the fiber cables to the door leads to a cycle of securing construction permits, digging and trenching streets, and disrupting traffic. The results are high costs and long provisioning times to businesses that need the bandwidth. To resolve the connection needs of a customer to access the Internet, the wireless optical networks provide the connection as shown in Figure 10-18. Here the wireless optical networks provide native LAN speeds to the Internet in a shorter provisioning time and at a more reasonable cost.

Changes occurred since the original publication that discussed the free space operation. First, significant improvements have resulted from the use of free space optics using infrared lasers and transmitting up to 155 Mbps at a distance of just under two miles. This is shown in Figure 10-19. A few companies were in the business at the time. However, many newer ones have seen the opportunity to jump into the business quickly and gain access to the customer's door around the local ILEC/CLEC twisted pair wires. The benefit here is that the frequencies used are in light and are not regulated or licensed in any way. This means that as long as we have line of sight, we can install. The disadvantage is the limited distances and the limit of line of sight. The other advantage is that these systems are becoming very reasonable to install for an OC-3 throughput for short distances.

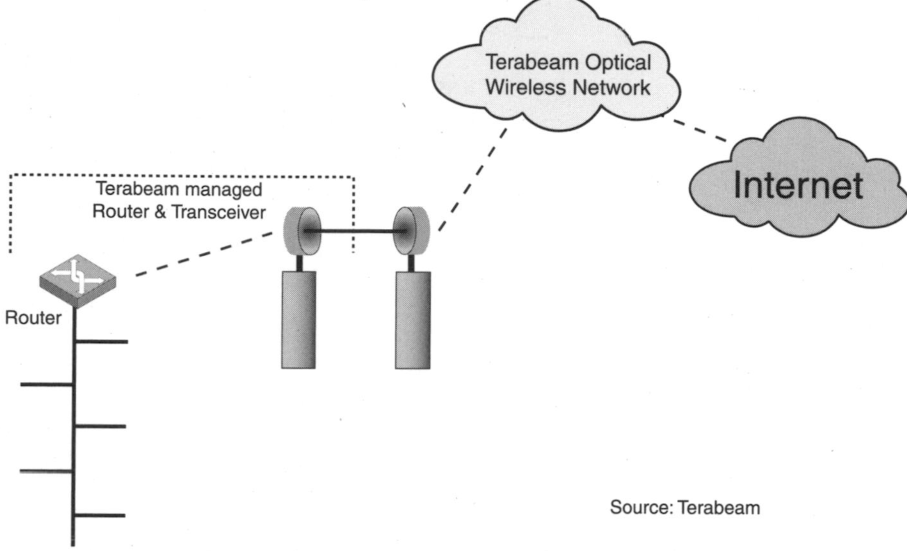

Figure 10-18 Accessing the Internet

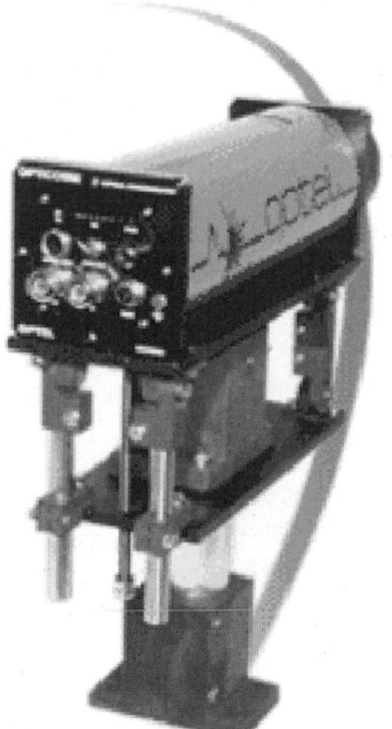

Figure 10-19 Infrared lasers that run at 155 Mbps

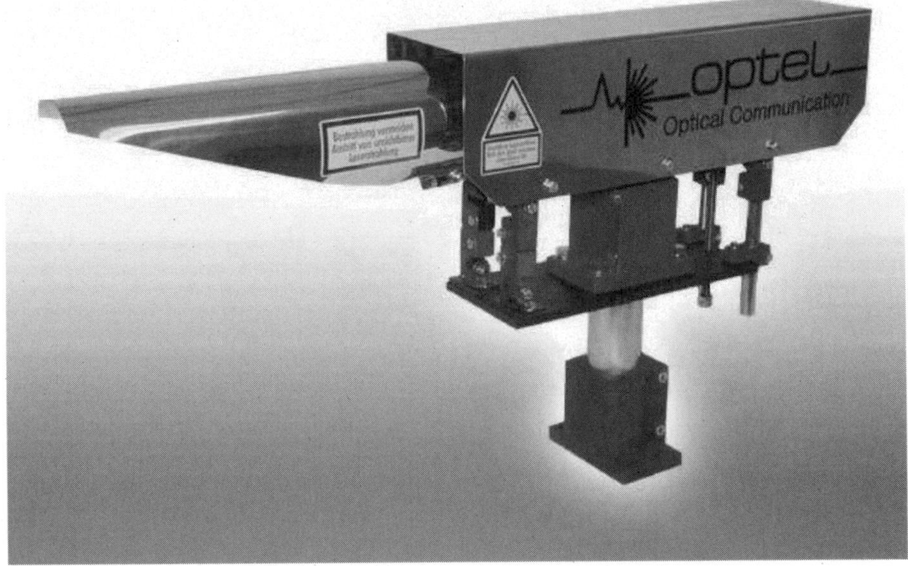

Source: Optel-Communications

Figure 10-20 These can be mounted side by side.

The glory of these systems is that no licensing is done, and the provisioning of 155 Mbps is fast. Systems can be up and running in a matter of hours rather than days. If 155 Mbps is not sufficient, then they can be mounted very close to each other, adding another 155 Mbps, as shown in Figure 10-20. The reason is that the "guns" have lenses that use tight angles.

Wireless Optical Networking (WON)

Wireless Optical Networking (WON) is a technology that improves upon the concept of free-space optics. A wireless optical link consists of two transceivers aimed at each other with a clear line of sight. Typically, the optical transceivers are mounted on rooftops or inside a customer's window. The optical transceiver consists of both a laser transmitter and a detector to provide full duplex capability.

Free-space optics enables fast delivery of high-speed access to buildings. The time and expense of digging up city roads is eliminated. The traditional approach is, however, problematic in that atmospheric conditions have an impact on the link performance. Availability is generally determined by the length of the link and fog conditions. Fog becomes a natural enemy of free space optics. If the light cannot pass through the air because of the fog, then the system does not perform.

A couple of companies are now building their networks on the West Coast to satisfy fast delivery in the local loop. AirFiber uses a mesh of short, redundant links between their optical transceivers. The mesh network functionality is provided by compact nodes mounted on the rooftops of various buildings and connected by line of sight. The short links yield high over-the-air availability, even in dense fog. The distances are extremely limited to start. However, redundant 622-Mbps links between optical transceivers provide much bandwidth. A representation of this is shown in Figure 10-21. The optical nodes are positioned on top of buildings.

The AirFiber network is installed on rooftops and aimed at building-to-building communications as well as in-the-window communications, as shown in Figure 10-22. Here the systems are shown in a community of interest to satisfy the short-haul communications in the city.

The final look at the AirFiber network is shown in Figure 10-23 where the components are separated from the backbone, the access, and the end-user premises network.

The second company to be aggressively involved is Terabeam. Their Fiberless Optical(tm) technology closes the last mile gap by linking customers to inter-city destinations and to WAN and Internet gateways via optical streams that travel through the air. Because they deliver bandwidth without laying fiber under streets, the optical bandwidth can be delivered quickly and cost-efficiently. This

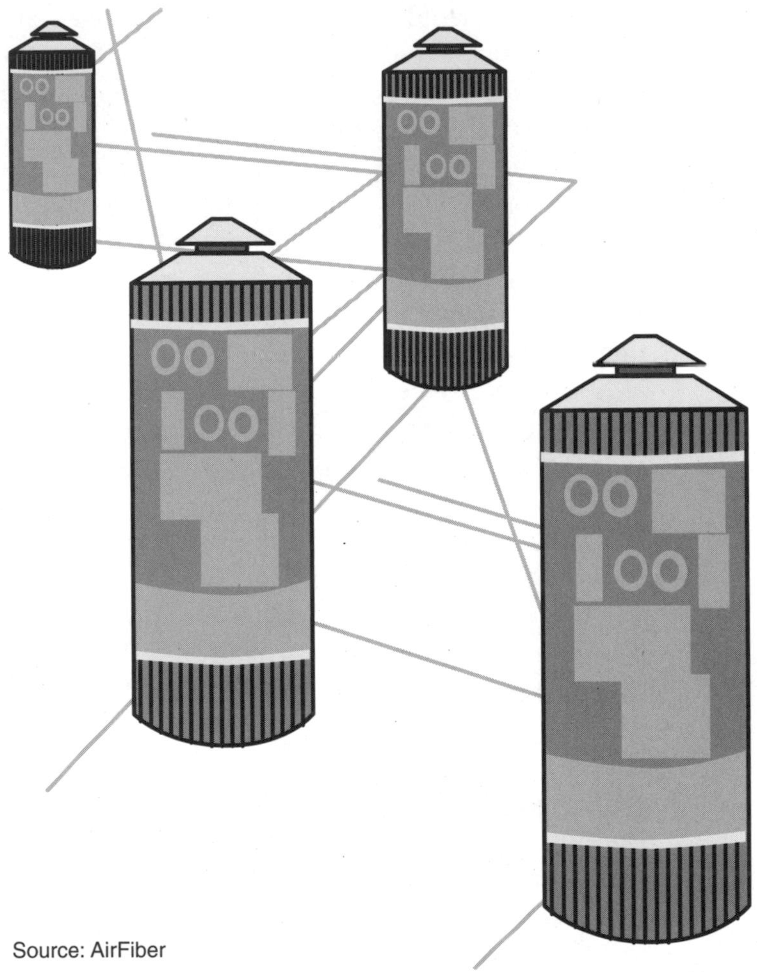

Figure 10-21 Redundant links are provisioned through the air.

Source: AirFiber

makes the bandwidth attractive. Their Metro Area Connection links LANs across a MAN using their backbone of wireless connections at LAN speeds. Replacing low-bandwidth and data protocols with IP over Ethernet enables transparent connections at speeds of five, 10, or 100 Mbps. This is shown in Figure 10-24 with the LAN-to-LAN connection. Using the IP over Ethernet service, the link is transparent.

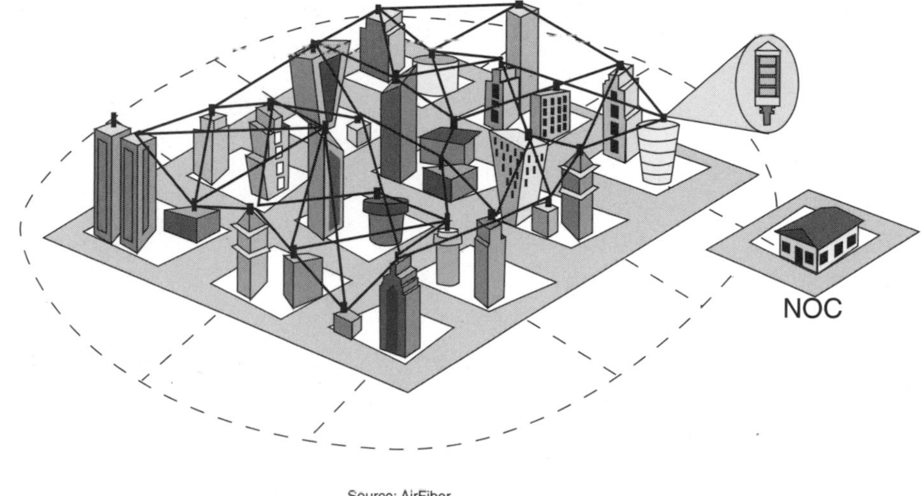

Figure 10-22 Building-to-building communications in a city

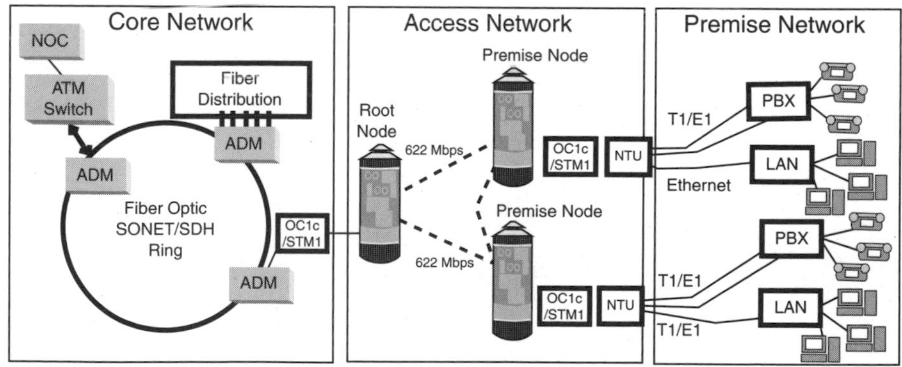

Figure 10-23 The components of the network

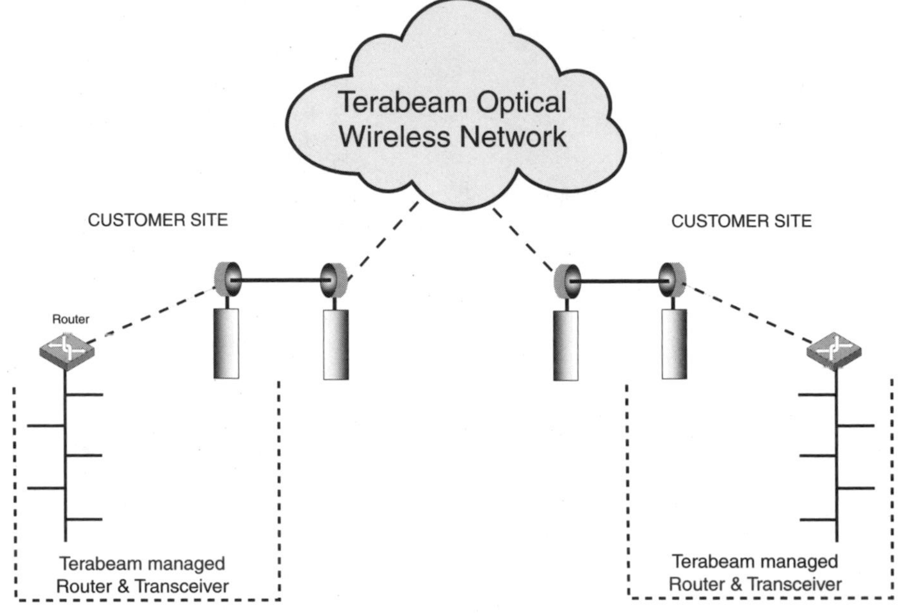

Figure 10-24 Fiber replacement enables interconnections at LAN speeds.

LAN-to-LAN connectivity can be installed in weeks, not months. The network runs on IP over Ethernet, eliminating training the IT staff on the complex data communications protocols. Terabeam employs *Multi-Protocol Label Switching* (MPLS) to provide QoS to low-latency applications such as video conferencing and remote server access. The QOS and the architecture is shown in Figure 10-25.

Final Thoughts

The optical edge of the network may take on several different looks from wired to wireless and from a new service provider to an old, such as the ILECs. It really doesn't matter who is providing the service, so long as the service is available. The architecture will change,

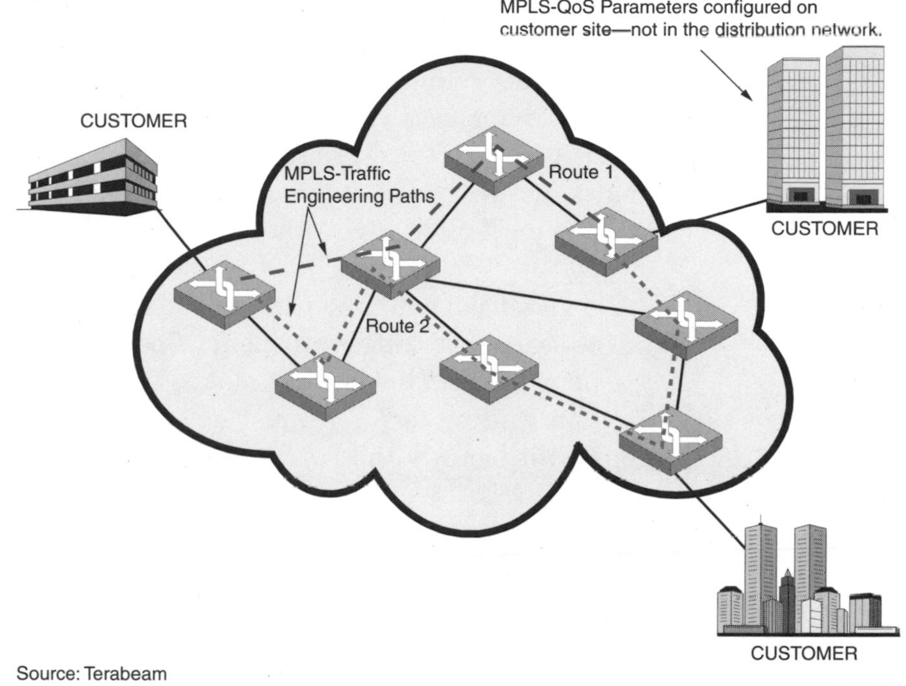

Figure 10-25 The use of MPLS guarantees QoS

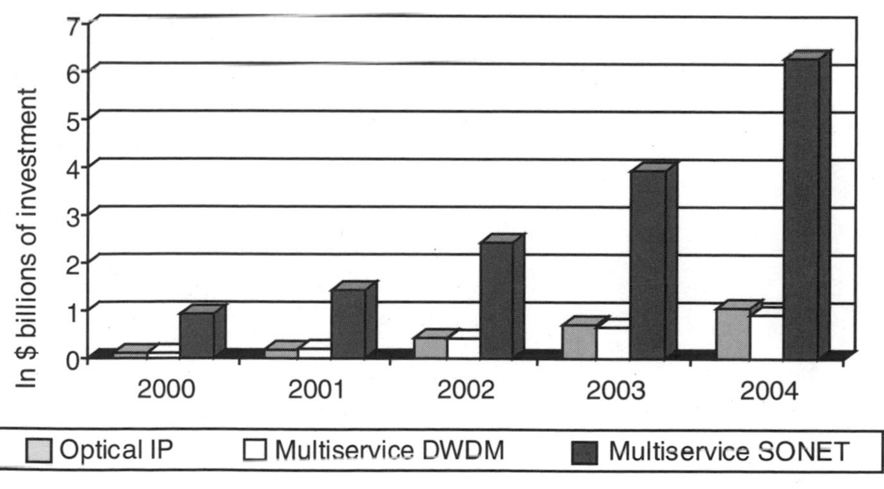

Figure 10-26 The investments for the future

the bandwidth will increase, and the ability to switch optically at the local and the long-haul networks is a given. Several factors keep the investments coming. These will see the growth in the Internet, the new killer applications (whatever they may be), and the multiservice provisioning by the carriers. Figure 10-26 is a graph of the investments market by the three areas described. This is a summary for the coming future where the vendors will keep their investments strong.

No slowdown will take place in the delivery of the provisioning of the optical networking components, fibers, and switching systems for the near future. This is what makes the industry so exciting. What are you waiting for? You must get your stake in this market and deploy the bandwidth in order to remain competitive in the market.

Good luck!

ACRONYMS

ADM	add-drop multiplexer
AM	Amplitude Modulation
ANSI	American National Standards Institute
ASP	Application Service Provider
ATIS	Alliance for Telecommunications Industry Solutions
ATM	Asynchronous Transfer Mode
AUG	Administrative Unit Group
BER	Bit Error Rate
B-ISDN	Broadband Integrated Services Digital Network
BRA	Basic Rate Access
BSC	Bisynchronous Communications (protocol)
CAN	campus area network
CATV	Cable television
CBCU	Centralized Broadband Control Unit
CCIS	Common Channel Inter-office Signaling
CCR	Customer Controlled Reconfiguration
CCS	Common Channel Signaling
CDMA	Code Division Multiple Access
CDPD	Cellular Digital Packet Data
CLEC	Competitive Local Exchange Carrier
CO	Central Office
CODEC	COder-DECoder
CPE	Customer Premises Equipment
CPI	Computer-PBX Interface
DCS	Digital Cross-Connect System
DLC	Digital Loop Carrier
DSL	Digital Subscriber Line
DSLAM	Digital Subscriber Line Access Multiplexer
DWDM	Dense Wave Division Multiplexing
ECSA	Exchange Carriers Standards Association

EDFA	Erbium Doped Fiber Amplifiers
EIA	Electronics Industry Association
ETSI	European Telecommunications Standards Institute
FDDI	Fiber Distributed Data Interface
FDM	frequency division multiplexing
FM	Frequency Modulation
FR	Frame Relay
FSAN	Full Service Access Networks
FSK	Frequency Shift Keying
Gbps	Gigabits Per Second
HFC	Hybrid Fiber and Coax
IC	Integrated Circuit
ICP	Integrated Communications Provider
IEC	Inter Exchange Carrier
ILEC	Incumbent Local Exchange Carrier
IP	Internet Protocol
ISDN	Integrated Services Digital Network
ITU	International Telecommunications Union
ITU-TS	ITU-Telecommunications Standardization Sector
IWU	Inter-Working Unit
IXC	Interexchange Carrier
Kbps	Kilobits Per Second
LAN	Local Area Network
LEC	Local Exchange Carrier
LMDS	Local Multipoint Distribution Services
LTE	line terminating equipment
MAC	Media Access Control
MAN	Metropolitan Area Network
Mbps	Megabits Per Second
MEMS	Micro-Electromechanical Systems
MMDS	Multichannel Multipoint Distribution Services
MOR	Multi-wavelength optical repeaters
MPLS	Multi-Protocol Label Switching

MSOH	Multiplexer Overhead
MTP	Message Transfer Part
NIC	Network Interface Card
NID	Network Interface Device
NIU	Network Interface Unit
NMS	Network Management System
NMP	Network Management Protocol
NNI	Network Node Interface
OADM	Optical Add/Drop Multiplexer
OAM&P	Operations, administration, maintenance, and provisioning services
OBLSR	Optical Bi-directional Line Switched Rings
OC	Optical Carrier
OEO	Optical to Electrical and Then Back to Optical Again
ONI	Optical Network Interface
ONU	Optical Network Unit
OSI	Open Systems Interconnect
OSNR	Optical Signal-to-Noise Ratio
OTDM	Optical Time Division Multiplexing
O-VPN	Optical Virtual Private Network
OXC	Optical cross-connect
PDH	Plesiochronous Digital Hierarchy
PM	Phase Modulation
PoF	Plastic Optical Fiber
POH	Path Overhead
PISK	Polarity Modulation or Polarity Inversion Shift Keying
PON	Passive Optical Network
POP	Point-of-presence
POTS	Plain Old Telephone Service
PSK	Phase Shift Keying
PTE	Path Terminating Equipment
PTTs	Post Telephone and Telegraph companies
QAM	Quadrature Amplitude Modulation

QoS	Quality of Service
QPSK	Quadrature Phase Shift Keying
RBB	Residential Broadband
RBOC	Regional Bell Operating Company
RF	Radio Frequency
RFC	Request for Comment
RG	Residential Gateway
ROI	Return on Investment
RSOH	Repeater (or Regenerator) Section Overhead
RSVP	Resource Reservation Services Protocol
SAN	Storage Area Network
SAR	Segmentation and Reassembly
SDH	Synchronous Digital Hierarchy
SONET	Synchronous Optical Network
SPE	Synchronous Payload Envelope
STS	Synchronous Transport Signal
STS-N	Synchronous Transport Signal level N
TCP/IP	Transmission Control Protocol/Internet Protocol
TDM	Time-Division Multiplexing
TE	Terminal Equipment
TIA	Telecommunications Industry Association
TS	Transport Stream
TUG	Tributary Unit Group
UNI	User Network Interface
URL	Uniform Resource Locator
VC	Virtual Container
VDSL	Very-high bit rate digital subscriber line
VoD	Video on Demand
VoIP	Voice over Internet Protocol
VPN	Virtual Private Network
VSB	Vestigial Sideband
VT	Virtual Tributary

VWP	Virtual Wavelength Path
WAN	Wide Area Network
WDM	Wavelength Division Multiplexer
WIXC	Wavelength Interchange Cross-Connect
WP	Wavelength Path
WSXC	Wavelength Selective Cross-Connect

GLOSSARY

Add/drop The process where a part of the information carried in a transmission system is demultiplexed (dropped) at an intermediate point and different information is multiplexed (added) for subsequent transmission. The remaining traffic passes straight through the multiplexer without additional processing.

Add/Drop Multiplexer (ADM) A multiplexer capable of extracting and inserting lower-rate signals from a higher-rate multiplexed signal without completely demultiplexing the signal.

Alarm Indicating Signal (AIS) A code sent downstream indicating an upstream failure has occurred. SONET defines four categories of AIS: Line AIS, STS Path AIS, VT Path AIS, and DSN AIS.

All-optical network (AON) A term first used to describe the world's first WDM network test bed that was architected and implemented at MIT's Lincoln Laboratory. Today the term is used to describe optical network environments that exploit multiple channel wavelengths for switching, routing, or distribution, using light to the almost total exclusion of electronics.

Alternate Mark Inversion (AMI) The line-coding format in transmission systems where successive ones (marks) are alternatively inverted (sent with polarity opposite that of the preceding mark).

American National Standards Institute (ANSI) A membership organization that develops U.S. standards and coordinates U.S. participation in the International Standards Organization (ISO).

Asynchronous A network where transmission system payloads are not synchronized and each network terminal runs on its own clock.

Asynchronous Transfer Mode (ATM) A multiplexing/switching technique in which information is organized into fixed-length cells with each cell consisting of an identification header field and an information field. The transfer mode is asynchronous in the sense that the use of the cells depends on the required or instantaneous bit rate.

Attenuation The reduction of signal magnitude or signal loss usually expressed in decibels.

Automatic Protection Switching (APS) The capability of a network element to detect a failed working line and switch the service to a spare (protection) line. 1+1 APS pairs a protection line with each working line. 1:n APS provides one protection line for every n working lines.

Bandwidth The carrying capacity or size of a communications channel; usually expressed in hertz (cycles per second) for analog circuits (the original meaning of the term) and in bits per second (bps) for digital circuits (newer meaning).

Baseband A method of communication in which a signal is transmitted at its original frequency without being impressed on a carrier.

Baud A unit of signaling speed equal to the number of signal symbols per second, which may or may not be equal to the data rate in bits per second.

Beamsplitter An optical device, such as a partially reflecting mirror, that splits a beam of light into two or more beams. Used in fiber optics for directional couplers.

Bending loss Attenuation caused by high-order modes radiating from the outside of a fiber optic waveguide, which occur when the fiber is bent around a small radius.

Bend radius The smallest radius an optical fiber or fiber cable can bend before increased attenuation or breakage occurs.

Bi-directional Operating in both directions. Bi-directional APS enables protection switching to be initiated by either end of the line.

Broadband Integrated Services Digital Network (BISDN) A single ISDN network that can handle voice, data, and eventually video services.

Bit The smallest unit of information upon which digital communications are based; also an electrical or optical pulse that carries this information. It is one binary digit, or a pulse of data.

BITE Built-in test equipment. Features designed into a piece of equipment that enable an online diagnosis of failures and operating status.

Bit Error Rate (BER) The number of coding violations detected in a unit of time, usually one second. Bit Error rate (BER) is calculated with this formula: BER = errored bits received/total bits sent.

Block Error Rate (BLER) One of the underlying concepts of error performance is the notion of Errored Blocks, that is, blocks in which one or more bits are in error. A block is a set of consecutive bits associated with the path or section monitored by means of an Error Detection Code (EDC), such as Bit Interleaved Parity (BIP). Block Error rate (BLER) is calculated with the formula: BLER = errored blocks received/total blocks sent.

Bit error versus block error Error rate statistics play a key role in measuring the performance of a network. As errors increase, user payload (especially data) must be retransmitted. The end effect is the creation of more (non-revenue) traffic in the network.

Bit-Interleaved Parity (BIP) A parity check that groups all the bits in a block into units (such as byte) and then performs a parity check for each bit position in a group.

Bit stuffing In asynchronous systems, a technique used to synchronize asynchronous signals to a common rate before multiplexing.

Bit synchronous A way of mapping payload into virtual tributaries (VTs) that synchronizes all inputs into the VTs, but does not capture any framing information or enable access to subrate channels carried in each input. For example, bit synchronous mapping of a channeled DS1 into a VT1.5 does not provide access to the DS0 channels carried by the DS1.

Bits per second (bps) The number of bits passing a point every second. The transmission rate for digital information.

Broadband A method of communication where the signal is transmitted by a high-frequency carrier. Services requiring 50–600 Mbps transport capacity.

Byte interleaved Bytes from each STS-1 are placed in sequence in a multiplexed or concatenated STS-N signal.

Byte synchronous A way of mapping payload into virtual tributaries (VTs) that synchronizes all inputs into the VTs, captures framing information, and enables access to subrate channels carried in each input.

Cable One or more optical fibers enclosed within protective covering(s) and strength members.

Cable assembly A cable that is connector-terminated and ready for installation.

Cable plant The cable plant consists of all the optical elements including fiber connectors, splices, and so on between a transmitter and a receiver.

Carrier class Carrier class refers to products designed specifically to meet the capacity, performance scalability, availability, and network management requirements of network service providers.

Community antenna television (CATV) A television distribution method whereby signals from distant stations are received, amplified, and then transmitted by coaxial or fiber cable or microwave links to subscribers. This term is now typically used to refer to cable TV.

CCITT The technical organs of the United Nations specialized agency for telecommunications, now the International Telecommunications Union—Telecom. They function through international committees of telephone administrations and private operating agencies.

Central office A common carrier switching office in which users' lines terminate. The nerve center of a telephone system.

CEPT European Conference of Postal and Telecommunications Administrations. The CEPT format defines the 2.048-Mbps European E1 signal made up of 32 voice-frequency channels.

Channel A generic term for a communications path on a given medium; multiplexing techniques enable providers to put multiple channels over a single medium.

Circuit A communications path or network; usually a pair of channels providing bi-directional communication.

Circuit switching A switching system that establishes a dedicated physical communications connection between end points, through the network, for the duration of the communications session; this is most often contrasted with packet switching in data communications transmissions.

Cladding Material that surrounds the core of an optical fiber. Its lower index of refraction, compared to that of the core, causes the transmitted light to travel down the core.

Concatenate The linking together of various data structures, such as two bandwidths joined to form a single bandwidth.

Concatenated VT A virtual tributary (VT × Nc) which is composed of N × VTs combined. Its payload is transported as a single entity rather than separate signals.

Connection-oriented A term applied to network architectures and services that require the establishment of an end-to-end, predefined circuit prior to the start of a communications session. Frame Relay circuits are examples of connection-oriented sessions.

Core The light-conducting central portion of an optical fiber, composed of material with a higher index of refraction than the cladding. The portion of the fiber that transmits light.

Cyclic Redundancy Check (CRC) A technique for using overhead bits to detect transmission errors.

Dark fiber Fiber-optic cables that have been laid but have no illuminating signals in them.

Data communications channels OAM&P channels in SONET that enable communications between intelligent controllers and individual network nodes as well as inter-node communications.

Data rate The number of bits of information in a transmission system, expressed in bits per second (bps), and which may or may not be equal to the signal or baud rate.

DB Decibel.

DBc Decibel relative to a carrier level.

DBu Decibels relative to microwatt.

DBm Decibels relative to milliwatt.

Defect A limited interruption in the capability of an item to perform a required function.

Demultiplexer A module that separates two or more signals previously combined by compatible multiplexing equipment.

Demultiplexing A process applied to a multiplex signal for recovering signals combined within it and for restoring the distinct individual channels of the signals.

Dense Wave Division Multiplexing (DWDM) An optical multiplexing technique used to increase the carrying capacity of a fiber network beyond what can currently be accomplished by time division multiplexing (TDM) techniques. Different wavelengths of light are used to transmit multiple streams of information along a single fiber with minimal interference. DWDM has been mainly deployed as a point-to-point, static overlay to the optical TDM network to create "virtual fiber." As such, DWDM is the precursor to optical networking. DWDM has drastically reduced the cost of transport by reducing the number of electrical regenerators required and sharing a single optical amplifier over multiple signals through the use of EDFAs.

Dielectric A material with both conductive and insulating electromagnetic properties. A dielectric thin-film material exhibits far more transmission than absorption at the wavelength of interest.

Digital cross-connect (DCS) An electronic cross-connect that has access to lower-rate channels in higher-rate multiplexed signals and can electronically rearrange (cross-connect) those channels.

Digital signal An electrical or optical signal that varies in discrete steps. Electrical signals are coded as voltages; optical signals are coded as pulses of light.

Dope Thick liquid or paste used to prepare a surface or a varnish-like substance used for waterproofing or strengthening a material.

DSX-1 May refer to either a cross-connect for DS1 rate signals or the signals cross-connected at DSX-1.

DSX-3 May refer to either a cross-connect for DS3 rate signals or the signals cross-connected at DSX-3.

Exchange Carrier Standards Association (ECSA) An organization that specifies telecommunications standards for ANSI.

Electromagnetic interference (EMI) Any electrical or electromagnetic interference that causes undesirable response, degradation, or failure in electronic equipment. Optical fibers neither emit nor receive EMI.

Envelope capacity The number of bytes the payload envelope of a single frame can carry. The SONET STS payload envelope is the 783 bytes of the STS-1 frame available to carry a signal. Each virtual tributary (VT) has an envelope capacity defined as the number of bytes in the virtual tributary less the bytes used by VT overhead.

E/O Abbreviation for electrical-to-optical converter.

Erbium-Doped Fiber Amplifier (EDFA) A key enabling technology of DWDM, EDFAs enable the simultaneous amplification of multiple signals in the 1,500 nanometer region, such as multiple 2.5 Gbps channels, in the optical domain. EDFAs drastically increase the spacings required between regenerators, which are costly network elements because they (1) require optical/electrical/optical conversions of a signal and (2) operate on a single digital signal, such as a single SONET or SDH optical signal. DWDM systems using EDFAs can increase regenerator spacings of transmissions to 500–800 km at 2.5 Gbps. EDFAs are far less expensive than regenerators and can typically be spaced 80–120 km apart at 2.5 Gbps, depending on the quality of the fiber plant and the design goals of the DWDM system.

Enterprise systems connection (ESCON) A duplex optical connector used for computer-to computer data exchanges.

Fiber Distributed Data Interface (FDDI) A dual counter-rotating ring local area network or a connector used in a dual counter-rotating ring local area network.

Far End Block Error (FEBE) A message sent back upstream that a receiving network element is detecting errors, usually a coding violation. *See* Remote Error Indication (REI).

Fiber The structure that guides light in a fiber optic system.

Fiber channel An industry-standard specification that originated in Great Britain that details computer channel communications over fiber optics at transmission speeds from 132 Mbps to 1062.5 Mbps at distances of up to 10 kilometers.

Fiber-to-the-Curb (FTTC) Fiber optic service to a node connected by wires to several nearby homes, typically on a block.

Fiber-to-the-Home (FTTH) Fiber optic service to a node located inside an individual home.

Fiber-to-the-Loop (FTTL) Fiber optic service to a node that is located in a neighborhood.

Fixed stuff A bit or byte whose function is reserved. Fixed stuff locations, sometimes called reserved locations, do not carry overhead or payload.

Framing A method of distinguishing digital channels that have been multiplexed together.

Frequency The number of cycles of periodic activity that occur in a discrete amount of time.

Gallium aluminum arsenide Generally used for short wavelength light emitters.

Gallium arsenide Used in light emitters.

Gigabits per second (Gbps) One billion bits per second.

Graded-index fiber Optical fiber in which the refractive index of the core is in the form of a parabolic curve, decreasing toward the cladding.

Grooming Consolidating or segregating traffic for efficiency.

Half-duplex A bi-directional link that is limited to a one-way transfer of data; that is, data can't be sent both ways at the same time.

Hard-optics The hardware technologies that create and transport light, such as DWDM, FEC, Raman amplification, tunable dispersion compensators, Variable Optical Attenuators, dynamic spectral gain compensators, Micro-Electro-Mechanical Systems (MEMS), and Optical Spectrum Analyzers (OSAs).

Index of refraction Also refractive index. The ratio of the velocity of light in free space to the velocity of light in a fiber material.

Infrared (IR) Light from the region of the spectrum with wavelengths between 750nm (red) and 0.1mm (microwave).

Intelligent optical network A dynamic flexible network of virtual lightpaths that is "light" from end to end and delivers an abundance of cost-effective, usable bandwidth.

Intelligent optical networking Bringing network intelligence to the optical domain; the creation, configuration, and management of virtual lightpaths within the optical domain. A new class of products for the development of an intelligent optical network.

Interleave The capability of SONET to mix together and transport different types of input signals in an efficient manner, thus enabling higher-transmission rates.

Isochronous All devices in the network derive their timing signal directly or indirectly from the same primary reference clock.

Jacket The outer, protective covering of the cable.

Jitter Small and rapid variations in the timing of a waveform due to noise, changes in component characteristics, supply voltages, imperfect synchronizing circuits, and so on.

Kilobits per second One thousand bits per second.

Lambda (l) An optical wavelength.

Laser An acronym for light amplification by the stimulated emission of radiation. A light source that produces, through stimulated emission, coherent, near-monochromatic light. Lasers in fiber optics are usually solid-state semiconductor types.

Light In a strict sense, the region of the electromagnetic spectrum that can be perceived by human vision, designated by the visible spectrum, and nominally covering the wavelength range of 0.4 μm to 0.7 μm. In the laser and optical communication fields, custom and practice have extended usage of the term to include the much broader portion of the electromagnetic spectrum that can be handled by the basic optical techniques used for the visible spectrum. This region has not been clearly defined. Athough, as employed by most workers in the field, it may be considered to extend from the near ultraviolet region of approximately 0.3 μm, through the visible region, and into the mid-infrared region to 30 μm.

Lightpath Analogous to virtual circuits in the ATM world, a lightpath is a virtual circuit in the optical domain that could consist of multiple spans, each using a different physical wavelength for the transmission of information across an optical network.

Line One or more SONET sections, including network elements at each end, capable of accessing, generating, and processing Line Overhead.

Line Terminating Equipment (LTE) Network elements such as add/drop multiplexers or digital cross-connect systems that can access, generate, and process Line Overhead.

Megabits per second (Mbps) One million bits per second.

Metropolitan Area Network (MAN) A network covering an area larger than a local area network (LAN); a wide area network (WAN) covering a metropolitan area. Usually, it is an interconnection of two or more LANs.

Micrometer One millionth of a meter. Abbreviated μm.

Multimode fiber An optical fiber with a core large enough to propagate more than one mode of light. The typical diameter is 62.5 micrometers.

Multiplex (MUX) To transmit two or more signals over a single channel.

Multiplexer A device for combining several channels to be by one line or fiber.

Nanometer One billionth of a meter.

Nanosecond One billionth of a second.

Narrowband Services requiring up to 1.5 Mbps transport capacity.

Network Element (NE) Any device that is part of a SONET transmission path and serves one or more of the section, line, and path-terminating functions. In SONET, the five basic network elements are

- Add/drop multiplexer
- Broadband digital cross-connect
- Wideband digital cross-connect
- Digital loop carrier
- Switch interface

Network Monitoring and Analysis (NMA) A fault management system used by RBOCs to perform network monitoring and surveillance. The NMA system has two types, facilities management and switch management. NMA is capable of performing an event correlation to determine the root cause, create trouble tickets, and track the status of outstanding tickets. NMA relies on topology information to perform event correlation. This information can come from TIRKS (via NSDB) or it can be manually entered.

Optical Carrier Level 1 (OC-1) The optical equivalent of an STS-1 signal.

Optical Carrier Level N (OC-N) The optical equivalent of an STS-N signal.

Opaque optical networks The current vision of the optical network whereby conversions from the optical to the electrical and back to the optical domain are required periodically. Such optical/electrical/optical conversions are required in order to retime the signal in the digital domain, clean up signal impairments, enable fault isolation, and provide performance monitoring (particularly of signal bit error rate). Today's optical networks take advantage of SONET/SDH frame structure for B1 byte parity checks, BER monitoring, and J0 byte path trace at a minimum. Opaque network elements will occur as gateways along extended backbones to limit the accumulation of analog signal impairments and enable performance monitoring and fault isolation.

Optical Add/Drop Multiplexer (OADM) Also called a Wavelength Add/Drop Multiplexer (WADM). An optical network element that lets specific channels of a multi-channel optical transmission system be dropped and/or added without affecting the through signals (the signals that are to be transported through the network node).

Optical amplifier A device that increases the optical signal strength without an optical-to-electrical-to-optical conversion process.

Optical carrier (OC) A designation used as a prefix denoting the optical carrier level of SONET data standards. OC-1/STS-1, OC-3/STS-3, OC-12, OC-48, and OC-192 denote transmission standards for fiber-optic data transmissions in SONET and frames at data rates of 51.84 Mbps, 155.52 Mbps, 622.08 Mbps, 2.48832 Gbps, and 9.95 Gbps, respectively. *See* SONET and STS.

Optical carrier (OC-x) This is a base unit found in the SONET hierarchy; the "x" represents increments of 51.84 Mbps (so OC-1 is 51.84 Mbps, OC-3 is 155 Mbps, and OC-12 is 622 Mbps). *See* Synchronous Optical Network.

Optical cross-connect (OXC or OCS) An optical network element that provides for incoming optical signals to be switched to any one of a number of outputs. Some OXCs connect fibers containing multi-channel optical signals to the input parts, demultiplex the signals, switch the signals, and recombine/remultiplex the signals to the output ports.

Optical fiber (a.k.a. fiber) A thin silica glass cable with an outer cladding material and a ≅ nine micro-meter diameter inner core with a slightly higher index of refraction than the cladding.

Optical network The optical network provides all the basic network requirements in the optical layer, namely capacity, scalability, reliability, survivability, and manageability. Today the wavelength is the fundamental object of the optical network. The long-term vision of an "all-optical network" is of a transparent optical network where signals are never converted to the electrical domain between network ingress and egress. The more practical implementation for the near term will be of an opaque optical network, that is, one that works to minimize but still includes optical/electrical/optical conversion. Optical network elements will include terminals, dynamic add/drop multiplexers, and dynamic optical cross-connects.

Optical networking The natural evolution of optical transport from a DWDM-based point-to-point transport technology to a more dynamic, intelligent networking technology. Optical networking will use any one of a number of optical multiplexing schemes to multiplex multiple channels of information onto a fiber and will add intelligence to the optical transport layer that will provide the reliability, survivability, and manageability today provided by SONET/SDH.

Optical switching products An emerging category of optical networking products that operate at the granularity of a lightpath and that provide the following functionality at a minimum: performance monitoring and management, restoration and rerouting enabled by inter-switch signaling, wavelength translation, the establishment of end-to-end lightpaths, and the delivery of customer services.

Optical transport products An emerging category of optical networking products that operate at the granularity of a lightpath and that provide the following functionality at a minimum: performance monitoring and management, restoration and rerouting, wavelength translation, and delivery of customer services. OADMs and DWDM terminals are included in this category.

OSI seven-layer model A standard architecture for data communications. Layers define the hardware and software required for multi-vendor information processing equipment to be mutually compatible.

Path A logical connection between a point where an STS or VT is multiplexed to the point where it is demultiplexed.

Path Terminating Equipment (PTE) Network elements, such as fiber-optic terminating systems, which can access, generate, and process Path Overhead.

Payload The portion of the SONET signal available to carry service signals such as DS1 and DS3. The contents of an STS SPE or VT SPE.

Photon The basic unit of light transmission used to define the lowest (physical) layer in the OSI seven-layer model.

Photonic A term coined for devices that work using photons, analogous to "electronic" for devices working with electrons

Plastic fiber An optical fiber having a plastic core and plastic cladding.

Plesiochronous A network with nodes timed by separate clock sources with almost the same timing.

Point-to-point transmission A transmission between two designated stations.

POP (Point-of-Presence) A point in the network where inter-exchange carrier facilities like DS3 or OC-N meet with access facilities managed by telephone companies or other service providers.

Polarization The direction of the electric field in the lightwave.

Port Hardware entity at each end of the link.

POTS Plain old telephone service.

Picosecond One trillionth of a second.

Pulse A current or voltage that changes abruptly from one value to another and back to the original value in a finite length of time.

Refractive index gradient The change in the refractive index with distance from the axis of an optical fiber.

Regenerator A device that restores a degraded digital signal for continued transmission; also called a repeater.

Ring network A network topology in which terminals are connected in a point-to-point serial fashion in an unbroken circular configuration.

Synchronous Digital Hierarchy (SDH) The ITU-T-defined world standard of transmission with a base transmission rate of 51.84 Mbps (STM-0) and is equivalent to SONET's STS-1 or OC-1 transmission rate. SDH standards were published in 1989 to address interworking between the ITU-T and ANSI transmission hierarchies. The European version of the SONET standard has two major differences: the terminology and the basic line rate in SDH is equivalent to that of the SONET OC-3/STS-3 rate (that is, 155.52 Mbps). SDH enables direct access to tributary signals without demultiplexing the composite signal. The compatibility between SDH and SONET enables internetworking at the Administrative Unit-4 (AU-4) level. SDH can support broadband services such as a broadband integrated services digital network (B-ISDN).

Silica glass Glass made mostly of silicon dioxide, SiO2, used in conventional optical fibers.

Single-mode (SM) fiber A small-core optical fiber through which only one mode will propagate. The typical diameter is eight to nine microns.

Slip An overflow (deletion) or underflow (repetition) of one frame of a signal in a receiving buffer.

Soft-optics The software technologies that package and control the light, such as the automatic power balancing of lightwave services, the auto-discovery of optical components and their capacities, fiber plant monitoring, signal equalization, path integrity verification, lightpath performance monitoring, dispersion compensation tune-ups, and optical fault diagnostics.

Splitter A device that creates multiple optical signals from a single optical signal.

Stratum A level of clock source used to categorize accuracy.

Superframe Any structure made of multiple frames. SONET recognizes superframes at the DS1 level (D4 and extended superframe) and at the VT (500 ms STS superframes).

Synchronous A network where transmission system payloads are synchronized to a master (network) clock and are traced to a reference clock.

Synchronous Optical Network (SONET) Standards for transmitting digital information over optical networks. Fiber optic transmission rates range from 51.84 Mbps to 9.95 Gbps. The base rate is known as OC-1 and runs at 51.84 Mbps. Higher rates are a multiple of this such that OC-12 is equal to 622 Mbps (12 times 51.84 Mbps).

Synchronous Transfer Module (STM) An element of the SDH transmission hierarchy. STM-1 is SDH's base-level transmission rate equal to 155 Mbps. Higher rates of STM-4, STM-16, and STM-48 are also defined.

Synchronous Payload Envelope (SPE) The major portion of the SONET frame format used to transport payload and STS path overhead. A SONET structure that carries the payload (service) in a SONET frame or virtual tributary. The STS SPE may begin anywhere in the frame's payload envelope.

STS Path Terminating Equipment (STS PTE) Equipment that terminates the SONET STS Path layer. STS PTE interprets and modifies or creates the STS Path Overhead. An NE that contains STS PTE will also contain LTE and STE.

Synchronous Transport Signal Level 1 (STS-1) The basic SONET building block signal transmitted at a 51.84 Mbps data rate.

Synchronous Transport Signal Level N (STS-N) The signal obtained by multiplexing integer multiples (N) of STS-1 signals together.

Terabits per second (Tbps) One trillion bits per second. An information-carrying capacity measure used for high-speed optical data systems.

Time Division Multiplexing (TDM) An electrical (digital) multiplexing technique used to enable multiple streams of information to share the same transmission media. For transmission at 155 Mbps or above, the electrical TDM signal is typically converted to an optical signal for transport.

Total Internal Reflection The reflection that occurs when light strikes an interface at an angle of incidence (with respect to the normal) greater than the critical angle.

Transmission The process of sending information from one point to another.

Transparent Optical Networks The original vision of the "all optical network" as a network in which a signal is transported from source to destination entirely in the optical domain. After ingress into the network, the signal is never converted to the electrical domain for analog operations such as amplification and filtering or any other purpose.

T1X1 Subcommittee A committee within ANSI that specifies SONET optical interface rates and formats.

Virtual Tributary (VT) A signal designed for the transport and switching of sub-STS-1 payloads.

Wide area network (WAN) A data communications facility involving two or more computers with the computers situated at different sites.

Wander Long-term variations in a waveform.

Waveguide A material medium that confines and guides a propagating electromagnetic wave. In the microwave regime, a waveguide normally consists of a hollow metallic conductor, generally rectangular, elliptical, or circular in a cross-section. This type of waveguide may, under certain conditions, contain a solid or gaseous dielectric material. In the optical regime, a waveguide used as a long transmission line consists of a solid dielectric filament (optical fiber), usually circular in a cross-section. In integrated optical circuits, an optical waveguide may consist of a thin dielectric film.

Wavelength A measure of the color of the light for which the performance of the fiber has been optimized. It is a length stated in nanometers (nm) or in micrometers (μm).

Wavelength division multiplexer A passive device that combines light signals with different wavelengths on different fibers onto a single fiber. The wavelength division demultiplexer performs the reverse function.

Wavelength-Division Multiplexing (WDM) Sending several signals through one fiber with different wavelengths of light.

Wideband Services requiring 1.5 to 50 Mbps transport capacity.

INDEX

Symbols

A

B

G

H

I

L

M

P

Q-R

S

T

U–V

W–Z